Being a Ballerina

UNIVERSITY PRESS OF FLORIDA

Florida A&M University, Tallahassee
Florida Atlantic University, Boca Raton
Florida Gulf Coast University, Ft. Myers
Florida International University, Miami
Florida State University, Tallahassee
New College of Florida, Sarasota
University of Central Florida, Orlando
University of Florida, Gainesville
University of North Florida, Jacksonville
University of South Florida, Tampa
University of West Florida, Pensacola

BEING A
Ballerina

The Power and Perfection of a Dancing Life

GAVIN LARSEN

DISCARD

University Press of Florida

Gainesville · Tallahassee · Tampa · Boca Raton

Orlando · Miami · Jacksonville · Ft. Myers · Sarasota

"The Eight-Year-Old, Part 1," "The Eight-Year-Old, Part 2," "Places," "Quivering," "The Drive Home," "The Time I Taught Someone Something," and a version of "The Triple" first appeared in *Oregon ArtsWatch* in August 2016. "Cinderella" and "Into the Night" first appeared in the Spring 2015 issue of *KYSO Flash.* "Helena" first appeared in *KYSO Flash,* under the title "Excellent," in Fall 2016. "The Human Monolith" first appeared in *The Threepenny Review*'s Winter 2013 issue. "No Tights" first appeared in *The Sunlight Press* on February 25, 2019. A version of "Scarred" first appeared in *The Maine Review.* "Meeting My Maker" first appeared in *Page & Spine* in January 2015.

All drawings by Wayne Rivard.

26 25 24 23 22 21   6 5 4 3 2 1

ISBN 978-0-8130-6689-9
Library of Congress Control Number: 2020944516

The University Press of Florida is the scholarly publishing agency for the State University System of Florida, comprising Florida A&M University, Florida Atlantic University, Florida Gulf Coast University, Florida International University, Florida State University, New College of Florida, University of Central Florida, University of Florida, University of North Florida, University of South Florida, and University of West Florida.

University Press of Florida
2046 NE Waldo Road
Suite 2100
Gainesville, FL 32609
http://upress.ufl.edu

For my parents, Anne and Eric,
with admiration, gratitude, and love beyond measure

Why dance? What is it about dance that makes us either awkward and uncomfortable to the point of paralysis or exhilarated, released, and able to fly? And, for the sliver of the human population that becomes addicted, compelled, to take "dancing" to the most highly refined level, to analyze, measure, and execute physical movements with a cellular level of precision, to devote life to the body—why? What is that sticky substance that pulls us deeper and deeper into this world of dance? The further we explore the peaks and valleys, forests and oceans of the dance world, the more lost we become. The pathway ahead gets smoother and yet more twisty and hilly the longer we follow it, and the end of the road will never appear.

Contents

Preface

Curtain Speech

On May 2, 2010, I retired. My life as a dancer, which had formally begun at around age eight, when I took my first fateful ballet class (although, according to my parents, I had been dancing for long before that), was officially over. Perhaps because I quite simply could not fear that which was incomprehensible, I was filled with joy and a surprising calmness on the day that was actually a small death.

In the ballet world, we grapple for an accurate descriptor of this inevitable, yet inconceivable, event: we say that a dancer is retiring or giving her farewell performance. It's her swan song, she hangs up her pointe shoes, takes her final bow. There's no reason why, for the dancer herself, there has to be one last finale, a triumphant conclusion after which there will be no more appearances onstage, in pointe shoes, in front of an audience. She will wake up the next morning exactly the same. The same body, the same talents, the same artistry, the same aches and pains, the same corns and callouses. Most of those things erode ever so slowly—though still more quickly than they were built—but her mentality, psyche, and her deep, deep body of knowledge live forever. This is part of why a final, "farewell" performance is such a conundrum for the dancer: it is the public declaration that tomorrow, I will not be a dancer anymore—but I know that is not true. I will be exactly the same, but my name tag will have been peeled off.

The retirement performance was a way of officially removing my ballerina identity, but tenderly, as one would carefully ease a Band-Aid off a child's scraped knee. No one, not even me, knew what would be discovered underneath. For all the years of self-analysis, of shaping and crafting my dancer's body, of delight and dismay in it, of gratitude, awe, and ambition for it, this was perhaps the moment of greatest revelation.

How It All Began

What has never been revealed to me, though, is exactly how all this—this slow but then sudden emergence as a dancer—happened. I can tell my life story easily, complete with names and dates, schools and teachers, ballets danced, companies joined, directors, tours, decisions. What I cannot explain is how I did it. The truth is, I feel I did nothing at all.

People often said to me that when I retired, I would "find myself," which I took to mean that I might discover other aspects of my spirit that had been squished down, that had remained hidden or dormant while I was busy being a dancer. But, as I suspected would be the case, the opposite has been true. I've always known who I am. Spending most of my time wrapped up in dance and all the peripheral things that it required did not hide me from myself.

But now, when I look back in time, what I wonder is just who, exactly, that dancer-person was. I'm in awe and even disbelief, sometimes, that she and I are the same being. My dancer-self really does feel like a "she," another person inside me, like a Russian nesting doll, uncovered then, but now sheathed in an outside layer that looks exactly the same but is just a shell.

The further I look back through the years, the more removed I feel from that person. The stories of my beginnings on the path of dance, particularly, seem just that—stories. Of someone else's life, only possibly my own. I don't know who that little eight-, nine-, ten-year-old girl was, but maybe by telling her story from my vantage point now, as a forty-five-year-old on the other side of a dancing life, we can figure it out together.

Being a Ballerina

Part 1

1

The Eight-Year-Old, Part 1

The New York School of Ballet

The noise and rushing current of Broadway disappear instantly once the old wooden door with its rattly glass window slams shut, sealing out the brilliantly sunny Saturday morning and crowds of Upper West Siders bustling about on their weekend errands. Inside, everything is gray-scale, muted, dusty, and chilly. A wide staircase leads straight up, enormously high and steep. At the top, far above the comforting familiarity of the sidewalk below, there's faded lettering on the door to the right: New York School of Ballet.

Through that door, a long hallway lined with pew-like wooden benches is softened by a big fluffy white dog lying in a pile on the bare floor, acting as foot rest and greeter. The air is hazy and musty, carrying a cold, sweaty stale smell, possibly left over from the generations of dancers before. Rows of ancient metal lockers fill a dressing room that is unlit, unkempt, uncleaned—and unused? Three doors along the hall open to cavernous studios with ceilings two stories high, so big their corners disappear into shadows, empty and forgotten. Rosin dust covers everything. Young children, talking excitedly, bring life to this museum that is the space itself. Their purple leotards are the only color in this movie.

To an eight-year-old, especially one there for the first time, the New York School of Ballet was confusing. Crowded into the big hallway cum lobby, there were certainly a lot of young children who looked like they were there for ballet class, but then there were also all these adults around—clearly dancers, real ones—who looked as old as parents, though they were, probably, late teenagers.

The procedures and expectations were confusing, too, especially to a timid, play-by-the-rules little girl, self-conscious, and terrified of doing something wrong. The laid-back attitude of the friendly (and gorgeously tall and glamorous) woman behind the front desk made it all more stressful, not less—was the handwritten ledger book an attendance sheet? If each page was a class, where was the eight-year-old's name? Why did the glamorous woman say it didn't matter and to go in anyway? The butterflies in the young girl's stomach made her yearn to follow her parents' shadows back down to the comforting warmth of their weekend routine of coffee and the newspaper in a nearby diner.

Most confusing of all was where to go and what to do. Nobody pointed the new student to the right studio. Wanting to get away from the crowd of loud grown-ups milling about by the entrance, she wandered down the hall to an almost-hidden studio that felt the safest—the most private, way down there almost out the back door. She could slip in unnoticed and blend in with the bunch of kids already there. *Just pretend to know where you belong,* she thought to herself.

Pretending soon became everything. Pretend to know where to stand, since the other children were already confidently lined up at the barre (which, she came to learn, was the proper name for the wooden railing bracketed to the walls), and obviously she should fit in there somehow, too. A woman strolled in with coffee cup in hand, her casualness only adding to the eight-year-old's anxiety: was this the teacher? Apparently so, since suddenly, without preface or introduction, or recognition of the terrified little mouse squeezed into line, she began to call out the names of steps and cued the music to begin. Pretend to know what the words mean, what the steps are; copy the girls on either side, mimic and shadow whatever they do. Play follow-along, but never think of speaking up—don't ask a question; they'll know you made a mistake—just stay quiet and hope no one notices. Blend in so you won't stand out, even though, as usual, trying to blend in makes you noticeable.

No one's being mean, so why so intimidated? Why so scared? Scared of what? Scared of being wrong, even if only because of others' benign oversights.

An hour of confused stumbling passed, and abruptly, class was over. The teacher caught the young little mouse, hanging back from the crowd of veteran ballet students rushing in a flurry for the door, finally allowed to resume their chatter. *How old are you? Eight. Aha—I think you're in the wrong class—have you ever taken ballet before? No. Oh, no wonder! But you know, it's fine—you kept up so well, and you'll catch up to everyone else quickly. Just stay here in this class, and come again next week.*

What? I kept up well? How is that possible? All I did was flail and vaguely mimic the fast-moving girls around me! How can I catch up to the middle when I don't even know where the beginning was?

——————

So it began. A lifetime—a ballet lifetime—that started off without a beginning but with a mandate to pretend that there had been one. Entering the race two laps past the starting line, hoping no one would notice.

Could it be done?

2

How to Be a Ballerina, Part 1

First, stretch. Gently but firmly, in every direction.

Get out of bed gingerly. As soon as your feet touch the floor, even before hauling yourself upright, carefully test your back for spasms: to do this, flop face forward over your mattress, legs hanging heavy over the side to make an L-shape with your body. Stretch your arms out across the bedsheet, feeling its softness against your cheek, and pause. This is only the first of many moments today when you'll try to imagine what's deep under your skin, listening hard enough to hear the inner mechanisms of your muscles and bones. The always-audible joint cracks and pops are meaningless chatter. Once your spine has unkinked, move immediately to a very hot shower.

Savor the strong pummeling of water as it starts to dull the brittleness of your body. Feel it tease your muscles out of their overnight grip, giving them a first taste of the possibilities—and tasks—of the day. Here's when you'll start to find out whether the crunchiness of your Achilles tendon is something to worry about, or if, with some encouragement, it will slide smoothly in its sheath. After drying off, layer on something soft and fuzzy, but unrestrictive, to keep in the shower's heat, and get down on the living room floor to begin your exercises: easily at first, a gentle prod to get your abs, hamstrings, adductors, and spine to engage, and then a second round, more businesslike. Push-ups to yoga poses will take you from flat on the ground to half-way up, and resistance-band exercises learned from your physical therapist will bring you to your feet. Now you'll be taking the temperature of your hamstring tear, or hip bursitis, or metatarsal inflammation, trying not to overreact if any or all of their temperatures are especially high. If it feels hard to get moving at first, know that energy begets energy. There's some time yet before you and your body must report for duty; right now, it's still just the two of you.

Accompanied by NPR's *Morning Edition,* do various stretches, take sips from the cup of hot tea next to you on the bookshelf, grab a few motivational glances at the clouds and sky outside the window—knowing that the point of this daily routine is to bring your instrument out of its case and pluck a few strings before the fine-tuning can begin. Rules: Do not think about the day ahead. Let your mind wander where it will, in and out of the morning's news, toward the drizzle outside, forward to the thick slices of hearty bread you'll toast for breakfast. Gradually, almost without your noticing, forty-five minutes will have passed and you'll be done with your last downward dog and feel your internal engine gently humming. Stretch your calves at the kitchen table while you enjoy that buttered toast with two hard-boiled eggs, make one more cup of tea, and spend a second or two staring wistfully out the back door, wondering what it would be like to just call in sick and stay home today.

Your mind and your body begin each day like this—cautiously eyeing one another, testing for grumpiness or moodiness or buoyancy, wondering why yesterday's work seems to have vanished and whether you can possibly do it over again. But it hasn't really vanished, at least not completely, and years upon years of habitual training make you pick up your bag, take two Aleve, and walk out the door.

3

The Eight-Year-Old, Part 2

The Greek

Now that she knew which studio to go into, the eight-year-old did return the following week, and the one after, and even more after that. As these weeks passed, she began slowly to gain, if not real confidence, then a familiarity with how things worked. She followed along. She watched, and copied, but just when she started to think she knew everything she and the other students would be told to do, the teacher called for a step or movement that was foreign. As before, momentary panic would strike— she was afraid no one remembered that she was the girl who was supposed to be given leeway, who was still catching up. She wanted to wear a sign reminding everyone she was new. Did she think of her newness as a defense—a justification for any mistake she might make? Was it becoming part of her psyche, her identity? Was she using it as a shield, so that she could fail without fear of shame? But the curse of being a good faker is that people begin to think you're for real, and then they expect things.

She was trying, and listening, hard, very hard. Every instruction that was given she multiplied by at least two or three. A straight knee was very, very straight. Shoulders down meant really, really down. "Point your toes" meant make your foot as strong as a dagger. "Stomach in" meant belly button to backbone.

Here's what she learned:

First position: heels together, toes pointing left-right.

Second position: same as first but heels apart.

Third position doesn't exist (well, not in this class, anyway).

Fourth position: one foot in front of the other, toes pointing left-right.

Fifth position: same as fourth, but feet smushed tightly together, toes of
one touching heel of the other.

Plié: bend your knees

Relevé: tiptoe, like when you reach for a glass on a high cabinet shelf.

Knees over toes at all times.

Stomach sucked IN at all times. ALL times.

But these were only the most basic of the basics. Beyond them, it was still mostly a game of quick-eyed copycat.

But even so, she began to fit in, a little bit. Still too shy to initiate any sort of real friendship, she did relax enough to join the other girls' chit-chat during the few minutes before and after class, trading those odd bits of information that eight-year-olds use to size each other up (What school do you go to? Are you allowed to take the bus by yourself yet?) while they were scrambling for socks and jeans to pull over their tights in the hallway outside. Those austere wooden benches didn't seem so cold anymore. They were just places to stow sweatshirts and sneakers, because nobody went into that dark and musty locker room.

After a while, there was a new teacher. Or an old teacher who was new to the eight-year-old, who was now nine. He was a man, who seemed to be ancient, with a disfigured foot and a severe limp, very thin wisps of silver hair, and sparkling blue eyes that betrayed the soft character inside his large, bellowing exterior. He didn't really know or care what had happened in any class or time before he arrived to teach, only that these girls should, at this point, by his judgment, know certain things and how to do certain steps. He was Greek, as he loved to remind everyone, with a robust temper and vocal cords to match. Everything he said was bellowed, and insults, even to young girls, were not off-limits. Shuffling into the studio that first day (his disabled foot seemed like a ball and chain that kept him, mercifully for the girls, from moving too fast), he immediately spotted the nine-year-old (did her inexperience show, even when just standing still?). *WHO ARE YOU AND WHERE DID YOU COME FROM?!?* he yelled across the room at her. Panic struck. Who *am* I? Where *did* I come from? She frantically searched for an answer, anything to take the attention away, but there was no deflecting him. Stammering her name three times, her tiny voice squeaking much too quietly for the Greek to hear, he scornfully gave up and hollered out the first exercise. For years to follow, he called her Anne.

As the weeks and months went on, the nine-year-old—by dint of doing everything with twice as much effort as was expected, by straightening her knees and pointing her feet and pressing her shoulders down impossibly hard and aiming her knees over her left-right facing toes at all times, by pulling her stomach in to her backbone—had started to look like she had actually been practicing ballet for a fair amount of time, not just a few months.

One day, the old Greek teacher had taken the class through their barre work and arranged them in lines in the center of the studio (this was the part of class when the nine-year-old had to be especially quick with her imitation skills). After he gave them a tendu exercise (she knew how to do tendus, now, but still hadn't figured out all the difficult words that went with the dozens of different directions and angles in which to do them), he said to do a pirouette. And he pointed at the nine-year-old.

SHOW ME!

She had not only never done or been taught a pirouette, she had only a vague idea of what it was. The image in her head of a pirouette came from photos or drawings in her collection of ballet books at home, or maybe from having seen Baryshnikov spin endlessly—amazingly—in a PBS broadcast of *Dance in America*. So she knew it was a turn and that the dancers in the pictures had their legs in passé (and luckily she did know that position by now—it was easy to remember because it made your legs look like a capital letter P). Thinking of the ballerina on top of a music box someone had given her for a gift, she desperately guessed at where to hold her arms.

The old terror and fear surged again—why she couldn't or didn't just say that she didn't know how to do a pirouette is unknown, but it was certain that scorn would fly, no matter what. So, reflexively and without hesitating (and thankfully able to move after momentary full-body freeze of panic), she threw herself into some sort of spin with her arms over her head, and the Greek wrath thundered.

What on earth is that?! Someone else—YOU! He swiveled toward another victim.

The other girl tried, maybe somewhat successfully, maybe not, but nonetheless, the class moved on. And the old man Greek teacher never did come back to the nine-year-old and teach her how to do the pirouette.

4

How to Be a Ballerina, Part 2

Once at the ballet studio, change into work clothes. A leotard is the base layer and can be chosen for its color, cut, or comfort level, according to your state of mind (or simply what's not in the laundry). Then a pair of tights (black or pink, or another shade if you're feeling frisky or bold), at least one more layer on your legs (baggy nylon running pants? Spandex yoga gear?), knit warmers for ankles and calves, a scarf or shawl wrapped around your waist (for lower-back protection and a hint of style), a form-fitting T-shirt or tank top on your upper half, and a sweater over that. Footwear is next, but you must protect your toes first.

The process of taping your toes will change as various wounds are incurred and heal. The basic line of defense, though, remains the same: white athletic tape encircles the boniest toes; gel-filled burn pads, held in place with more tape, cushion your toe knuckles that are so prone to corns. Plain masking tape over it all reduces friction inside your pointe shoes. By the time you're done, your toes look like mummies in their protective cocoons of tape. There may be a need for a metatarsal pad, which you will have cut carefully to size out of thick moleskin, stiffened with glue, and fit squarely under the ball of your foot. It's important to be assertive with this toe-taping routine. Your feet are your soldiers, unseen but not unheard, and this armor is their only protection from hour after hour of confinement, pressure, heat, and sweat. Squeeze your feet into a soft pair of pointe shoes (starting the day in already-worn shoes helps ease the shock). You know from long experience that, ironically, they feel the worst when you first put them on. As always, movement helps everything. Walk upstairs to the studio. The burn in your quads makes you unable to believe that those legs will, later today, propel you through the air. But give it time.

These past three hours have been the day's overture. Now, with fifteen minutes left until class starts, here's what you do: head to your regular spot in the corner, where the barres affixed to the studio walls meet. Some of the other dancers in the company are already in the studio, most of them stretching out on the floor near their own preferred barre-spots, isolated with headphones on or exchanging a few comments quietly with each other. Others trickle in, some visibly dragging, as the clock ticks toward class start time. Avoid conversation or even eye contact. Too much energy required for that, yet, and you need all you have to get into first position: perfectly straight knees, your heels touching each other, toes and kneecaps pointing east-west, rotating each leg outward from its hip joint and holding it all with the strength of your inner thighs. Test out your pointe shoes with a few careful relevés, rolling smoothly up onto the tips of your shoes and back down, now bending your knees into demi-plié. Do several of these, gradually sinking deeper into your plié, coaxing it to cushion your descent. Gradually lighten your grip on the barre. Allow, and encourage, your feet to make friends with your shoes.

Now, turning away from the barre, find yourself in the mirror on the studio's far wall and consider the next stage of your body's work—pushing, wrapping, arching, extending, contracting, lifting, shaping, reaching, and recoiling. Today's teacher enters the studio and immediately the tone of class is set: if they stroll in casually, making warm eye contact with a few dancers or chatting with the pianist, the room's slightly tense aura of expectation relaxes and you know you'll be given psychological space to work your own way. But a brisk, businesslike entrance signals that the teacher is going to push you, and the others, to follow their agenda today. They won't want to let you take class wholly inside yourself. You'll be performing for the teacher's fulfillment, too.

Class officially starts with the demonstration (or maybe just the verbal explanation, illustrated with vague hand gestures) of the first exercise and the pianist's first notes, musically corralling us, kindly, into the first semblance of unison for the day. Some free license is given (only during class) to modulate how closely you match your movement to the music, but even still, rhythm and melody are the singular voices we all follow. The pianist's mood, too, affects the room—the energy, passion, even humor of what they play will either buoy you up or weigh you down or bring a collective laugh. Something as simple as a heartfelt rendition of *Hallelujah* brings a surge of renewed motivation.

Now that class is under way, you're scrutinizing your shape and form and relieved when the leaden feeling in your muscles starts to dissipate. Your spot at the barre lets you face a large pair of windows. Outside, tree branches sway in the wind and people come and go from the coffee shop across the street, leaving with lattes and little white paper bags in hand. You feel an intense but brief desire to go and get a cheese danish.

The reassuring layers of warm-up clothes you put on earlier have been a kind of protective shield, keeping you from working too hard, too soon. But with each barre exercise, your body begins to respond more nimbly, and the thickness of your warmers becomes a hindrance. Off they come, but be sure to shed them strategically, one piece at a time, starting with the bulkiest outer sweatshirt, being careful not to overestimate your confidence.

Ronde de jambe *en l'air*. Four, and then four more. Reverse directions. Repeat on demi-pointe, heels pushed up as high as they will go and calves engaged rock-hard. Grab every muscle you have to do this not just adequately but also faster, with a more pointed foot and turned out leg and without giving in to a hint of strain or fatigue. An impassive, expressionless face gives you strength of will and perhaps also of body. Stare ahead with a piercing gaze and channel everything into an intense compulsion to finish this ridiculously difficult series without a wilt.

(Continue this approach through the rest of barre, with pockets of relief in between exercises. The joker at the barre-spot a few feet away likes making caustic comments to whoever's nearby. Even if you don't have the levity to respond, try, at least, to smile at his brash way of coping.)

5

The Triple

The next year, the girl, now ten, was moved up into the next level of ballet classes. She'd faked it well enough, copied well enough, worked harder than regular eight- or nine-year-olds would and, unsurprisingly, come to seriously love going to class. The ritual was fun now. Her family, a foursome, escorted her downtown quite early on Saturday mornings, where they all encamped at a table inside Burger King, half a block away from the rattly wooden front doors of the ballet school. They'd get cheese danishes wrapped in airtight plastic bags, or Styrofoam plates of scrambled eggs, sausage, pancakes, and maple syrup, and her parents would drink coffee. When it was time, she'd set off to walk by herself the half-block to the ballet school, open those front doors, and leave Broadway behind to climb the mountainous flight of stairs. Her parents, pretending to be calm and casual, watched anxiously until she'd crossed the street, passed the candy store, and disappeared into the building.

The fun of the Saturday morning ritual, though, was only because it led up to the dancing-time. And it wasn't just that the dancing was less terrifying. She felt its pull now, its compulsion. And that was because of the music.

There was a pianist who played for class every week. She was a tall woman with a puffy halo of tightly curled brown hair and a sort of drooping posture, as if she was ashamed of her height or was apologizing for being physically present. But she was not apologetic musically. When she played the piano, she didn't hunch. Her music drove, lifted, propelled. It danced, and it probably was her way of dancing, too.

The ten-year-old pinned her spirits on the sight of the pianist, who she came to see as an angel, slinking in through the studio door, always at the very last minute, juggling and dropping binders of sheet music as she murmured apologies and hustled to the piano in the corner.

No exercise was hard with music like that. It magically made the ten-year-old able to hold her leg up higher and longer, straighter and more proudly. In fact, the music itself was doing the work for her. It took over. Now she had learned some jumping steps, simple ones designed to build strength in the legs and lungs, and the pianist played hornpipes and mazurkas and marches that pushed her, pulled her, carried her along—she could practically see the notes dancing alongside her, teasing her to keep up as fast as they were going, holding her hand as they flew through steps and left muscle burn behind them.

Along with those moments of pure, ecstatic joy, though, there were still valleys of shadow. The Greek teacher would spring verbal pop quizzes about the French names of steps, their translations, and ask to see them demonstrated—and then done in reverse. He'd pick a student and ask if they knew who Nijinska was, and if they didn't, he'd say they had about as much right to be in ballet class as an elephant.

The ten-year-old lived in fear of being called on to answer a question or translate a step she didn't know. There was no forgiveness for never having been taught or told something. All were expected to *know*, somehow, whatever the Greek teacher thought they should. Pirouettes had still never been taught to the ten-year-old, but by now she had watched and tried enough times, had learned the position—and held it twice as hard as necessary—to have something of a grasp, though uncertainty still ruled.

Cracks, however, were beginning to show in the Greek teacher's crusty exterior.

One day, during the summertime, the number of students in class was small, maybe because some had gone off on family vacations or to sleepaway camp or weren't interested enough in ballet to keep coming to a musty indoor studio in beautiful weather. The Greek teacher gave the class a pirouette exercise. By now, the class had advanced enough that many of the students were doing double pirouettes, rotating two times around instead of just one. The command on this day was for all doubles, from everyone. Ever timid, the ten-year-old held her breath and her position as hard as she could until it was over.

Come here. The rest of the class cleared to the sides and back of the studio, and the ten-year-old, very nervously, stepped forward.

Do a triple. Having no mechanism to defy her instinct to obey an order, she took the preparation position. And did a triple pirouette.

Now, just for fun and games, do it to the left. So she did.

Somehow, she did.

6

How to Be a Ballerina, Part 3

Soon (or maybe not soon enough), the portion of class done at the barre will be over. Forty-five minutes of near-continuous movement, however small and controlled, brings blood and oxygen to those previously bound-up muscles, and the excited hint of maybe, just maybe, being able to dance again cracks the room's tension. Up to this point, all of you, some thirty-odd dancers, have been practicing the same exact steps, in near-unison, yet absolutely alone. You've all been faced with the same tasks, but you must struggle to complete them in isolation: no one can help another, no one can join forces or share tools. At barre, each body is on a solitary quest, surrounded by others with the same frustratingly elusive goal. The buzz of chatter that erupts as soon as the last exercise at the barre (*grands battements*—straight-legged kicks requiring abs of steel and perfectly pointed feet, with not even a quiver of movement in the midsection or upper body) is finished pulls you out of your shell, whether or not you're ready. It's 10:15 A.M. and the studio windows are covered in steam.

Each dancer needs his or her own piece of territory, a work space of roughly four feet in diameter. It's understood that this buffer zone is personal space, not to be violated, so when class is crowded, portable barres are arranged in rows in the center of the studio. There's a comforting symmetry to this arrangement, and in their inevitable way, the dancers disperse themselves evenly between the wall-mounted barres and the center ones so that everyone has their own spot. After barre, the security of this tidy geometry dissolves as the guys hoist the barres and move them off to the edges of the studio, where they won't be in the way for center work. Most of the women have slid to the floor and are rummaging in their bags for a flattering skirt to add to their outfit, or maybe a different pair of leggings, while others are either, trepidatiously, pulling on a brand-new pair of pointe shoes that needs breaking in before today's rehearsals or calculating which of her old ones can be used up in class. It may take one or two changes of pairs to decide.

During the barre work, the only sounds had been the pianist's music accompanying the exercises after the teacher had named the steps to be done, explained and demonstrated their combination, and offered occasional corrections. Now, in the few minutes' break before center, everyone feels free to talk if they like, and the noise level rises. The men, unconcerned with shoe or clothing choices, are generally the most convivial chatterers. Someone looking into the room might think they were observing a cocktail party: small circles of friends, hugs, greetings, laughter, small talk, a few loners avoiding the others, but with the guests wearing pointe shoes instead of high heels and stretching into splits on the floor. It's pleasant to enjoy the moment of camaraderie and ease, even though at the same time you're thinking mostly about what's ahead.

The teacher will cut this intermission short by signaling the pianist to start playing for the first combination—tendus in multiple directions, or a slow, controlled adagio of high-leg extensions—the equivalent of rapping a knife on a wine glass to cut through the din. It takes a moment or two, but a hush falls and a momentum toward work is slowly regained. The energetic ones are up on their feet, in the front line and ready to go, setting the pace for others still struggling with shoes, aches, injuries, or the fog of mental fatigue. My advice is to find yourself a spot in the middle of the pack, a comfortable compromise between prominent and invisible. Inescapably, there's a performance aspect to center work. The blinders are off, for the most part, and now you can and do watch each other—you're dancing each exercise in groups, large ones at first, then smaller and smaller until you're traveling across the floor four, three, two, or even one at a time. It's impossible to work in privacy. The journey you started early this morning, right out of bed, was all for you and you alone, but now you're being looked at, and that makes an extraordinary difference. The intensity isn't as high as it will get later on, but if you're not ready for even this much exposure, go to the back corner and fuss with your shoes. You're not onstage, yet.

Or, even better, concentrate on your balance. Challenge yourself to make a perfect, tight sous-sous, your feet firmly glued into fifth position on pointe, your legs fitted together like two pieces of a jigsaw puzzle, your arms as engaged as your legs, reaching proudly into a broad oval shape overhead. Drill the tips of your pointe shoes even deeper into the floor, pull your waist in and up under your ribs until your balance is so secure that you step out of it only when and because *you*—not gravity—decide to. *This* is the fine-tuning you've been looking for all morning—the precision you thought you'd lost overnight.

7

The Eleven-Year-Old, Part 1

The Audition

The eleven-year-old stood in fifth position, with her back to the barre, facing out into the center of the room. A few feet to her right, and a few feet to her left, on and on down the length of the barre, more legs were pulled into fifth positions, some clean and tightly crossed, some uncomfortably strained. She'd never been told to start class like this before, but nothing about this afternoon was familiar, except the fact of being inside a cavernous ballet studio, lit only by daylight from big windows way up high by the ceiling, allowing only a view of the sky.

A gaggle of Russian women, maybe a posse, all of them older ladies, chattered in a huddle in the front of the studio. Their voices overlapped like a bunch of political pundits arguing on a news talk show as they stood peering at each child. They spoke in low tones, but each one insistently, persistently, demanded attention. The six of them—three teachers, the regisseur, the school director, and a secretary, all stern-faced and dressed in conservative, old-world clothes—pointed, commented, scribbled on clipboards. They began to make their rounds, moving in a group from one end of the barre to the other, stopping in front of each child for one of the teachers to take hold of the child's foot and lift it as high as the leg would go, both in front of her nose and to the side of her ear. More comments and more scribbles were made. The group moved on down the barre to the next child anxiously hoping to be admitted to the School of American Ballet.

The eleven-year-old was used to following along. Used to pretending she knew what to do. The Russians' designated spokeswoman started barking instructions that the eleven-year-old could tell were as confusing to her fellow auditioners as they were to her. They exchanged befuddled, nervous glances—no ballet exercises were set or demonstrated, just individual steps called out. In this lineup of young bodies and brains as shaky as hers, she felt less terror than usual of making a mistake. There was no music, no indication of how many tendus to do, which made her feel, strangely, that it didn't seem to matter. The band of women absorbed in their clipboards and conversations seemed to have stopped scrutinizing each child like a scientific specimen. If they were still watching, they did so quite covertly.

Before very long, the eleven-year-old and three others were told to leave the barre and come forward into the center of the studio. Those uncalled hovered off to one side, close together as if for warmth, unsure if their fate had been determined, and if so, which way.

The spokeswoman's job was taken over by the youngest-looking of the Russians, the one who had been doing the least talking and the most scribbling.

Do you know 'balancé'? Good—show me. Do you know tombé pas de bourée? Show me. Pirouette en dehors? Do. Sautée? Echappé? Assemblé? Entrechat quatre? Go.

The eleven-year-old and her small group did each step, first all together and then one by one. More, and more, and more scribbles . . . and still, no music.

The next Russian to speak was the oldest, grayest, smallest but fiercest one. She pushed her way out of the circle and limped over to the eleven-year-old.

Brisé? Brisé? You know brisé?

Having seen a brisé once or twice and being afraid to say "no," the eleven-year-old nodded.

With a jut of her chin and a flick of her hand toward the eleven-year-old's feet,

Do!

Apparently, the eleven-year-old's memory of what a brisé looked like was fuzzy, and since she had never tried to do one before, her approximation of the step was a fumble. The fierce Russian's face turned from stern to scornful and this time, the flick of her hand was dismissive as she sputtered some sounds of rejection.

Brisé did not turn out to be so important, after all. The eleven-year-old and her mother were summoned into an office.

She's very nice. She'll be in Children's Fourth Division and wear a dusty mauve leotard. She will start tomorrow.

There wasn't any discussion. The information was issued, not offered, the barest facts laid out, and the rest—if there was anything else—would be revealed in its own time. There was no reason, clearly, why a child would *not* start the very next day in Children's Fourth Division. In a mauve leotard.

8

The Eleven-Year-Old, Part 2

Madame Dudin

I think I will always be intimidated by Russians. The day I auditioned for the School of American Ballet engraved in my mind an impression of the old-guard, traditional Russian ballet master as all-knowing and strict. Because such people held in their brains and blood the experience, wisdom, and history of ballet, they were not to be messed with or doubted. As teeny and uninformed as that made me feel, it also made things simple—there was no reason to search further, because these people could teach me all I needed to know, if they so chose. And luckily for me, by accepting me into their school, they did.

The next day, a Thursday, the eleven-year-old arrived back at the scene of the previous day's audition with absolutely no more confidence than she'd had before, despite having been described as "very nice" by the secretary in the brief and businesslike acceptance meeting. Like her previous school, this one was a hubbub of activity, but here the energy was electric. It was focused and important. The students stretching in the hallways (dark floors of cold, hard, black stone) seemed to have dual purposes of warming up and posturing for those who walked by. There were no friendly smiles at the front desk, no casual welcome, no fluffy white dog asleep on the floor.

The eleven-year-old, after following the only possible route down the hall from the front door, ended up in the girls' locker room. This locker room was actually *used*—it was brightly lit, overheated, and packed with girls of all ages, buzzing with conversation and crowding around banks of mirrors to fix their hair. Endless rows of lockers were crammed full of leg warmers, tights, shoes, many with pointe shoe ribbons hanging out the bottom of the door like a badge of expertise. It was impossible not to stare at the teenagers with leg muscles as taut as ropes, wet with sweat and faces flushed bright red with exertion from the class they had just finished. The school year had already been in session for a few weeks. The eleven-year-old was starting late.

Spotted instantly as a newcomer, she was surrounded by other eleven-year-olds—veterans, her new classmates—and herded toward the studio where their class would be held. Random nuggets of information and curious questions came at her from all sides. *Where are you from? How old are you? This is where we have class on Saturdays, that's the bulletin board where Nutcracker casting goes up, Madame Dudin teaches on Thursdays, soon we start pointe, why are you wearing a black leotard? We stand in height order at the barre but she'll tell you where to go . . .*

The eleven-year-old newcomer didn't want to be picked out of this huge class of girls and noticed for anything, though that was impossible owing to the fact that she was, as already pointedly questioned by one of her classmates, in a black leotard instead of the class's required dress code of dusty mauve. (There'd been no time to go to the dancewear store in the twenty-four hours that had elapsed since the audition the day before.) As the sweetest-looking of the Russians from the audition posse opened the studio door, the twenty young student dancers scurried instantly into their preassigned order at the barre. The eleven-year-old squeezed in between two of them and held her breath.

Madame Dudin tiptoed across the room to the piano. She set down her large black purse and looked around, surveying the room, as if she could smell a new girl.

Excruciatingly slowly, with a strange, extremely pronounced limp that looked like one foot was frozen on tiptoe, she made her way over to the eleven-year-old, took her hand, and moved her one spot farther back at the barre, trading places with the girl behind. The height-order lineup must be perfectly precise, right down to the quarter-inch.

Then, class began. Quietly, and quickly. Even for the sharpest pair of eyes, keeping up by imitation was very, very hard. The exercises were given in Madame Dudin's tiny, whispery Russian-French-English voice, barely decipherable. Even her hand gestures indicating the steps were vague. The eleven-year-old just kept paddling, as fast as she could, to stay afloat.

9

How to Be a Ballerina, Part 4

From the first tendus, class has progressed to adagio and pirouettes and eventually to *petit allegro*—small jumps are fun, a relief from the tricky showmanship of pirouettes and the agonizingly hard, yet beautiful control of adagio. But temper your exuberance—the fleet, bouncy steps drive you to move faster and faster, but then there's less time for your brain to keep pace with your legs. Be cautious with, and conscious of, every tiny move you make, of which there are a million per second. Your creaking Achilles, jammed-up ankle joint, your strained and taut hamstring . . . all can explode from a worry into a crisis in an instant.

But you *do* need to push, just enough to give your joints a taste of some force and impact. You need to test your nerves, the ones in your legs and feet as well as your head, for quick, nimble reactions. Your heart, too, and your lungs want to pump and move fast, to get you fully and truly warm with blood and oxygen.

You could stop now, bow out with grace, go change your leotard and pointe shoes and turn your mind to the rehearsal that'll be starting soon. You've done all the exercises your body needed, you've gotten yourself to the point of preparedness, ready for the most important work of the day. The teacher has just given grand allegro, the last combination of jumps before class ends, and dancers are flying across the room's long diagonal in pairs and trios to a big, soaring waltz. It's a bit of a reward, a child's ice cream treat for finishing their homework, but it's also what audiences most often like to see. Grand allegro ties together all the steps you've taken so far today, from pliés and tendus to turns, balances, and extensions.

You know you can defy gravity, though—you have so many times before. You know that when the time comes, when the choreography calls for the power of a grand jeté and saut de basque, or *tour jeté* and cabriole, your body will remember how to spring from the floor and automatically rebound—you've adjusted your arms' coordination carefully, so they'll help you lift, and your knees, ankles, and feet know just how to cushion your landings with soft, strong, catlike deceleration.

So, quietly weave your way through the crowd of sweaty dancers to the corner of the studio where you stashed your bag at the beginning of class. Pull on some leg warmers, socks over your pointe shoes, and your fleece warm-up jacket. Grab your water bottle and slip unobtrusively out the door, leaving behind the studio's bright, hot energy for the chilled air and soft light of the hallway outside.

10

The First Nutcracker

I have always been a performer. I have (very fuzzy) early memories of demanding to "put on a show" for my parents' friends when they'd come over for dinner, prancing and twirling around the coffee table to whatever music happened to be on the stereo, finishing with a grand exit through the double doors. Those childhood performances were the first way I found to satisfy the weird combination of shyness and show-off that shapes my personality. The theatricality made it feel safe, the music made me feel exuberant and free, and I didn't have to look anyone in the eye.

When I was an eleven-year-old student at the School of American Ballet, just weeks after my very first class there, I spent a long Saturday afternoon auditioning (along with every other student under age fourteen) for The Nutcracker. I was still a foreigner to the complex operations of this highly structured ballet school, but that would change very soon. After the day's audition, I was cast in the New York City Ballet's production of George Balanchine's The Nutcracker. I would be a boy Polichinelle in act 2 and a baby mouse in act 1. The experience was transformational. Years later, answering the question of why I decided to try to be a dancer, I realized that my very first Nutcracker was when I knew—I felt, without a shadow of a doubt, that I was home. The theater was my home, as much as my parents' apartment was. If I could re-create my train of thought during one of those revelatory days in the theater, this is what it would sound like.

We go everywhere in herds, we Polichinelles. When it's time to go to wardrobe to get into our costumes, of course we all need to go together. It's funny seeing how closely we stick by each other just to walk down the dimly lit, cement-floored hall in the theater's basement. I feel like I'm squished in a pack of fast-moving cattle, carried along by the other girls jostling shoulder-to-shoulder and stepping on each other's heels, rushing so fast to get there. I'm excited to get ready, too, though, and even though we're all playing it sort of cool, I think everyone has the same fluttery-stomach feeling. Every show feels like Christmas Eve, which is funny because that's when the ballet is supposed to take place. For me, it's real!

We'd been hanging out in this big room in the basement (euphemistically called the "lower concourse") for what seems like hours before it's time to get into costume. When it's not overtaken by *Nutcracker* children, it's the orchestra's rehearsal room, so there are music stands and folding chairs scattered all around. Each of us commandeers a music stand to use as a makeup table. I always get here as early as we're allowed to—most everyone else does, too. No one waits until "half hour" (which is actually thirty-five minutes before the curtain goes up and is our official call time) to arrive—that would practically be late, even though we don't go onstage for a long time. The lucky girls who are in Party Scene in act 1 show up with their hair in curlers and spend the time before the show starts combing out their curls and putting in their bows. Since I'm a boy Polichinelle, my hair needs to be up in a bun. The girl Polichinelles get to do curls, just like the Party Scene kids, because they wear their hair down for our dance, with a little cap pinned on top of their heads. Even though my bun gets covered with a hat and no one will see it, I want it to be perfect. What if my hat fell off during the show and suddenly everyone in the audience saw messy hair? I want everything—*everything*—to be perfect when I go onstage.

We all get to put on some makeup, which is kind of fun but a little nerve-wracking because I don't really know how to do it. Some of the other girls who've done *Nutcracker* before act like old pros, so I just try to watch what they're doing (without looking like I am) and copy them. My makeup collection is pretty haphazard, just some almost-used-up eyeliner and rouge I found in my mother's makeup case at home. Now that we've done a bunch of performances I've gotten the hang of it, I think, but last time Wilhelmina (she's like the commander in chief of all the children in *Nutcracker*) yelled at me because I had put on too much blue eyeshadow. Well, she didn't *really* yell, but she sounded very exasperated and said little girls should not have bright blue eyeshadow and to take it off! So I just tried to wipe off as much as I could and felt really embarrassed . . . how was I supposed to know? The one part of the makeup we don't do ourselves is our "cheeks." Polichinelles and Hoops (their official title is "Candy Canes," but they dance with these striped hula hoops so that's their nickname) get these perfectly round, bright red makeup circles pasted on our cheeks so we look like toys. Some of the older girls who are our chaperones/shepherds (they're advanced students in the School who are too old for the kids' roles but not in the company yet) are also in charge of putting our cheeks on. They use these round makeup sticks—sort of like an oversized lipstick—to press them on, and then we have to be really careful to remember not to touch our faces—but every time, someone smudges their cheeks and either goes onstage messy or, if there's time, gets them redone. And the costume people are always telling us not to get check-smudges on our costumes, but it's impossible not to! Red streaks are kind of everywhere, but I think mostly the audience is too far away to see.

Okay, okay, let's go, let's go! It's intermission, act 1 is over, and that's our cue to line up to get our costumes on. The women in the costume shop are so particular about how dancers get their costumes on—you can't pull them up by the shoulder straps because it'll stretch them out, you can't let anything touch the floor, you definitely can't fasten the hooks on the back of your friend's costume. They're always talking about how old and fragile and delicate the costumes are, but even though there are some frayed edges at the hems and they smell a little musty, I don't care. My costume is not exactly beautiful—it's not a tutu—but when I put it on, somehow I feel really important.

So now we're hanging around AGAIN, waiting for the "Onstage" call from the stage manager so we can go upstairs to the stage and act 2 will start! Now everyone's getting really tittery and the chaperones keep telling us to be quiet. Especially when that call comes down from the stage manager (well, it's really over a loudspeaker system so everyone in the whole entire theater—except the audience, of course—can hear it) for

"ONSTAGE, PLEASE! ONSTAGE FOR ACT 2!" and we scurry to the elevator—they make us take the freight elevator so we don't crowd out the company dancers—and ride up a few flights to "Stage Level," the most exciting and important floor in the theater. I get kind of nervous just looking at those words on the elevator button panel.

We're here, Stage Level, and as soon as the elevator doors open, you can smell and hear and feel the stage—I love this part! It's as though this floor is alive and the rest of the theater is taking a nap. We've been totally isolated down there in the basement, but now that we're up here onstage, we're really, truly, a part of this whole big, beautiful, important, REAL thing. It seems as businesslike and serious and energized as a hospital or airport control tower. There's a calm urgency in the air and in everyone's voices and faces. All the principal dancers' dressing rooms are along the hallway from the elevator to the backstage area. Walking by and reading the names on the doors is like being in Hollywood. Those dancers are bigger than movie stars to me, and being that close to their dressing rooms is unbelievable!

Once, one of the doors was half open and I got a glimpse inside of a jewel-box room, warm lightbulbs around a big mirror, bright costumes hanging, toe shoes all over . . . just like a tiny magic kingdom.

We're heading into the wings (again in a tight little clump, because our chaperones are hyperalert to keep us as unobtrusive as possible—they're terrified of getting yelled at for letting us kids be in anyone's way). It's still intermission, and the company dancers are all either onstage practicing steps, or at the portable barre on each side of the stage warming up, or at the prop table fixing up their hair or costumes, or at the rosin box on the floor getting their pointe shoes on. Some are just milling around talking to each other, looking super casual (I always try to overhear what they're saying), but some others look really serious. Are they maybe even a little nervous themselves? No, that's impossible. They're probably just concentrating.

It's getting really close to time now. They just turned off the work lights and popped the bright stage lights on and suddenly, everything feels a little hotter but also as though we've sealed out anything having to do with the regular world and are in a different place: the theater world, the ballet world, where the stage lights are the sun and time is suspended.

All of us are grouped on stage left, because that's where we enter from. After all this waiting, I almost don't believe that the curtain will actually go up, but—after the conductor enters the orchestra pit, the audience applauds, and the music starts—it does. And this is amazing—before our entrance, the Sugarplum Fairy does her variation and we get to watch! Well, we HAVE to, right? We can't leave the wings and possibly miss our entrance, can we? There's a different Sugarplum almost every show because they have so many casts. I wonder how and when they all rehearse? They all seem to appear out of thin air, looking perfect. I love watching each one and seeing how different they are. We do sort of pick our favorites . . . mine are the ones that I want to be like someday. We've all seen the Sugarplum solo so many times now that we've learned some of the steps—we actually try to do them, downstairs while we're waiting. In fact, we do that a lot . . .

She's done—applause—that means it's our time! Okay, we've got to hurry up and make sure we're lined up in the right order for our entrance. I want to rush to the edge of the wing and be ready to go, but there are all these other dancers that go on before us, so as awful as it feels, we have to stand back. But as soon as the Sugarplum gestures to the first group of dancers to run onstage and greet her, everyone moves really quickly, and it happens so fast: in a millisecond, I'm out here under the lights. The music is so loud it vibrates in my chest, and the audience is so real I can feel them breathing, and I am *performing*—this is IT—and it feels somehow like being more alive than life itself. I'm here, onstage, right next to dozens of real, true, professional dancers—amazing dancers, the best in the world—right next to them! And it doesn't matter that I'm just a kid—I'm a Polichinelle, and Mr. Balanchine put us in this ballet because he thought we were just as important as everyone else. This is my world—our world—the real world. I'm home.

Not long after my first Nutcracker season, I was cast as a bug in New York City Ballet's production of A Midsummer Night's Dream. We child-bugs were meticulously rehearsed with no concession given to how young we were, just as we had been for our Polichinelle roles. We took our responsibility as seriously as the professional adult dancers

*with whom we shared the stage. And at last I was up there onstage
again, standing in my bug pose, watching the curtain rise. Hearing the
orchestra play Mendelssohn's soul-stirring, heart-wrenching overture
for the first time, I thought there could be no better place in the world
than right there, right then. The music was so elating, I thought I might
actually lift off and take flight. Thank goodness I had steps to dance
that gave me an outlet for that magnificent feeling.*

11

Waving Goodbye

By this time, the thirteen-year-old was in pure heaven: she had class every day of the week except Sunday. Now that she was in the higher of the two intermediate levels, her weekday classes were, on certain days, not until the late afternoon, leaving her time to go home after school instead of straight to ballet. The walk from school to home was short, fifteen minutes at most, and the route was as familiar as the inside of the apartment where she'd grown up and her family still lived. She'd walked that pathway twice a day for nine years: to the corner of Ninety-Ninth Street, down Broadway to Ninety-Fourth, left and uphill to Columbus Avenue, and then either straight ahead another half block to the lower school entrance or a right turn to Ninety-Third Street, left toward Central Park West and the upper school. And then, of course, the reverse on the way home.

The landmarks changed over the years, some of them, but many remained: the bodega where she and her best school pal, in the years before her rush to make it to ballet class made her scurry on by, stopped for Twinkies; the brownstone with soft green moss growing on its front steps; the housing project and its strangely institutional facade; the pizzeria; the old man sitting on a patio chair on the sidewalk in front of his apartment building with his two little dogs, taking in the afternoon sun.

She'd tripped and fallen on the uneven sidewalk here and there, scraped her knees and braced against fierce cold winds in the winter, pulled off sweatshirts and windbreakers and tied them around her waist on the first warm days of spring, swung her knapsack full of textbooks from shoulder to shoulder.

Before she was old enough to make the trip alone, her dad walked her to and from school. The weight of students' book bags was, at that time, a big issue with the PTA, and her dad in particular couldn't bear the sight of his little daughter listing to the left or right with a huge sack off one shoulder (balancing a backpack as it was meant to be worn was very, very uncool). He'd always take her bag from her and sling it over his own shoulder as they walked side by side and talked about this or that, usually about the sights they were seeing along the way, stopping to pet the moss and check on the newly planted flowers in one brownstone's front box. When she was very young, well before homework or after-school ballet was a factor, there was often a stop at the long, narrow coffee shop just around the corner from home. Whether the stop was a treat for her or a needed break for her dad, she didn't consider until much later, but at the time it was just regular. Plain days meant a small cup of orange juice for her and coffee with milk for her dad while they sat on swivel stools at the counter (no tables in this sliver of real estate), watching the gruff, short-order cooks work the flattop grill right in front of them. She saw how they scooped hash browns with a spatula, fried eggs, burgers, and bacon, dipped baskets of potatoes into the fryer full of hot oil over and over again. Everything was cooked on that griddle, and everything smelled, deliciously, of grease. The doughnuts, though, were at the front of the shop, just inside the front door and visible from the street, three or four sloped tiers of trays full of different varieties. The sugary smell competed with the savory greasy one, but to her senses, they ended up melding nicely.

Some days, their orange juice and coffee were accompanied by a plain, cake doughnut, a small, perfectly round one with a dryish, powdery and cinnamony coating and an even drier crumbly inside. She loved the dryness, how the cake sort of became chewy in her mouth and wasn't very sweet. They shared it, cut up into bite-size pieces with a knife and eaten with forks.

On special days (which she never knew were coming or what made them special), her dad ordered her a Coke, which came in a wider, taller plastic cup, with crushed ice, than orange juice did—AND her choice of doughnut. She always got a bowtie. An airy, fluffy-inside and sugar-iced outside, figure eight–shaped thing that left her fingers and face sticky, clumps of iced sugar clinging to her lips.

At thirteen, coming home after school was just a quick stop to drop off her school bag, fill her ballet bag with slippers, pointe shoes, lamb-swool, extra hairnets and hairpins, hair spray and a navy chiffon skirt, and change into her navy blue leotard (the dress code for her level) and pink tights. She put her jeans back on over her tights and a sweatshirt over her top, so as soon as she'd arrive at the ballet school, she could quickly strip down and be ready for class.

There wasn't much time, but there was enough—and her dad wouldn't let her go otherwise—for something to eat. Changing clothes down the hall in her room, she smelled melting butter, reminiscent of the coffee shop. Ready for class, she came out to the kitchen to watch him lay two slices of American cheese onto buttered bread, slide it into a greased frying pan and top it with another piece of Home Pride Wheat. They watched until a peek underneath showed the perfect shade of golden brown, and Dad expertly flipped the sandwich over. Little trickles of melted cheese started to ooze from in between the bread slices. Done. She ate at the kitchen table, gooey bites of grilled cheese and toasty bread. Time to go.

Dad walked her downstairs to the bus stop and they stood waiting for the M104 to take her straight down Broadway to Sixty-Sixth Street. Here it came. Not too crowded today, easy to find a window seat. *Have a good class,* Dad said, and waved his arm high as the bus pulled away.

Early one Saturday morning, she arrived early for class. No one else was in the studio yet, and the hallways were empty except for a couple of older students stretching silently in their wool leg warmers and a receptionist still flipping on light switches and unlocking doors. The heat had not come up yet, and sitting on the cold black tiles of the hallway floor, she shivered in her little leotard and tights. She stood up and pushed open the enormous, heavy black door into the studio where class would be held.

Inside the studio was hazy, lit only by daylight from the windows up near the towering ceiling. The door slowly whooshed closed with a click as it latched. She felt like a mite sealed inside a huge, glass-covered box, seeing only sky through those high windows. All sounds from outside were dampened. Sealed off from the outside world, it was a secret moment to have the vast, treasured studio space all to herself. Freedom to fly with only the walls, barres, and well-danced-on floor to witness. She did soaring grand jetés, over and over again, from corner to corner, bursting out of her skin, truly feeling flight until she was gasping for breath—and then the door cracked open, other students peeked in, and she pulled herself back down to earth. Soon, class started, at the barre, in first position, with minute precision.

12

Detective Work

The class exercises became, increasingly, devilishly hard, not just on one day but every day thereafter. They were more challenging than the nearly fourteen-year-old had ever imagined they could be. But—in increments so tiny she was oblivious to them—she started to get stronger, more pliable, and more sure of herself. She analyzed the other girls in her classes, not with judgment but with the eye of a detective searching for clues. *Her legs are long, her feet look nice, her jump is high, her arabesque is so smooth. . . .* She analyzed her own equipment, too, also without judgment, introducing herself to every inch of her body's lines, every degree of movement in her joints. But she was unable to settle for its being, or doing, anything less than the ideal. And now, as she learned what that model of perfection looked like, she also began to discover how it could feel.

Occasionally, pointing her foot as hard as she could, examining and scrutinizing her arch in the mirror, she thought it looked all right. Stretching to create that look was addictively satisfying. *Very* occasionally—pulling her leg behind her, reaching it farther and farther away, sucking her belly button to her backbone, lifting her chest to the sky, and then glancing at the mirror across the room—she caught a glimpse of an arabesque like the one she'd seen in the photographs of famous dancers. One day, gluing her feet into fifth position with such fierce determination she thought she would explode, her double pirouettes took off and landed with an ease and control that shocked her. It was as if another being had taken hold of her insides and was working the controls instead of her. There was a momentary touch of pride as others noticed what she'd done, but then she got self-conscious. *I didn't really do that, it wasn't really ME—but what was it?*

13

Stretching

The now fourteen-year-old had discovered how to stretch. A startling observation one day that her friends could do the splits more easily than she could alarmed and unnerved her. At home one night, before bed, she anchored one foot on the edge of the waist-high dresser in her room and started bending and straightening her leg, bending forward with each straightening to bring her nose to her knee. It felt good. Her nose came closer to her knee, and closer. And the next day in Madame Dudin's ballet class, having forgotten all about last night's experiment, her legs went higher than before, felt easier to lift, and were happier to be stretched in an arabesque. Such freedom! Like her hamstrings had been unlocked and her hip joints released from a cage.

Madame Dudin tottered around the room, moving from student to student, as the fourteen-year-old and her classmates strained to hold their legs and backs, interminably, through an adagio exercise. The one moment of respite was a huge *attitude derrière*, a position that the fourteen-year-old couldn't see herself do in the mirror but somewhat enjoyed—she had the sense of her leg fitting perfectly into her back, her knee lifted right up to her shoulder, her neck and foot arching together, arm curved to match the line of her torso, her face inclined, her eyes open and bright.

Later that afternoon, as the fourteen-year-old was awkwardly slurping at the hallway water fountain, there was a feathery tap on her shoulder. Madame Dudin had silently tiptoed up behind her.

You take such nice steps in class. Very good girl.

14

The Fifteen-Year-Old and Mr. Rapp

He had a mustache, a coffee mug, and a pack of Halls cough drops. His entrance was businesslike and purposeful, yet not rushed, and always exactly the same. He'd pad through the studio door in his soft white jazz shoes, plain black trousers, and knit polo shirt with an upturned collar and walk directly to the piano, which was also his desk, or cubby, or coffee table. Peeking around the room from behind his mug, he surveyed the teenagers standing ready at barres lining the walls. He swiftly unwrapped the white tennis sweater from around his shoulders, folded it loosely, and heaped it on the piano's lid. After a few muted pleasantries with the pianist (he was politely mannered with all of the accompanists), Mr. Rapp covertly popped a Halls lozenge into his mouth and cleared his throat. It was time for class to begin. The fifteen-year-old, one of two dozen eager, ambitious girls in level six, was ready. She was ready to try, yet again, as she'd done yesterday and as she would tomorrow, to understand what Mr. Rapp wanted and to get it right.

The fifteen-year-old was fascinated by Mr. Rapp and hung on his words. He interested her because he seemed, despite his plain, even-keeled Midwestern exterior, to be a bit mysterious, even secretive. There had to be something colorful behind his reserved speech, conservative clothes suitable for a Florida country club, and poker-faced demeanor. She couldn't stop trying to imagine what his life was like—his *real* life, the one he led before and after he taught ballet classes at the School. Where did he live? What did he have for breakfast, for dinner? Who were his friends, and what did they talk about? Mr. Rapp's teaching was so matter-of-fact, so organized and assured that it clearly came to him with no effort, leading the fifteen-year-old to speculate that he must have an outside life completely unrelated to ballet. She pictured gatherings, like retirees' weekly bridge games, or golf—but for some reason she hoped he gambled at cards and occasionally stayed up late, if only to prove that a quiet person could be daring, too.

She also felt drawn to Mr. Rapp because his personality, and hers, were perfectly aligned. He was firm and direct, but not overbearing, and, without any of the tactics or histrionics or volume that were so expected in other teachers' classes, his messages to the fifteen-year-old got right through: *Separate your fingers. And curve your neck.*

There was a lot more, of course, that Mr. Rapp taught during a year's worth of classes. One day, the students stood in fifth position in center, ready to repeat the adagio exercise for the second time through. The pianist played the four-count introduction, but Mr. Rapp stopped her before the row of teenagers in front of him had barely even moved.

Go back to fifth. Tighter. More crossed. Hold it. Now, begin the développé—*without moving your back foot. DO NOT LET IT GO.* The fifteen-year-old, and possibly others in the class, instantly learned the most basic of lessons, one that should have been instilled years before but somehow hadn't been. *Never let your turnout go. Never relax it. The leg you stand on has to be the strongest one, and turnout is strength.*

And then, he pointed at the fifteen-year-old. *Try it.* Concentrating only on her back leg, the one that needed to be like the trunk of an oak tree, while she drew her other foot up her shin, past her knee, and extended it high in front of her nose, the fifteen-year-old drilled her turnout muscles into the floor and, astonishingly, felt the oak tree's sturdiness—and saw her front leg floating lightly into the air.

All right. Now, curve your neck.

It was never-ending, Mr. Rapp's quest to get the fifteen-year-old to bend. She was reedy at that age, long-torsoed, long-necked, long-fingered. Even her toes were unusually long—sometimes she thought they looked like frogs' toes. But lengthy extremities and appendages—hers, particularly—make long, subtle curves, not the tightly arched, exciting shapes that were considered the most aesthetically interesting.

For years, going back to her days as an eleven-year-old, she'd been trying to hold on—extra tight, extra hard, to get the firmest grip and farthest reach she could on these impossible-feeling ballet positions. She felt she was still making up for some unknown information she'd missed by stumbling into the wrong class that very first day as an eight-year-old, into a level advanced beyond her. So she grasped, almost desperately, with every muscle she could find and every one she could control. And she did advance and did get stronger. But she was, at the age of fifteen, only able to be strong in one solid piece, making her entire body sturdy as if bracing herself against hurricane-force winds.

Yet, of course, dancing is about movement. The tree that survives the hurricane is the one that bends with the wind. Earthquake-proof skyscrapers have flexible steel beams. The dancer with control, with speed, with precision, with expansive freedom, is the one who can both hold on and let go, at the same exact time.

And the very first step, for the fifteen-year-old, was learning to let go of the weight of her head, allowing it to be off center, tilting her cheek slightly upward, as if asking for Grandma's kiss, and curving her neck.

Mr. Rapp's cues—several times per class—to do this, his demonstrations and explanations and analogies, weren't easy for the fifteen-year-old. Her balance felt more controlled with her head neatly centered on top of her body, no matter if it looked rigid. Equally persistent were his patient, calm, often wordless corrections on the placement of her fingers and the shape of her hands. Time after time, week after week after week, as he softly moved—almost floated—around the studio, making adjustments and murmuring directions in an unexcitable, placidly determined tone of voice, he stopped in front of the fifteen-year-old. Paused the entire class to fix her hands, precisely arranging the curve of each finger and its exact spacing from the others, angling her thumb to reach gently away from her palm. He painstakingly sculpted her hands and told her to memorize the shape. Finger muscle memory.

It wasn't hard for the fifteen-year-old to accept the importance of such details, but her brain was preoccupied with her legs, her feet, her back, her turnout—she was already multitasking and barely keeping up. It took a year. A full year of near daily admonitions, reminders, explanations and, demonstrations over and over again. Her hands learned, like a dog learning a trick, what to do when given a command to "separate"—her fingers and thumbs would bloom into the delicate flowerlike shape Mr. Rapp was cultivating—but they could not, exasperatingly for both the fifteen-year-old and Mr. Rapp, stay there on their own. The commands, though, gradually became quicker and quieter. A word instead of a phrase, a nod instead of a word. She was almost there, almost had her fingers trained to stay put even when her active thoughts turned to *grands battements* and *tour jetés*. Mr. Rapp suggested that practicing in class was not enough.

Walk down the street with your fingers separated. And never wear mittens. Imagine you have a fresh manicure and are letting the nail polish dry.

This was the kind of project she really liked. It made her feel as though she had a secret from the rest of the world, just between her and Mr. Rapp—something that she held in plain view but that only the two of them could understand. She walked down the street, waited for the bus, rode in the elevator, all the while sculpting her hands and separating her fingers.

It worked.

———————————

Years later, memories of Mr. Rapp came flooding back when a choreographer said to her, moments before the curtain went up on the premiere of his ballet: "Pretend you have a fresh manicure. Use your hands like your nails are wet with polish, and you are letting each finger dry in the air."

15

The Sixteen-Year-Old's Epiphany, Part 1

The sixteen-year-old knew that the way she had just danced was not quite right. She knew because the reaction she got from her teacher—a perky, curly-haired former dancer whose thoughts came out in her gestures more than in her words—pushed what had been a deep down, gut-level unease way up into her throat.

She, the sixteen-year-old, had been cast to perform a solo variation in the School's upcoming year-end showcase. Rehearsals, which had begun months ago, were fraught with anxiety. Envy, outright jealousy, and competition made the air in the dressing room, hallways, and studios thick and tense. The stakes were high. The students analyzed the casting of every role, from the leads to the ensemble, with the depth and detail of a science project, trying to discern which of their peers were thought most highly of. Who were the favorites, the most promising, the ones with the rosiest futures? They dug for meaning in every decision.

But at this moment, despite the relative self-confidence she gained from having been cast in a solo, the sixteen-year-old felt mediocre. She knew she was a good student. She worked hard, was responsible and sensible and smart, had a strong body with at least a few enviable balletic qualities. All this must have meant she had a certain level of talent, putting her somewhere in the upper-middle of the pack. She was always in class, always knew the exercises and never did anything wrong, but . . .

But there was a dark cloud. For some time, it had been hovering off to one side, slowly growing in mass and density. She'd felt it there but tried to ignore it. And now, it moved in with an undeniable presence.

It had been nicer, and easier, to prance around under a pale blue sky without doing much real thinking—or questioning. It had been nicer not doing much more than what came naturally and was familiar, regular, and fun. Go to class obediently, every day, along with your friends. Know what's right and wrong, in general, and strive for the same things everyone else does—higher leg extensions, more turnout, pointier feet, more flexible limbs. It turned out, however, that there was more to be learned about dancing than the things most teenage ballet students fixated on and obsessed over. This was the fact that the sixteen-year-old had somehow sensed and had subconsciously pushed aside. It seemed too vague and amorphous—and too risky—for an adolescent girl whose strongest need was to conform.

Along with the Curly-Haired Teacher, another teacher in the School had tried, hard, to show the sixteen-year-old that there was more, so much more—what it meant, and what it took, to be better than mediocre—and that sixteen was much too young an age to be complacent already. This particular teacher always wore bright, shimmery unitards in pastel colors, sometimes with a flowered chiffon skirt over the top, but unlike the Curly-Haired Teacher, whose reaction on that fateful day would rock the sixteen-year-old to her core, this Pastel Teacher's manner was more reserved, matter-of-fact, and direct. The sixteen-year-old listened obediently and thought she understood, but sometimes being a model student is not helpful. Having always been praised for being correct, proper, precise, for following directions exactly, she did not comprehend that the Pastel Teacher's attention to her was not merely an affirmation of her talent. It was that, but it was also a push. A challenge. It was an open door, with an invitation to walk through it into the *real* world of dancing, where a person—even a sixteen-year-old person—could start to learn how to become an artist. It was an attempt to inspire her to be something she didn't already know.

But the sixteen-year-old ignored the signals and hints. The corrections she got—to do steps a little differently, more energetically, to dance more expansively, to bend farther and throw caution away—became urgings and even pleadings. She, the obedient sixteen-year-old, *did* do those things when she was specifically asked to, but then she went right back to her old normal ways, sticking with what felt safe. And eventually, the Pastel Teacher either gave up or needed to take a break. She stepped away and let the sixteen-year-old continue alone down her predictable path, perhaps hoping she'd see how gray it was and turn back.

The sixteen-year-old noticed, of course, that something had changed. The Pastel Teacher's interest in her was suddenly diminished—there were no more individual corrections in class—and although she still lived for classes each week (the exercises were fun, with lots of big expansive steps that compelled the students to fly across the floor, eating up the space and soaring on top of music), the sixteen-year-old felt a chill, as if she had done something wrong or offensive but didn't quite know what. At first, the thrill of having a solo role to learn comforted her—maybe this sudden disinterest was just a mirage, a trick her mind was playing on her. But it wasn't. And, finally, today, with the dismissiveness of the Curly-Haired Teacher, her noncommittal comments and quick gesture brushing the sixteen-year-old aside as soon as she finished dancing, all these were undeniable. They were louder than any harsh words that could have been said. Being uninteresting was worse than being wrong.

The Pastel Teacher had been watching from the doorway. Rehearsal continued, and she disappeared down the hall.

16

The Sixteen-Year-Old's Epiphany, Part 2

Soon after that unsettling and disorienting moment, rehearsal ended and classes were finished for the day. The studios emptied out. As the confused, dejected sixteen-year-old made her way to the locker room, the Pastel Teacher waylaid her in the hall. *What are you doing right now? Come here for a minute.*

Having a feeling that this might be more important than the dentist appointment she was supposed to be headed for, the sixteen-year-old followed. Suddenly they were alone, the two of them, in the largest of the School's grand studios.

Without any music, the Pastel Teacher took the sixteen-year-old through her solo, step-by-step, moment-by-moment, piece-by-tiny-little-nuanced-piece. The Pastel Teacher had patience but made it clear that this was it: the sixteen-year-old's last chance to get serious and either make something of her dancing potential or just coast along in the sea of mediocrity. There was no more time to waste.

Take off those silly, ridiculous warm-up shorts—you have a beautiful body, why cover yourself up? And the epiphany began.

One detail at a time, the Pastel Teacher explained every arm gesture, head placement, and foot articulation. How to angle her body differently to create a more interesting shape (echoes of Mr. Rapp's admonitions to "curve your neck" rang in her ears). How to lift her arms higher in order to accent her jumps, and how to relax her elbows so she didn't look stiff like a scarecrow. Why bending at her waist before a soutenu turn would link the preceding steps smoothly together. Most of all, she needed to *give* more. Give more energy, attack, more life, more bravery. To dance with her brain instead of just her body. These were all things she—the Pastel Teacher—had tried, time and again, to get the sixteen-year-old to do. In class, so many precious minutes spent showing her how to do these exact things, which had then seemed vague or scary, or even silly. But now she saw how to really *use* them, in real choreography, not just routine classroom exercises, and a breathtakingly cold burst of air hit her in the face. This was what real dancing was.

It was finally clear to her that she had two choices, and that they really weren't choices at all. One was incomprehensible and absolutely unacceptable, because it would indicate that she had failed at, or given up, something that she had declared to be her life's passion. And the other— the inevitable, only path she could take—was what she'd always known was her destiny, what she was born and made to do, even before she knew what "it" was. Her innate stubbornness—one of her most valuable assets—had been temporarily lulled into a confused teenage ambivalence, but now it was back full force.

Knowing that she had backed down the moment the Curly-Haired Teacher showed doubt, that those suspicions of mediocrity could conceivably have been proven true, was, after the initial sickening feeling of horror, infuriating to the sixteen-year-old. Plus, it would be, it *was*, embarrassing to submit to a label of mediocrity when she was surrounded by prodigious talent. There were dozens of girls in the School who were already in line for success—*NO!* She wanted to scream. The dancer-beast stuffed down inside her came roaring out. She would let it push her, now, but also train it, watch it grow, and ride it for the rest of her life.

17

Tumey

No wrinkles in your leotard, she barks. *No wrinkles!*

Take an impossible directive and make it happen. There's nothing weird about that. Nothing irrational. Just make it happen. Do it.

She—Madame Tumkovsky—is, in a way, a beast tamer. She has a herd of hardworking animals, well-made, well-meaning, very eager to please, very young. They reflexively follow commands. They think for themselves, a little bit, though the real Thinking comes later.

The herd, however, shape-shifts when she is not present. They start out in human form (a gaggle of teenage girls, sprawled around on the studio floor, chatting, primping, stretching in pools of sunlight from the way-up-high windows). Out of her presence, they even affectionately nickname their fearsome leader "Tumey" and anticipate the painful drills about to come their way with a mixture of trepidation, acceptance, determination, and camaraderie. But—since they can sense her approach from well down the corridor—they are never caught off their feet. In an instant, and in communal silence, the girls effortlessly spring up from their lounging and are lined up in formation at the barre, in uniform, as if they'd been standing at attention for Madame Tumkovsky all morning.

Her outward appearance is stern, though there are accents of lightness. She dresses in all black, but there is a colorfully patterned silk scarf draped across her shoulders like a shawl. Perhaps it's a keepsake from Russia, the home she fled decades ago? She's rotund and walks with a limp, but the cane in her hand seems as much a warning as an aid and is often used as a tool to clear a path through the crowded lobby or point out something (or someone) across the room, as if it were an extension of her index finger. Her face is small, with distinct features as sharp as she is fiery. But she wears bright red lipstick, and her eyes, which are icy blue and deeply set, sparkle.

She knows that her dancers-in-training are hanging on her every word (though those words are often very hard to understand, owing to her thick accent). She utters her commands in fragmented phrases, rarely in a voice lower than a half-yell. When she becomes very tired from many hours of teaching, or when leading a class of much older, seasoned students who know her exercises inside out, her tone occasionally slips to a murmur, almost as if she is communing with them. But in every class there is a sort of secret dialect, unrecognizable to an outsider, that bonds Madame Tumkovsky and her followers.

She also knows that her silence is as powerful as her commands, so as she enters and makes her ungainly, erratic way across the length of the studio, she eyes the girls lined up at the barres and exchanges a few words in Russian with the pianist, her compatriot. She lets the anticipatory air in the room hang for a moment, emphasizing the contrast between that stillness and what is about to come, and then unleashes a madcap ninety-minute boot camp/ballet class with one bark and a terse gesture. Everyone knows what to do. Giving further instructions only wastes time.

Every exercise is fast, even the adagios, but because of their speed, there is time to do them multiple times over during the span of class. Barre work is over in twenty-three minutes, half the time of a regular class, but contains 50 percent more exercises and three times as much sweat.

She's not modern and doesn't know or care that in America teachers aren't supposed to have favorites. All she wants is for her girls to become full-fledged dancing machines—pristinely tuned, hyper precise, supremely strong, sinewy as racehorses that could do anything asked of them and more. Anything less is pointless, a waste. Strength-building is the foundation of her methodology. Follow her instructions, do not deviate from them, overrule your body's pleas to rest, and you will grow into a product of which Madame Tumkovsky is proud, and your legs will be supremely muscular.

Certain students take naturally to this training, or almost, but for most others it is a massive struggle. To focus hard enough to keep jumping when the lungs and legs burn, to have the mental and physical will to prove wrong Madame Tumkovsky's expectation that you will fail or give up, takes a defiance of human nature and (this is not an exaggeration) the inner strength of a Navy SEAL. The brain must be stronger than the body will eventually become. These young innocents aren't beasts or racehorses at first; they are otherwise average teenage girls. But a few of them do have stubbornly militaristic mindsets. And those are the ones that can be spotted by Madame Tumkovsky's icy blue eyes as she surveys the room and limps across the floor.

With time and perseverance, and likely a few tears of frustration and agony, those few stubborn minds will eventually notice that their legs and arms, feet and backs, have become accustomed to being challenged like this so frequently. They're used to it, though not complacent in the least (for Madame Tumkovsky sees when that starts to happen and demands an even higher level of difficulty), but they grow familiar enough with the dialect and rhythm of the hour-and-a-half-long drill cycle that they can, and maybe do, let their mind's focus drift, ever so slightly, one tiny second during the entire length of class. Perhaps it is a moment of confidence or pride, a brief reflection on how far one has come and excitement at how much has been achieved, or just pure exhaustion—mental as much as physical.

The lapse might not show, but if it does, it will appear as a misplaced arm at the end of an exercise, or fifteen tendus instead of sixteen, a foot placed in *coup de pied* rather than the slightly different *sur le coup de pied* position, a balance released a moment too soon, or the omission of the final pose after a series of turns. Any of these would be huge errancies to Madame Tumkovsky, almost as huge as stopping in the middle of an exercise—the most egregious and appalling act of all.

Today, it was winter, it was cold outside, it was midway through the school year. There were no sunny patches on the floor before class in which to warm up, and some moods were dark as well. In this class (the middle level of the three advanced divisions), most had been studying with Madame Tumkovsky for only a few months, maybe a year or two at most. The prestige of this school drew advanced students who were talented enough to move to New York after getting their elementary training elsewhere. The top levels were predominantly composed of students from other states, and even other countries, while the beginner and intermediate classes were mostly full of New York–area kids. Only a few of those persevered through the ranks and reached the advanced classes. They caught on fast but still had all their senses on high alert to catch, interpret, and execute Madame Tumkovsky's cues as fast as possible so as to avoid the startlingly loud yells that could emanate from this small woman. A few of the teenagers, though, maybe two or three, had been with her for years—essentially grown up under her eyes—and were approaching, perhaps, the level of being called examples of her method's success.

And one of them lapsed.

She ended a barre exercise in a position unlike everyone else's, not out of deliberate defiance or inability but merely from a momentary slip of concentration, from complacency, from mental weariness at putting up such a fight on such a dark day. From a flash of angry obstinance at *having* to put up such a struggle, day after day, year after year.

WHAT YOU DO!?!?!? WHY YOU NOT TAKE STEPS LIKE OTHER GIRLS!?!?

Normally, a tirade would stop there, the object of it withered and remorseful, Madame Tumkovsky turning away with a dismissive wave of the hand and a scornful comment in Russian to herself or the pianist, then the resumption of class. But this time, maybe Madame Tumkovsky herself was feeling dark and especially obstinate and saw this moment of laziness as a challenge. Or maybe, just maybe, she was truly, genuinely disappointed. Maybe she was saddened that this one girl, who had been learning to hold her leg in développé for impossible lengths since she was eleven and who had previously satisfied Madame Tumkovsky by jumping with the stamina of a marathoner and the spring of a gymnast, had slipped. Maybe she saw it as an example of a general malaise throughout the class, or the School, or the youth of this generation. Maybe it reminded her of how easily standards could be allowed to erode, and her own fiery stubbornness was stoked—the future of ballet was dependent on each and every exercise in class, and there would be no complacency on her watch.

Whatever the reason, the tirade was violent and did not stop. It went on and on, barely understandable through Madame Tumkovsky's fury. There were references to how long the Lapser had studied at the School, why she should know better, how terrible an example she was, and much more. The One Who Had Lapsed became unhinged but did not cave in. Eyes filling and then overflowing with tears, she stood straight and strong and didn't look away. Did not breathe. Her face was as sturdy as she could make it, despite the redness and wetness. And she waited.

Finally, Madame Tumkovsky grunted at the pianist to continue. The teenagers, all stunned by this exceptional display, meekly turned to complete the exercise they'd been halfway through. Class continued, and the tears ebbed and flowed as the Lapser wavered from indignant, to fearful—had she permanently fallen from grace?—to embarrassed.

The humiliation turned into determination and won out over the rest.

Ready, now, to prove Madame Tumkovsky wrong, a sort of superhuman strength came into her. She almost literally growled. She hit every exercise as if it was a punching bag and took a sick pleasure in how painful those punches were. Nuclear energy propelled her, and she kicked fatigue aside by speeding up even more.

Madame Tumkovsky, still on fire herself, challenged the One Who Had Lapsed with her eyes, waiting to see how she would react, how she would continue—if she would pass the test.

Perched on her chair in the front of the studio, smack in the center of the long mirror lining the wall, her head and eyes directed straight ahead, she slyly watched the Teenager Who Had Lapsed and who was now busting out of her skin with furiously red-hot technical prowess.

Class was at its end.

Tumey nodded.

Good.

18

Making Shapes

Not long after she'd lapsed in Madame Tumkovsky's class, the teenager found herself, on another gray, cold, dreary weekday morning, frustrated and grumpy. The Curly-Haired Teacher was leading class that day, but her spritely, bright, pixie-like appearance and demeanor weren't encouraging to the teenager. She still had the sense that she wasn't fitting into the mold and that she couldn't fit into it, ever. She felt mad. Mad at her body for not having the shape she wanted.

The Curly-Haired Teacher was upbeat, but she was always that way. The teenager knew, now, that underneath her niceness was a strict, practical, unrelenting analysis of which students "had it" and which didn't. If you "had it," the training was just a matter of refinement. If you didn't, you were welcome to learn just like everyone else, but your innate building blocks were only very slightly malleable. Your eagerness might be appreciated and rewarded, but the real prize was out of reach.

There were favorites in the classes, no denying it, and the girls all knew who they were. Amazingly, the favorites were not only the "perfect" physical specimens—some of those with drool-worthy bodies weren't among that group. There was Joy, for example, and also Elizabeth.

Elizabeth was a beautiful girl. Her prettiness was the gentle, blue-eyed and rosy-cheeked farm girl kind. She never used hair spray, so her wavy blonde hair was fuzzy even when pulled into a bun. She was sweet in voice and personality, loved animals, and had gorgeously arched feet. She carried an LL Bean tote as her dance bag, never wore makeup, and liked to snack on organic granola.

She didn't have, aside from those lovely arches, a great body for ballet. In fact, it was a hard one to work with. Her torso was long in relation to her legs, which didn't have much natural rotation in the hip joints, therefore limiting not only her ability to turn out but also to get her legs up very high in extensions. But, somehow . . . every shape she made, every position she assumed, was beautiful. Just visually lovely and pleasing, like a Rodin sculpture or Impressionist painting. The teachers loved her and gave her much attention in class and lead roles in the ballets they cast. She worked very, very hard, and during class, her rosy cheeks would get rosier and rosier, adding to her adorableness. She could do things well, technically, but it was her presence that was so captivating, not her legs, feet, or pirouettes.

On this day, the teenager (still brimming with fire from the sting of the day she'd lapsed in Tumey's class) watched, along with everyone else, while the Curly-Haired Teacher used Elizabeth to demonstrate a correction she was trying to explain to the class.

Even with less-than-full turnout and an only moderately high développé, Elizabeth looked, well, just magnetic. She somehow exuded an aura. Of peace, of happiness, of completion. Elizabeth was trying, and trying hard, and knew what she lacked, but she didn't hate herself for it. She didn't strain to make herself something she wasn't. Instead, she inhabited her own shape.

The teenager stared and made a decision. Why couldn't she do that, too?

19

Crumpled

What made this particular episode so jarring to me was that as a seventeen-year-old student, I had not yet tripped over the line where conviction and determination meet physical reality. It was the third of three performances of our graduation showcase at the School, a prestigious event that was seen as the world's chance to spot tomorrow's potential stars, and I was flying high on the thrill, the buzz, the excitement all around. The year before, through my own complacency and blindness, I'd nearly lost my chance at my dream, but now I had worked my way back, proven I was more than average. I had a leading role and was a star for the night. My adrenaline must have been pumping since ten o'clock that morning, and by the time I got onstage it's no wonder my youthful legs, coltishly strong but clueless and giddy, gave out. Poor things were just plain old tuckered out, like a little kid who's played too hard and falls asleep in their dinner plate. I was met with sympathy all around afterward, of course, and attempts to boost my devastated ego, but none matched what was in the paper the next day. A mention in the New York Times, which noted that George Balanchine famously approved of a dancer's fall, for it showed energy, verve, and total commitment. Those I had, certainly. But now I also had fear of weakness and the disturbing knowledge that I could not always control my body. The shock of the moment etched it on my brain with a clarity and realism that endures to this day. This, I know for sure, was me.

It happened absolutely out of the blue. Everything was going just fine—I was dancing, breathing, moving my way through the perfectly choreographed steps with joy and the strangely normal sense of being slightly outside of my own body. That's what happens during the rush of a live performance, but this was an intensified experience: I was only seventeen years old, dancing my first principal role. And there I was. I'd clawed my way to the top of the class from the middle of the pack in my last year of schooling and somehow found myself center stage, under a spotlight, in a stylish sequin-covered demi-tutu and pointe shoes, dancing the work of George Balanchine to the music of George Gershwin in one of Balanchine's most famous and crowd-pleasing ballets, *Who Cares?* Six months of rehearsal had led to this moment.

As I calibrated every muscle fiber's contraction and coordinated them from the farthest reaches of one extremity to the other—literally, from tip to toe—I felt as if I were occupying a thin shell around my own physique, perhaps because of being so utterly inside it. There was no buffer zone between me and the abyss, no safety rail, and absolutely no holding back. That is the only way to perform—to dance with your truest heart means to balance on pointe on the thinnest razor's edge. Only technique, grace, and sheer trust keep you from falling.

But then, with no warning, my legs crumpled underneath me, buckling like the legs of a card table with flimsy hinges, and I collapsed in a heap on the stage. Momentarily, I was out of control. To go from sixty to zero in no time flat is shock-inducing. Thoughts do not have time to come into play. Reflex and instinct dictated what happened next, which was that I popped up and stepped right into my role again, back into the groove. My legs were heavy now, though, my muscles spent from the panic of trying to save myself and straining to the extreme in the moment of terror.

Now I was distracted, my sense of automatic control over my body shattered. My brain was in chaos, unsure of what had happened and what to do next, a confused tangle of commands and reflexes. All I could feel was the heaviness of my thigh muscles, overly contracted and completely maxed out. There was nothing more for them to give, having already been pushed to their limit and gone into overdrive. The stage floor was sucking me down like quicksand. Gravity's force shackled me with ankle weights, but I kept trying to jump, to finish my solo's last sequence of sissones and grand saut de basques, spinning leaps that were meant to look insouciantly gleeful and sassy.

I made it almost to the end, took one large step that was just too deep for my poor legs to handle, and stumbled to the floor yet again. This time, the audience gasped and I could hear them. There was also a perceptible, sympathetic sigh. Pity filled the auditorium. Those are comforting sentiments, but they made me mad. I was harshly snatched back from the threshold of artistry. Pulled down to earth with a stern reminder that I was still a kid and everyone knew it.

I did finish the solo. The conductor never stopped the orchestra, of course, but even if the music had silenced I would have kept stumbling my way through to the final pose. The applause, then, was a human response, not an otherworldly one. I had become normal, mortal in the audience's eyes. Was that slightly satisfying to them, in a strange way even reassuring? To have watched a daredevil young dancer teeter on her way toward professionalism, testing the limits she didn't yet know were there, and then get rocked back into the world they could relate to—error-prone, clumsy humanity—must have eased a small fear that the child they saw onstage had been about to actually, possibly, potentially, touch the sun.

My falls, maybe, reminded them—and taught me—that boundaries crop up where moments before there'd been nothing but open space. That electric fences might stun you for exploring. But dance on over the line anyway and expand beyond the borders of your own skin. Let your muscles recover, and you'll find your edge once again.

20

Turning Point

Just a couple of months before, in early spring, the day that the teenager had marked on her calendar arrived. She was in her senior year of high school. It was time to get a job.

She had been training for nine years, seven of them at the School of American Ballet. Somewhere along the way, it just became a known fact: she was going to be a dancer, a professional one, and that was that. There was no moment of decision-making, no heart-to-heart discussion with her parents (though surely they'd had several of those on their own, full of the common and reasonable worries parents should have about a child wanting the life of a professional artist). Later on, people inevitably asked, "Why did you decide to be a dancer? When did you decide?" She never had a satisfying answer. She couldn't even recall a moment for herself when she knew; it had sort of evolved and swelled, like a gradual change of the seasons, or like the dawn breaking. The inevitability of the thing was there, growing bigger and closer; it curved into existence. There's no sharp corner to turn. The closer you get, the more clear it is you're not going back and there's only one place to end up.

Along the way, though, there *had* been some corners. Looking back on her journey, years later, she realized that her childhood *Nutcracker* and *A Midsummer Night's Dream* performances had flipped a switch in her soul. The fire had already been there, but those first exposures to being on the stage, in the theater, dancing in costume next to real professional dancers, fanned the flame. The sights, sounds, feel, even the smells of the dancing life were all so natural to her that there was no need to question that the theater was her home. Out of either naivete or deep instinct, she didn't worry about whether she could or would "make it." She was going to be a dancer. She *was* a dancer.

It helped that all her friends had the same intention. The ones who didn't, well, they'd realized that they were surrounded by kids and teachers with drive stronger than their own, and one by one they fell away. They had other interests on par with but completely different from ballet, but that concept was bizarre to this teenager. She could not have cared less about going to a high school prom, or playing a sport, or even going to college. She was very good in school—after spending her freshman year at a highly competitive math and science high school, she had transferred to a small, private school for children whose professional aspirations already took up most of their time—and she did dedicate herself to academics, but it was almost out of habit. Habitual work ethic, habitual diligence, and a personal, inviolable rule to be good. Also stubbornness. A refusal to let something, anything slide. She was the girl who did things right and did them well, got praise for them, and was responsible and correct. Not one with failures or slipups, and that extended to schoolwork as well as ballet. At home, too, she was fastidious. She liked things just so: everything neat, tidy, in its place. Messes were exasperating and needed to be cleaned up immediately, or better yet, prevented in the first place. She wanted her life to be storybook, classic, correct. Holiday traditions, particularly, she wanted honored and unvaried, year after year.

This day in March of her senior high school year was another turning point, but this was a very concrete one. It marked a new step on her ascent to dancer-hood. The audition for Pacific Northwest Ballet (PNB) was held at the School on a Saturday afternoon. Since she was already there for her regular morning class, she was one of the first in line to register. Her audition number, which she pinned on the front of her leotard, was 2.

The audition was crowded. Lots of aspiring dancers wanted to be seen by the directors of PNB, as it was known. Many of them were her classmates, but there were equally as many from out of town, other schools, even some who were already professional and looking to switch companies. The studio was so packed that when auditionees lined up at the barres, they were like sardines in a can, so close together there was barely one leg's length between them. Développés and grand battements had to be angled away from the barre so the dancers' legs could rise above hip height.

In the center, although they were divided up into several groups to do each combination, the seventeen-year-old wondered how anyone could really be seen. She felt lucky, though: she knew the directors of the company already, and they knew her. She'd gone to their summer school three years in a row and had attracted their attention, and at her end-of-summer conference a few months ago, they'd even told her that they were interested in her for their company someday. Even so, this was far from any sort of guarantee. She had no idea what was going to happen and fretted that they'd forgotten about her, or that they'd changed their minds about her potential, or that she'd flatlined instead of improving since they'd last seen her the previous summer. She didn't even know for sure if they had any available jobs to offer.

So she pushed to dance her best despite the conditions and to shine from within the crowd. The class was not hard, but it felt that way to her. She concentrated on finishing each exercise with precision. She tried to perform as if she was on a stage, projecting her gaze up and out through the mirror, moving with as much fullness and energy and dynamism as she could even though there were dancers within inches of her on all sides.

The class audition ended. The directors, seated with the company's ballet master, school director, and the company manager at a table in the front of the room that was covered with papers, headshots, resumes of all the auditioning hopefuls, huddled their heads, whispered together, and tried to hide who they were pointing toward and looking at. The dancers were told, "Thank you, please stay here and give us a moment." They stood nervously, shuffling around, stretching a bit, relieved it was over and that there was nothing more they could do. After having gone through the audition ordered in lines according to the numbers pinned to their leotards, now they relaxed into shapeless clumps.

After a few awkward minutes, the company manager stood up with a sheet of paper in her hand. "We'd like to speak with the following people. Everyone else, thank you," and proceeded to read a list of numbers.

"Three, seven, nine, ten, fifteen, twenty-two, twenty-three, thirty-one . . ." and on and on. With each number she spoke, those whose number had been passed by felt their hearts sink and, one by one, stopped holding their breath. A small buzz of sighs and shuffling feet grew as more and more people realized they'd been passed over.

When her number wasn't called, Number Two felt like her chest was suddenly full of lead. She couldn't move. The group of dancers who had been called went eagerly, excitedly, up to the directors' table, while everyone else made for the door. There was a current rushing around her, but she was frozen in place. Disappointment, heavier than she'd imagined she might feel, hit.

But, before she recovered enough to move her feet: "And Number Two. Please stay."

The group who'd been called were all being spoken to en masse by the school director, but the company manager signaled Number Two to stand back, away from them. The larger group were being told something about leaving their resumes and being in touch at a later date. There were smiles but no exaltation. That group cleared away, and Number 2 was beckoned.

"You look wonderful, and we'd love to have you in our company."

The teenager was stunned into silence. She didn't know how to respond to those words, what she was supposed to say or expected to do. She must have said "thank you," but that was probably about it. She could not, later, recall what else the director said to her, but she knew it was a very short conversation, and she left the studio not knowing what was going to happen next: apparently, she had a job, and for now, that was all that mattered. It didn't occur to her to ask about anything beyond that— rank, pay, starting date.

She trotted straight to the pay phone in an alcove off the lobby and dialed home. Her mother answered. "I got in!" was all the teenager remembers saying, but that was enough of an explanation.

That night, the whole family went out to their favorite Indian restaurant to celebrate. The four of them sat at a round table in the warm, elegant, dimly lit room, secluded from the evening bustle of Broadway, as they had so many times before, talking, laughing, exclaiming over the flavor and intoxicating aroma of the chicken tikka masala, the satisfying oily crunch of the onion pakoras, the warm, soft, buttery naan bread's impossible perfection. The attentive, dignified waiters discretely swept crumbs off the white tablecloth with their special little tool and brought two little boat-shaped dishes of coconut- and cardamom-scented rice pudding for dessert, on the house.

So it began.

Part 2

21

The Summer of 1992

In the summer of 1992, I thought I had been duped.

I was naive, even for a seventeen-year-old. But as it became clear that I had failed to notice a huge, crucial, completely obvious basic fact about being a dancer, I was rocked absolutely to the core. I'd been oblivious to something everyone else got but didn't bother to tell me about because it was so commonly understood. I was terrified. And I feared I just might have made a terrible mistake.

It was as if, after desperately wanting and hoping to be granted membership into a special club, one whose members I idolized and that was my ticket to the dreamed-of life of a dancer, I had finally been allowed to join—but once I was inside, the expectations and assumptions and responsibilities were completely unlike anything I had envisioned. They were dauntingly difficult and stunningly painful. There was no rulebook, and nothing was explained. The price of membership in this Professional Dancer Club was a test of toughness, adaptability, and stoicism. It required worldly wise savvy, of which I had none. The other members were welcoming enough, even accepting, but their blasé air of capable professionalism was intimidating. I was much too embarrassed to ask a question that might reveal my shocking lack of preparation—my reflexive instinct was that I should hide my struggle or I would be branded as inadequate, not up to the task. I was in completely over my head.

What scared me most during that summer of '92 was a startling feeling that I *should have known* what this was going to be like—I should have known what to expect when I graduated from ballet school into this life of a professional dancer. I should have known that I would be in pointe shoes for eight hours a day—and my feet should have been able to handle it. I should have been able to learn the choreography for three different ballets, and understudy three other dancers' roles, and been able to step in without warning to any other dancer's position whether or not I'd learned it. But I hadn't even known how long the rehearsal days would be, and I definitely did not imagine they would leave me feeling desperate from pain and fatigue.

Those days were more than long; they were endless. Each hour was filled with the anxiety of uncertainty, starting with company technique class first thing in the morning. Just walking into a studio filled with professional dancers was utterly forbidding, as I, fresh out of school, felt so green and self-conscious I could barely see where I was stepping, let alone find an appropriate barre-spot. Needing to be as inconspicuous as humanly possible, I hovered in the no-man's land in between two barres until the last moment before class began and then slipped into a space that no one else seemed to want. If no senior dancer (and they were all senior relative to me) looked peeved, then that obscure spot I'd chosen along the side wall, putting me miles from the mirror and awkwardly straining to see the teacher's demonstrations, was safe.

Once class started, I breathed. My nervous guessing game of figuring out where to stand was temporarily resolved. And once the music began for *plies,* the risk of possibly being spoken to by one of these supremely confident, old-pro dancers—and the pressure to respond appropriately and cleverly—also disappeared. For the forty-five minutes of barre work, I was on safe ground. Everyone in the studio did the same exercises, which were, while unusual to me in style and presentation, basically familiar. For this brief time each morning, I had a bit of confidence. This was something I'd done millions of times before. I could just hide in the solitude of barre work, knowing there'd be no surprises and I wouldn't have to interact with anyone.

That sense of safety evaporated when barre neared its end. The second half of class was a huge minefield, an obstacle course I felt I was navigating with an eye patch on. No longer tethered to their barre-spots, the dancers swarmed into the center of the studio. It seemed too dense to possibly allow anyone room to dance. There was constant movement. Groups of dancers quickly formed and reformed for each exercise, leaving me no time to gauge where I might fit in—so I clung to the back of the crowd, where I was camouflaged and happier anyway. I was more nervous about bumping into someone or stepping on their toes (literally or figuratively) than actually dancing, but no matter how keenly I watched to avoid collision, I felt clumsy and slow. I was inevitably in someone's way.

If class every morning was a study in the social workings of a ballet company, the rest of the day was physical boot camp. Up until this point, I'd never worn pointe shoes for more than three hours at a time, but now I was called to rehearse for six hours a day—after the hour-and-a-half-long class. I had never known such foot pain. I began to live by the clock, counting the minutes until another hour had passed and we were given our union-mandated five-minute break. I searched for ways to stand that might give my feet some degree of relief. I rocked back and forth from leg to leg, giving each one a chance to be pressure-free while the other took all my weight for a minute. The glory of sitting down—oh, it was pure nirvana. Even kneeling felt blissful. I would happily, joyously, gratefully spend five minutes on my knees if the choreography called for it. Anything, anything, to get off my feet.

Every dancer knows, soon enough, that standing still is remarkably more tiring, and painful, than moving. The blood pools in your feet and lower legs, which swell and throb. And when you are in the corps de ballet and learning new choreography, you spend much more time standing in the back of a studio than you do dancing. The cursed burden of being an understudy. And as the newest of the new, I had a lot of understudying to do.

A new ballet was being created that summer with twelve couples in its corps de ballet, and I was half of one of those pairs. Rehearsals ran for three hours at a stretch, then an hour lunch break, followed by another three hours of rehearsal. It was July, there was a heat wave, the studio was not air-conditioned, and I thought I was going to die.

I did have a few blisters, but even worse were the "zingers," the electric zapping sensations that shot through my toes and couldn't be taped or padded. The inner sole (the shank) of a pointe shoe is slightly smaller than the length of the dancer's foot, and the places where my heel over-hung the shank burned so much I expected to see blood, but the skin wasn't broken. My big toenail became bruised, and I started my lifelong battle with soft corns, which formed in between my knobby toes on moist skin that never had a chance to dry out.

The first of the three hours did not necessarily pass the most quickly. When the zingers start early, and you see by the clock that there are six hours and forty-five minutes left of the day, it's hard to put on a sunny face. The choreographer of this new ballet was also the artistic director of the company, but any eagerness I might have had to make a good impression on him (who doesn't dream of being Esther in *A Star Is Born*?) lost out to my instinct for survival. I didn't care if my face betrayed my exhaustion, or if he thought I was lazy for sitting down at any opportunity or unambitious for hiding behind other dancers (so he couldn't see me wince). It was all I could do to stay standing and not cry tears of frustration at the incredible discomfort I was in. At my worst moments, I felt flares of outrage at the inhumanity of it all—to treat people this way, to expect them to endure such hours in such conditions, did he not know how awful it was? Not care? As I lost a sense of perspective, I started to feel trapped and even slightly panicked. This was slavery, forced labor, torture! And no one seemed to care! I thought about the people outside on the streets, in their offices, working normal jobs, going through daily life in the regular world, what they would do or say if they knew what was happening in this stuffy, moist, torture chamber of a ballet studio. They would be outraged, surely, and rescue us! No one could allow their fellow human to suffer this way. . . .

But no rescue came. When the one holy hour each day that was my lunch break finally arrived, all I could do was lie on my back with my legs straight up in the air, feet overhead, and wish upon wish that I didn't have to put my pointe shoes back on. I didn't know how the day could be only halfway over, how I could conceivably do this for another three hours. The rumble in my stomach forced me to stand up, barefoot, and even as much as I wished I could levitate to the dressing room to retrieve my lunch instead of walking there, feeling the spread of my feet on floor was amazing. It may as well have been a deep-tissue massage for the pleasure it gave.

In stark contrast to the interminable hours of rehearsal, my lunch hour passed faster than sixty minutes ever should. Delaying the inevitable moment of putting my pointe shoes back on was always a mistake, since the initial few minutes inside them was the worst. At ten minutes before four o'clock, I re-taped my toes, vainly hoping that fresh athletic tape and corn pads would magically alleviate the pain. I gave my arches one final stretch and pulled each pointe shoe back on, almost stunned at how disgusting it felt. Awkwardly standing up, I could not conceive of dancing, or doing any ballet steps at all, but luckily, walking was harder than dancing. The choreographer was already back in the studio, talking to the pianist, and was about to resume work on the latest section of his ballet, picking up where we'd left off an hour before.

He placed us twelve corps de ballet girls in a circle, sort of—it was more like a loose amoeba-shaped formation, with all of us joined hand to hand. He wanted unspecific, continual movement, an undulating wave from girl to girl through our linked arms, without ever losing contact with one another. Our bodies were positioned in a vague half-curtsy, no one standing fully upright, but our backs would rise and fall as the wave passed through us. The undulations started with one girl and came to me, back around and through us all again and again and again, until I was not an active part of the chain anymore—I just couldn't be. My arms were being jerked and practically yanked out of their sockets, I was bobbing up and down obediently, my feet were throbbing. Suddenly, the ridiculousness of what we were doing, in juxtaposition to the degree of physical pain it was causing, was hilarious—I was struck with pure disbelief that this was my job, my exalted career. At another moment, my emotions would have erupted in tears of exhaustion and frustration, but now I was past that point. From way, way down in the pit of my stomach, giggles bubbled up—I stared at the floor, trying desperately to sober up, but this sudden giddiness was uncontrollable. It was like I'd let a release valve open a millimeter, and the steam pressure that had been building up all week came rushing out.

I was one week into my fabulous professional ballet career, and I was being pulled limb from limb and told to move like a single-celled organism wearing soggy, putrid pointe shoes in a 100 degree studio. We must have looked like eight-year-olds on a playground. My giggles turned into full-throttle gasps for air the harder I tried to hold them in. Unfortunately, the choreographer called us to stop moving the amoeba—my paroxysms might have been camouflaged by the swarm of moving bodies if he hadn't—and in the stillness I tried desperately to calm myself with humungous deep breaths, pretending to have been working so hard I was winded.

He ended up choreographing a section for us that involved a snaking conga line around the room, and, although it felt equally ridiculous to be shuffling behind another dancer with my hands on her waist and I still had to squelch the occasional guffaw, my meltdown in the amoeba circle had been a catharsis. Even in my desperation, I'd acknowledged to myself the absurdity of the moment, and suddenly the fog of desperation lifted. I could possibly, just possibly, be able to handle this. The other girls were hurting, too; they were just more used to it than I and had accumulated a tool kit of tactics and strategies to help them cope. They had figured out the best corn pads to use, what kind of tape held them in place, how to position pieces of SecondSkin on a blister. Their legs were stronger than mine from years of work, and they knew how to pace themselves psychologically through long hours of rehearsal. They were acclimated to this life, and they knew the answer to the question I was afraid to ask: Is it always going to be like this? Is this all there is?

Rehearsals ended at seven o'clock and thankfully never ran late. The choreographer was as tired as we were, and the heat in the studio felt soul-sucking to everyone. As the afternoon wore on, intense sunlight beamed directly in through the open windows and door, bringing smoldering heat from the black tar of the parking lot directly inside. My skin was tight, caked with salt. Nine hours of sweat had dried, layer upon layer, but now that the day's end was at hand, it felt good, like evidence of my membership in the club of the hardworking corps de ballet. Sitting down to take my shoes off, I didn't let myself think about tomorrow—at that moment, I almost relished the ache in my legs, the pins and needles in my feet, the open blister on my heel. I could walk barefoot to the dressing room, stick my feet under a stream of cold water, and listen to my comrades laugh and chat and commiserate about the day, feeling light about it now that we'd pushed through to the finish line. I might even confess that I'd thought I'd be fired on the spot for my outburst or ask someone what to do for my ingrown toenail. The hours had worn away my self-consciousness, and I felt the glow of pride and camaraderie.

I got a ride home that night from Catherine, another girl who was almost as new as I but had a year of corps de ballet experience under her belt. *How long would this last?, I asked her. Were the days always going to be this hard? Was this normal?*

Her answers weren't very reassuring, but I did learn that no, it was not always this hard, this long, this hot, or this exhausting. But often, it was. There would be periods of respite when we'd learn different ballets and eventually I'd not have to understudy so much, and in a few weeks, we'd be performing. That would change everything, of course. That would be the payoff.

But for now, I'd begun to earn my stripes as a professional dancer. I had the battle wounds to prove it, and next week, I would have my first paycheck.

As we pulled out of the studio's parking lot, Catherine put the air-conditioning on full blast and I sank into the soft comfort of the bucket seat. On the way to the freeway, she stopped at a McDonald's drive-through for a Diet Coke. I got one, too. I wondered what the woman at the window would say if she knew what we'd been doing all day, while she'd been serving up fries and shakes to normal people going through their daily lives. Imagining her reaction if we described our day didn't make the prospect of tomorrow's pain any less heavy. But I secretly loved knowing that in the sea of cars in rush-hour traffic, we were two absolutely normal ballet dancers, making their way home from the office like everyone else, earning a living one tough day at a time.

No Coke ever tasted so good.

22

Chateau Ste. Michelle

My Big Break

Toward the end of my first weeks as a professional dancer, the tenor and energy of those rigorous rehearsal days changed. The performances that had loomed for four weeks were suddenly imminent. With my focus on simply surviving hour by hour, they'd seemed almost hypothetical. The starkness of their reality, when it hit me, felt almost playful in contrast to the overwhelming stress of the weeks I'd been trapped inside.

The ballet company had an annual gig at the breathtakingly beautiful Chateau Ste. Michelle winery in Woodinville, Washington. The winery's extensive grounds included an expansive lawn that made a perfect natural amphitheater. Every summer, a covered stage was set up, rigged with lighting and wing space, and a series of outdoor concerts was presented. The ballet was on board along with classical musicians, pop singers, and bands. It didn't occur to me that making my professional debut in such a relatively relaxed setting lessened the pressure that the landmark occasion usually brings. The flood of new experiences flustered me as much as a performance at Carnegie Hall.

The program we were presenting at Ste. Michelle that summer included excerpts from *Swan Lake* (act 2, with the ending of act 4 blended in), as well as a neoclassical ballet choreographed by the company's artistic director, in which I had understudied a "short" corps spot. (Corps de ballet dancers are forever classified as "short" or "tall" for general ease of assigning roles.) I was also, of course, a swan in *Swan Lake*. The setting at the winery was incredibly scenic: the stage looked out over a long, sloping expanse of lawn with trees in the distance, mountain ranges beyond, and vineyards on either side. It was also, for a performance venue, makeshift. Instead of dressing rooms, we huddled in curtained-off areas in the winery's barrel room, adjacent to its tasting room. To get to and from the stage we had to walk through the barrel storage area—which was concrete, chilled, and very aromatic of wine, of course. From there, we trudged outside and up some rickety stairs to get "backstage," a misnomer because it was in nearly full view of the audience. Needless to say, the atmosphere was casual, jovial, and felt a bit like summer camp without the campfire songs. Each day before making the journey out to Woodinville, I stocked my dance bag full of every conceivable amenity I might need. Water and food, of course, but also extra toe tape and warm-up clothes, waterproof booties for walking through the barrel room and across the grass, a blanket, sunglasses (to wear during late afternoon warm-up class, when the sun blazed directly onto the stage), gloves (it got really cold after sunset)—basically packing as if I was going to a remote land, unsure of what I might encounter. After the first evening's rehearsal left me mosquito-bitten, I added bug repellent. I would have taken bear spray if I'd had any.

We ran through the program on our first afternoon at the winery, working out our spacing on the cramped stage and negotiating entrances and exits in the absence of any real wing space. It was determined that the sixteen swans awaiting our single file entrance would have to spill down the stairs and partially out onto the lawn. It was an accepted fact that the magic of the theater would be compromised here. We swans were a true flock, huddling closer together than we'd ever done over the past weeks of rehearsal. There was a short break (spent watching tourists taste wine as we ate our lunches on the lawn) before the full dress rehearsal that evening. Dress rehearsal went fine, from my point of view— I made no mistakes, which gave me enough confidence to start feeling excited about performing—and the next morning I went to class full of anticipation for opening night. After class, we were to have a two-hour rehearsal to go over notes from the dress rehearsal, beginning with the artistic director's ballet. Since I was only an understudy for that ballet,

I stood in the back of the studio ready to review the part I covered. The ballet master stopped the music. Lost in thought, I barely noticed—until I realized she'd walked over and was leading me by the hand to the line of "tall girls" ready to make their entrance. "You're learning a new spot." Um . . . *What?!*

Yes. A girl in a different section of the ballet had, unbeknownst to me, thrown her back out during dress rehearsal, and for some reason that to this day I am not clear about, it was decided that I would be the one to replace her. Not only had I not learned this particular section, but I had barely even watched it in rehearsals, needing to save as much memory power as I could for my own parts. And now I had to learn, essentially, an entirely new ballet—and the performance was only a few hours away.

So the ballet master began to teach me my new part, one step at a time, with an amazing amount of patience and calm. The rehearsal went beyond the scheduled two hours and into "spillover," which meant everyone in the room was suddenly earning overtime. I don't recall how long rehearsal went, but for once I didn't want it to end—because although I got the entire ballet crammed into my head, I knew it wasn't very secure there. The dancer whose part I was stepping into was amazing. She drove me home after rehearsal, while I ceaselessly reviewed the steps in my head and out loud, asking her for prompts when I hit a blank. She made me lunch while I kept reviewing, and we kept at it during the hour's drive to the winery. I tested my memory by quizzing myself on what came right before or right after various moments in the ballet. I knew the only way I'd be able to manage this was by blocking out every other thought, running a tape of the choreography in my head until the curtain went up.

At the winery, I tried to stay calm, but inside I was tipping into panic mode. Anytime someone spoke to me, it was as if their voice was coming from far away—I could barely hear anything but *"sauté, pas de chat,* step cross lunge, pose B+ hold, seven, eight, nine, kneel . . ." Someone wished me "merde" ("good luck" in dancer-speak) but I couldn't even say thank you—my eyes filled with tears of anxiety. After putting on my makeup, I found an empty space in the barrel room to go over the ballet one more time. I hit a blank spot—no idea what came next—and realized my chances of getting through this without messing up were slim.

The ballet started, and something took over—I suddenly had a fearlessness that surprised me. My brain was running a mile a minute, but the previous five hours of intense learning had worked, and although I couldn't stop reading from the script in my head, I did know what steps came next, and next, and next. I danced big, fully and with energy. Subconsciously, I must have thought that even if I made a mistake, I'd already succeeded and no one could really criticize me. The only thing I could do wrong would be to hold back or look timid or unsure. My first step onstage was a humungous sauté arabesque out of the fourth wing, by myself (each dancer entered on their own phrase of music, one from each of the four corners of the stage), and I relished the moment to say, "Here I am!" The other corps dancers onstage with me were immensely supportive, whispering cues throughout and sort of nudging me into the right spot if I started to go astray. I remember the finale of the ballet the best, because the music was so rousing, the choreography so exhilarating, and the dancer next to me in line practically shouted prompts: "Sailor step! Crossovers! Lunge! Paddle turn and kneel!"—even though I proudly discovered I didn't need the help. I was so happy that this was nearly over I thought I might explode.

And then it WAS over. Relief and almost desperate gratitude at having made it through without disaster washed over me. Finally I could hear clearly and see straight again. People congratulated me on my professional debut, which I had totally forgotten about—my first time onstage as a professional dancer hadn't been anything like I'd imagined or anticipated. I'd rehearsed for weeks, only to do my first performance in a part I'd learned in the last five hours.

But the night wasn't over yet. *Swan Lake* was still to come, after a short intermission. I raced back to the dressing room/barrel room/makeshift tent where our white tutus were lined up for us to pull on as fast as possible. Towels and tarps lined the runway from stage to dressing room in an attempt to keep us from tracking mud onto all that white tulle. I tore my hair out of its high bun and whipped it back into the low swan hairdo, someone helped me pin on the feathered headpiece, I jumped into my tutu and, with a deep breath, took my place in the line of swans on the grass outside upstage left to enter in Swan Lake: arabesque, emboîté, arabesque, emboîté, arabesque, emboîté . . .

23

Making a Living Being Tired

As a little girl, my fascination with the physics of ballet naturally led to a fascination with my body. Studying the design of my fingers, hands, toes, legs—the easiest parts to see on oneself—without judgment or opinion, seemed to occupy a lot of my time. I hadn't yet learned what was considered ideal, nor what a "ballet body" really meant. I just looked at the shape of my own extremities, almost with detachment, no particular pride or distaste. It was an initial assessment, though I did not know it at the time, of the sculptor's clay I'd be working with for the rest of my life.

Making a living being tired is hard for people to understand. Family or nondancer friends suggest a good night's sleep as the solution. But when your body is your tool, your instrument, your product, your advertisement, when it is absolutely indispensable for doing your job, *and* also must carry you through daily civilian life, it is rare to feel completely and totally rested. When I did, I feared I was out of shape.

I still am a dancer, but since I don't do it for a living anymore, I have a bit of perspective on the life that some people thought was crazy, a little twisted, or self-centered. Many others recognized it as one of the closest things to sublimity that there may be. The human body is too phenomenal to have been intended as merely a shell for our internal organs. It must be *used*. The things our bodies are capable of are astounding, and virtually nobody comes close to tapping into that potential. As a race, we are much more focused on pushing the limits of our brains, and as a result, our bodies get treated as suitcases for our mental capacity. My obsession was, and is, learning what my muscles, tendons, and nerves could do and then honing and developing their potential until I could wield power over every cell. The most beautiful feeling in the world is having the sensitivity and strength to use your feet, fingers, neck, legs, back, arms—and every fiber within them—like a fine-haired paintbrush.

But in addition to self-awareness, and yes, compulsion, this requires energy. Interestingly, though, some of the hardest things to master in classical ballet don't take that much wattage. The subtleties and finesse that create an artistic performance are learned less through rote repetition or exercises of brute strength than by observation, thought, and analysis. I know: this sounds too intellectual for what's stereotypically thought of as a light art form for less-than-genius young people who may be avoiding college. And no, not all dancers—not even all professional ones—dig deep enough into ballet to truly *study* it. When you first start out, there is an endless repetition of dry exercises, which are essential to developing the basic strength and coordination for the mechanics of ballet. This formulaic practice becomes so familiar over the years, so regular and everyday, that it fits into a dancer's day right along with toothbrushing. At the beginning, though, it's the kids who have ballet in their blood who don't find it boring. Instinctively, without making a conscious decision to do so, they push themselves, somehow already knowing that every hour spent in class, every basic step or position learned, leads the way to thrilling discoveries. To these kids, even the simplest steps are fascinating and fun to experiment with. I remember as a child not being able to restrain myself from tendu-ing constantly—any structure approximating a barre compelled me to plié, rond de jambe, développé, fondu. The washing machine in the kitchen was perfect, as was the back of the living room sofa and the wooden frame of my bed. Stretching and molding my limbs was like an itch that I had to scratch. That endless, automatic energy of youth fades, but for real dancers, the itch doesn't really go away. Their mental will to keep going remains, even once batteries inside the Energizer Bunny peter out. The brain and body start slipping out of sync, and that's when things get really hard. That's when momentary doubts can start to show up.

24

Ballerina Doll

It is an absolutely crushing blow, and a confusing one. The rehearsal casting has been posted on the bulletin board. Last year, as a first-year dancer in the corps de ballet, I was cast in this ballet, in a small solo role normally only given to senior corps women and soloists. I learned the part, rehearsed it, and performed it onstage several times. People said I was good. My friends, dancers and nondancers alike, congratulated me, but I got no comments from the artistic staff of the company—no praise, no criticism. I hadn't known whether to expect any, so the absence of feedback didn't bother me too much. If I had done badly, I wouldn't have kept seeing my name on the casting sheet, I figured. But now, a year later, my name is not listed, although others' names—my peers' names—are. It makes no sense. What could be the reason? Could it be a mistake, an oversight? It takes immense courage for me to ask someone in authority what's happening. But I do, in a quivering voice that reflects the fragility of my self-possession. "Well, you know, it was a little poker-faced last year," says the kind but frank ballet master. But . . . then why didn't anyone tell me that last year?

The lesson I'd learned earlier, back in my teenage years, with the Curly-Haired Teacher's dismissive wave of the hand and the Pastel Teacher's determination, had given me a second chance. Ballet is a business, and time is money in the studio and onstage just as much as anywhere else. Don't wait for someone else to fix you; do it yourself. What this situation revealed was that no news is bad news.

Shocked and scared at this realization that I was on my own, I ask permission to come to rehearsals for the Ballerina Doll anyway and to be reconsidered for the part. Granted. Armed with indignation that anyone might have doubted me, my determination explodes exponentially and I vow to prove them wrong. I go to rehearsals and scrutinize the soloists doing the role, watching their expression and quality, and then dancing it myself with more abandon and crisper technique than I had before. I think about my face, where my eyes are focusing at each moment and how that could brighten the positions I make. I move with more fullness and authority now that I know what is on the line.

And when the performance casting goes up, there is my name.

25

Orange

I am clad entirely in orange. From my neck to my ankles and out to my wrists, I am orange. On my feet are little white anklet socks with sticky nonslip pads on the bottoms. I am about to go onstage to perform in *Artifact II*, by the great choreographer William Forsythe, and I am mortified.

I hide. For as long as possible, I stay alone in my dressing room. When the stage manager's "PLACES, PLEASE!" bellows through the loudspeaker, I scurry down a flight of slippery concrete stairs and take cover in the darkness of backstage, where, in the last seconds before the curtain goes up, the work lights have been killed.

I have company, though they are not all as bashful as I am, or they cover it with bravado. Twenty-some orange people have assembled onstage, where the jokesters flaunt their Creamsicle costumes as if to prove their superiority over this indignity. We're an asexual bunch, a classless mob, and—almost—lawless. Men and women are exactly the same. The braggarts, the machos, the petite ladies, the newbies, and the seniors, we're all glommed together for effect. The sight of the coolest, most unflappable guys in the company swaggering around in pumpkin orange suits and little white socks is hilarious—ridiculous! It's enough to shake me out of my funk, but I still want to cover my behind. The snarkiest fellow of all stands right in front of me in our opening formation, a huge V shape that takes up the entire stage. He keeps sarcastic comments and rude jokes coming, under his breath, every time I'm in earshot.

This ballet is controlled anarchy. We appear, to the audience, to be moving in preordained choreographic patterns, but much of what we do is a sort of structured improvisation. We have a leader. She is the very small woman standing smack at center stage, with her back to the audience, as far downstage as possible without falling backward into the orchestra pit. She is not one of us—she is not in orange. Muddy gray paint covers every inch of her body, including her face and hair and fingernails. A leotard, also covered in the drabbest dark grayish brown paint, is all she wears. She is barefoot.

This Mud Woman is, discreetly, giving us cues, and clues. She signals us with sharp, semaphore-like arm movements, and we have to mimic her immediately with no discernible delay. She continues in whatever pattern she wants, for as long as she wants, until her "end" cue sends us—the orange mob—running as fast and unballetically as we can into a new formation. We're not supposed to be dancers. We are, literally, human scenery, and at certain times, we're percussion. We've been instructed to run without a care for grace or lightness, to pound our feet into the floor and hurtle ourselves through space (thus the nonslip pads on our socks). The wings have been lifted up to the flies of the theater, out of the audience's view, so the stage appears endless, like an infinity pool. There is no back, no sides, no ceiling. We race from edge to edge of the vast space making diagonals, Xs, Vs, going from shapeless clumps to sardine-tight lines. We flop on our stomachs and then jump up like marines into formation while the principals dance in front of us. Their choreography is the antithesis of ours. It's on pointe, very tightly wound and even more tightly stretched, stressful and wiry and taut, highly technical. The principals disappear from time to time, melting into our mass as we swallow them up in a swarm. The lighting is dark and shadowy, ominous, and our orangeness pops out startlingly.

The Mud Woman moves with us, or ahead of us, running from spot to spot, but she must always be visible to every orange person onstage. When we form a gigantic box rimming the stage, no one may turn their head to see her. We keep our noses straight ahead, eyes peeking to the side, and copy the movements we see in our peripheral vision, mentally translating them to our own bodies with insane speed. Those facing her have the easy job of being her mirror image. The Mud Woman begins to move faster, though in rehearsals, we pleaded with her not to. Furiously trying to keep up, groans of frustration and nervous giggles start to be heard all around, but the recorded music—a Bach Partita for solo violin—is so loud, it more than covers our eruptions. Just as we become frantic and hover on the edge of falling too far behind—revealing to the audience that our choreography isn't memorized—the Mud Woman signals us to halt and regroup. At one point, she steps out of the way for the "Sprint-Race": we cram, shoulder to shoulder, in a starting line along one side of the stage. There are way too many of us to fit comfortably, so our bodies overlap and some are squeezed out altogether. When the violin solo reaches a specific note, each of us silently begins chanting a rhythmic recitation of the months of the year. *January . . . February . . . March . . . April . . .* When the month of your birthday is reached, you're off—tearing as fast as you can to the finish line on the opposite side of the stage, where those with earlier birthdays and a head start have already won.

There's more shape-shifting, then, including a spell of lying flat on our backs staring straight up into the flies. We lie in two staggered rows, pointing upstage so the audience sees only the tops of our heads. Our arms become visible, too, because now we get to pick and choose our own favorite gestures from the Mud Woman's vocabulary, doing as many or as few as we like, fast or slow or not at all (a few mavericks lie motionless, adding empty space to the collage we're making). Arms that *are* in motion must stay perpendicular to our bodies, and to the floor, so the effect is of random, spiky spears jabbing the air. Every move has to be staccato and angular; our hands must stay perfectly flat, with fingers glued together like spatulas. Or knives. I'm beginning to enjoy the freedom of being one in a herd and the bravery of anonymity.

By the end of the ballet, our volume overwhelms and takes over the stage. We're released from the Mud Woman's spontaneous commands and her control. There are no traffic patterns anymore as each of us carves our own road around and around, zig-zagging or not, any which way and at any speed we choose. Nearly fifty pairs of arms maniacally chop and slice as we stride about; there are near-misses and some full-on collisions.

Each orange person is their own master now. We rule together but alone, isolated without words—and invisible in front of two thousand people.

My timidity returns the moment the curtain falls. I am just another body, clad all in orange.

It's a minute or so away from my entrance and I'm standing ready, about two or three feet back from the edge of the wing from which I'll enter. The stage lights are starkly bright in comparison to where I stand in relative darkness. I always leave my leg warmers on until the last possible moment, and now the time has come to take them off. I peel one down from the top of my thigh and pull it off, and then peel the other but it gets stuck on my foot. Without thinking, I give my leg a shake to get it free, and it flies off—landing one inch from the edge of the wing. A big, green, woolly leg warmer nearly made an unplanned entrance.

26

Cinderella

It's Cinderella's grand entrance to the ball in act 2. We courtiers have already danced our sweeping waltz, elegant in red velvet Romantic tutus, our gentlemanly partners in matching tunics and tails and, in the style of the fairy-tale era, with little ribbon-adorned ponytails pinned to the hair at the napes of their necks. Chests still burning from exertion and exhilaration, we move from our triumphant final pose into a long V formation to frame the approach of Cinderella's coach—but where is it? The Prince, waiting expectantly on center stage, peers curiously, eagerly, and then anxiously toward upstage right where the coach is supposed to enter behind the raised balustrade. The six supernumerary guards standing at attention between the ornate columns of the stage set don't flinch at the sight of the coach as it finally appears—aslant, lurching forward strangely as if its horses were old and drunk. The conductor (a veteran of ballet performances) senses trouble and slows the orchestra down to a liturgical pace—the music sounds unrecognizable for its slowness. A courtier positioned at the top of the steps near the guards is able to see behind the balustrade: her view is of four sweaty, heaving stagehands on hands and knees pushing and pulling the carriage, straining to keep it upright and cursing out loud, the waistband of one's pants well below where it should be. Up above, Cinderella grips her stomach muscles and prays for dear life.

Entranced, the audience cheers.

27

Rejected

*After seven seasons as a dancer with Pacific Northwest Ballet, I was
still a courtesan at Cinderella's ball, an anonymous body clad in orange, a swan in the flock, yearning and hungry for any small Ballerina
Doll moments yet knowing that there was more, much more, than that.
Daily company class was the only time I got to dance the same steps as
the principals and soloists—class being the equalizer, when ranks are
erased and everyone works on the same level, side by side—and was
freed from the restrained choreography of the corps de ballet. One day,
an allegro combination full of swirling, dynamic changes of direction
just begged me to play, teasing and tempting me to sweep through every
curve, peak, and valley in its phrases. I launched into it with the glee of
a little girl in the playground but then let myself stretch out nuances of
the movement as if, as the saying goes, no one was watching. Briefly, I
was alone with that very thing that compelled me to dance in the first
place and that was, as ever, in my core, as strong as a steel rebar both
grounding me and holding me up, the pilot light ready to ignite at any
opportunity.*

*After I finished the exercise, high with the joy of flight and feeling
fulfilled enough to face the rest of my day, I walked to the back corner
of the studio to wait while the other groups of dancers took their turns.
Suddenly, a friend of mine, a soloist, spun around and grabbed my
arm, stopping me in my tracks. "We have to talk," she said, glaring
at me—and I froze, paralyzed with panic at what I might have done*

wrong. Did I trespass on her (or another soloist or principal's) space in class? What horrible, unintended thing had I said or done that made her so inflamed?

"That was fucking amazing," she said. "Whatever 'it' is, you have it. You have to get out of here. Find someone who appreciates who you are." I needed no convincing.

Her words were validation of what I'd felt in my gut: that this wasn't about prestige or pride but about a barely tapped reserve of dance inside me that I was desperate to use. What my friend was talking about was that indefinable "thing" that makes a person a dancer: it's an urge that won't be satisfied unless the body is in motion, that refuses to move meekly, that has an inborn, silent agreement with the musical rhythm inside her to never be silent.

Too young to be worried about the folly of leaving a stable union job in a notoriously cutthroat industry, I had no qualms about walking away in search of my dream. At first, with a glorious image in mind of quitting my job with another contract safely in hand (and confident I could get one), I tried auditioning in secret. Eventually, time ran out—I had to sign my agreement for the following season with Pacific Northwest Ballet or have nothing. But soon after, with my heart in my throat and my blessed parents on my side, I asked to be released from my contract, essentially stepping off the edge of the cliff while hoping there would be a branch to break my fall before I hit the ground. Here is the seven-month journey I took from one audition to the next, to the next, to the next, and the unexpected destination I found at the end.

When I was twenty-four, I went to Pittsburgh to audition for a ballet company. It wasn't my first audition, but I was inexperienced—and naive—enough to still think that chances were in my favor.

I wasn't unemployed at the time; in fact, I had a very good and enviable position with another ballet company. But knowing that lots of other dancers would love to have the job that I was ready to give up wasn't enough to make me any happier with it. I was potentially throwing away a valuable object—a ballet job of any sort will always be ridiculously hard to find—and any reminder of that *did* give me twinges of guilt and feelings of irresponsibility. But I kept my eye and heart set on the dream of being more than a corps dancer, somewhere . . . anywhere. I wanted to open a new chapter of my own life, one that would eclipse even the best things about the previous seven years.

I arrived in Pittsburgh from London, by way of New York City. I had been on tour with Pacific Northwest Ballet, performing at Sadler's Wells, and after that two-week adventure, which gave me plenty of time to question why it was I wanted to leave this company, our return flight to the West Coast had a layover at Newark. My parents lived in New York, and I told the company manager a lie. I asked to get off the plane during the stopover so I could join my family for a memorial service for a recently passed grandparent. I was the one who always played by the rules and never asked for anything special. Making up this story, and then having to say it out loud, was in itself quite nearly enough to make me chicken out. Some actress with my name took over when I sought out the manager to have this conversation, and that actress gratefully thanked him for granting her permission to take a few days off for this sad family event.

So when we landed in Newark, I hopped off the plane, grabbed my luggage and a cab, and in a bleary state of jet lag, sped to the Upper West Side.

My father had drawn the shades in my old room and opened up the sofa bed. I went straight to it and slept. Four hours later, after a meal at the Greek diner on the corner, hugs with my parents—what oddness, such a short visit home—I caught another cab and went to LaGuardia for a flight to Pittsburgh.

The tiny commuter plane took off late in a raging thunderstorm and landed late. It was full of business travelers, and I startled myself by realizing that I was one, too. I felt like a traveling salesman with my suitcase full of tools of my trade: pointe shoes, leotards, tights, exercise bands, protein bars, arnica cream, résumé, headshot, a video of myself in performance. I was in full work mode. My commodities were my body and my energy, and my mission was preserving, protecting, and ultimately presenting them. Once the plane touched down, the order of priority was eat, stretch, organize, and sleep.

My mother had made a reservation for me at the Hampton Inn, because it had been recommended for its generous free breakfast. During the interminable shuttle bus ride from the airport (the thunderstorm still going strong), I counted backward from tomorrow's wakeup time to calculate how many hours of sleep I could possibly get and grew anxious at how late it already was. Finally, finally, I was at the hotel . . . but my relief at finding my room to have a refrigerator and enough space to easily stretch out on the floor with my yoga mat was outweighed by one big inconvenience—the only ice machine was in the lobby. Extra time spent fetching buckets of ice for my feet and ankles just wasn't something I had. And with legs already worn out from two solid weeks of touring, I was intent on minimizing their use for anything other than dancing.

That night, jet lag and anxiety canceled each other out and I was able to sleep solidly, but for too few hours. The prospect of class at the ballet company—at 9:15 A.M., unusually early for me—was eating away at my hopes of staying calm. I clung to my habits like an animal, nestling in their security despite my foreign surroundings. As much as I could manage, I re-created my regular morning routine: a few stretches in bed as soon as my eyes opened, more stretches in a hot shower, a mug of tea while I did my yoga, Pilates, and physical therapy exercises. I put on makeup, twisted my hair up into as perfect a twist as possible, swallowed Aleve and vitamins, and ate breakfast. Protein bar and a banana (snuck into my pocket from that fabulous free buffet downstairs, along with a few other portable goodies I knew would be handy later—packets of peanut butter, hot chocolate mix, instant oatmeal), a few more sips from my mug of tea, teeth brushed, and one last check of my supplies for the day (the carefully chosen leotard and tights, three pairs of pointe shoes and one of ballet slippers, leg warmers, chiffon skirt, sweater, warm-up pants, toe tape, and my "promo pack" of photos, résumé, and video). Plus a water bottle, emergency Power Bar, lipstick, needle and thread . . . my bag was big and heavy.

The hotel receptionist called me a cab. The company's main studio, where class took place, was enormous. It was the size of two studios, which in fact it was, with an accordion divider that could be pulled across the middle of the room to slice it in half. This meant that everything in the studio was doubled—two pianos in opposite corners, mirrors on both front and back walls, and a dancing space twice the size of anything normal.

I was not here for an open audition, the kind where dozens of hopefuls pin numbers on their leotards and jockey for position, trying to edge out their competition. The alternative route for job prospects, considered a likelier one toward the ultimate goal, was to snag an invitation to join the company for their daily warm-up class. During audition season—between January and April or so—it was expected that a nervous stranger or two would show up nearly every day, tiptoe into the studio and awkwardly try to act casual while figuring out how both to fit in and to stand out at the same time. I was just another one to be eyed, assessed, and pitied. These dancers already had jobs—I was only competing with myself.

Every ballet company in the world is the same, and every ballet company is different. A thousand small details can be relied upon—class will start at the barre, there will be music to accompany it, someone will teach or lead the class using the language of classical ballet—but there are at least two thousand more variables that are unpredictable. Things that define the culture, the aesthetic, the principles of that group of dancers and its artistic director. Do the women wear pointe shoes for class—maybe for part of class but not all of it? What's the trend in outfits—are there a lot of cover-ups, or do they strip down to streamlined leotards and tights that show off their legs? The amount of chitchat is a good barometer of the company's personality. Sometimes it's like cocktail hour once class gets rolling, but in other places only quick, whispered comments are exchanged, with tension and nervousness, even insecurity, in the air.

The way the class will be taught, the arrangement of the steps, how complicated or challenging they'll be, how fast, how slow . . . all are unknowns. There are protocols to be followed, too: Do the dancers divide into groups for center work? How many? Are the exercises done once, twice, or as many times as possible? Walking into that bizarrely large, two-piano-ed, double-mirrored studio that day, I again made like a creature in the woods and buried my nose in the security of routine. With that much barre space, it was easy to find a place for myself without fear that I'd trespassed on someone else's property. I did my usual pre-class warm-up, lying on the floor for stomach, hip, back, and foot exercises. *Just close your eyes, don't stare around the room, pretend not to eavesdrop, concentrate on yourself* . . . As a result, when I stood up, ready to start pliés, I saw that I was the only one with pointe shoes on.

I managed. There was no time, once I'd realized that every other female dancer in the room was in soft ballet slippers, to take my pointe shoes off. The ballet master was already showing the first exercise, and to sit down and change my shoes would have been not only disrespectful and odd, but I'd miss learning what the exercise was. So I had to muddle through, despite the fact that barre work, designed for feet unencumbered by the rigid blocks of pointe shoes, was full of controlled relevés, both fast and slow. I mangled my way through barre, kept my eyes wide open and my antennae alert as the class moved on to center, and caught my breath when the artistic director appeared in the doorway. In my struggles to deal with the technicalities of the class itself, I'd forgotten about the reason I was here.

He hovered for a while, perhaps even for the duration of the class—my overstressed brain had clouded my gauge of time at that point. Torn between the risk of stepping over the invisible boundary lines of another dancer's space or getting hidden in the back of the crowd, miles away from the front corner where the director stood, I compromised and hovered in the middle ground somewhere near the equator of this planet-sized studio. The space was so deep from front to back that some dancers even used the rear-wall mirror as the front, essentially turning their backs on the teacher and going into their own world.

People were friendly, though, and a few even offered welcoming words, making small talk in the brief lulls between combinations. They seemed sympathetic to this latest poor soul going through the de-personalizing rigor of job-seeking, interested in who she was and where she was from, looking for common ties and calculating degrees of separation. I'd relaxed by the time we were doing grand allegro, the big traveling jumps across the studio's runway-long diagonal.

My nerves returned, though, and multiplied as soon as class was over. The scariest, most unknown, but most important part was about to happen. The Conversation.

I thanked the ballet master who had taught class, having already introduced myself to her before class began. I was hoping for some guidance on what I should do next, but she offered none, and the artistic director had disappeared from the doorway. I asked a secretary-type person near the front door what to do and was sent to a maze of office cubicles in the far wing of the building. Asking one person what was expected of me created a domino effect of sorts, a chain reaction of instructions leading into others. *Wait here, wait there, wait while I find out for you, this person will tell you, but she's at lunch, this other person knows, go wait outside.*

I waited outside the office maze in the lobby and practiced deep breathing. I distracted myself by reading every word on the large, framed publicity posters lining the walls. This company had toured to some interesting places over the years. I tried to figure out what the German and Russian posters said, picking out a few words here or there.

It was like waiting for test results at a doctor's office; or, although this has never happened to me, for a jury to issue its verdict. Absolute limbo. I'd presented my case, done my act, put myself on the catwalk to be seen from all angles, and now was powerless and information-less. I imagined standing there in that lobby for the rest of the day.

But I didn't. He—the director—opened a door and came out to get me himself, apologizing for the wait. He'd been on the phone, he said, ushering me into his office. Inside, I thought I'd walked into Teddy Roosevelt's study. Warm and wood-paneled, it was more of a den than an office, with leather armchairs, a huge wooden desk, an Oriental carpet, and bookshelves all around. Missing only was a moose head mounted on a wall. The fluorescent-lit, rosin-dust-covered, linoleum-floored, bare bones studio couldn't have felt farther away.

My résumé and photographs were on his desk, and he picked them up as he began to talk. What he said was not important, until a certain point.

You're really quite wonderful.

Spontaneously, my hands automatically started rubbing my Achilles tendon, the one that had been so injured for so long and was never far from the top of my worry list. I had no idea what to say.

I waited a month, or more, before calling to find out. There were several back-and-forth phone calls, messages left on my answering machine about the uncertainty of how many available contracts there would be, about current dancers' letters of intent still being unsigned, the company's budget-cutting, their need to promote from within. As my own employer's deadline for giving notice loomed, I saw my window of opportunity closing.

I never got a definitive "no." I just never got a "yes."

A few weeks later, I was in an uncannily similar setting: *I respect your talent. I just don't know right now what I have available.*

And a few days after that, I sat nervously across a desk in yet another artistic director's office, this one housed in a strip mall deep in the sprawl of Southern suburbia. *Well, you're well-trained and have a nice body. Pretty face.* Months later, a form letter arrived: *Thank you for your interest . . . not suited to our needs . . .*

Above a street-level studio, facing a well-trafficked pedestrian mall, after being shown a scale model of the not-yet-under-construction, multi-million-dollar, state-of-the-art facility planned for . . . sometime soon, I was told: *I kept trying to trick you in class with those complicated combinations, but you kept right up!* (Wink, wink.) *While you're here, make sure you get to the beach, and the best café con leche is from this bakery, have you been shopping yet?* The tourist advice was nice but wasted. I didn't care about suntanning; I just wanted to know if he would hire me.

After a class taught at lightning speed by a man who mumbled his words and gave no demonstration—I frantically tried to keep up, yet always fell behind—nothing. No "yes," "no," or "maybe." The director had watched me flail through class—other dancers told me that was remarkable; he never watched an entire audition class—but when it ended, he disappeared down a hallway. I wandered through office cubicles, looking for an assistant or secretary to tell me how to follow up, but all I got was a street map and a subfreezing afternoon spent wandering around a desolate downtown.

But then, months later, on a broiling hot afternoon in New York City, as I was on the Broadway bus heading uptown from the Capezio dancewear store where I'd treated myself to a new pair of tights, my (newly acquired) cell phone rang. It was my father, calling to tell me that the director of Alberta Ballet in Calgary, Canada, had called our house and left a message for me. My résumé, one of dozens I had sent to directors of companies across the country and Europe, had landed on his desk that morning. And that same afternoon, one of his dancers had asked to be released from her contract. Their season was starting in two weeks and he suddenly had an open position—could I send a video overnight? Of course I could, and I did. Two days later: *I like your work and am excited* *at the potential I see—the job is yours, if you want it. But I can only pay you $450 a week.* I took it. Two weeks later, I packed my car with luggage and essentials to live with until a moving truck could follow me to Canada and drove over mountains and prairies to my new life. It was acceptance, sight unseen, after months of what now felt like the pursuit of rejection.

28

Glace Bay

Arriving in Halifax, an insistently rumbling stomach becomes a desperate hunger—no food all night long on the red-eye flight from western Canada—but thirty people flooding into a hotel lobby all at once is as slow as molasses. By the time a room key has been obtained, a dash upstairs to deposit luggage accomplished, and a frantic race back to the hotel restaurant won, a plate of scrambled eggs is the most delicious, and fastest-disappearing, food on earth.

The scene: a small ballet company's bus tour through the Maritime provinces of Nova Scotia and New Brunswick, to St. John's, Moncton, Sydney, and Glace Bay. The landscape through the bus window is lunar and endless. Springtime here feels cold, glacial, and much farther north than the map says. Snow's on the ground, ice patches, hardly any signs of civilization, yet a ballet company is on the marquee of the old vaudeville theaters in each town. Would puffins come from their roadside nests to see the show?

Glace Bay, Nova Scotia, is the first stop. The town's theater is rich with history, no doubt, but what were its stories? Who else tripped over the trapdoor ridges on the stage floor? The flouncy crinoline cancan skirts of the old days would have been as wide as our tutus—and as unwieldy in the narrow, steep staircases leading up from the dressing rooms directly beneath the stage. Performers from decades past would also have had to turn sideways to shuffle behind the backdrop and get from stage right to stage left. Who else looked up from the deck to the people sitting mere feet away, in velvet box seats precariously overhanging the stage? Who were the other performers who felt the garish footlights' heat under their chins, who bowed to a front row audience so close their heads tipped backward like Pez dispensers to see the dance?

A twenty-first-century ballet company's one-night stand quickly adds a short chapter to a very long story.

*Intermission. Racing the twenty-minute countdown from curtain
on one ballet to "Places" for the next. Run up the stairs, frantically
peel off the layers of costume, tights, and pointe shoes (the next ballet
requires a different pair), quickly pull hairpins out and shake loose
the hairpiece, chug some water—is there time to go to the bathroom?
Struggle to pull on a different costume and tights over sweaty legs, ap-
ply a dusting of face powder, fix smudged lipstick, shove another pair
of pointe shoes on halfway, pull on leg warmers and socks and a scarf
around my waist to hold in my muscles' warmth, the briefest glance in
the mirror, and one deep breath . . . a fleeting moment's thought of the
chicken teriyaki meatballs waiting at home for dinner . . . "ONSTAGE,
PLEASE" . . . quickly, but grabbing the handrails on those slippery
stairs, back downstairs to the stage.*

29

Vertigo, Part 1

For a dancer, times of injury, illness, or any physical instability at all are panic-inducing. For me in particular, the first sign of pain sparked a flash of fear—not fear of the pain itself but of the what-ifs: What if this gets worse? Can I dance through it? How bad will it be? Can I stand it? What if I can't? The sickening feeling in my stomach was not so much an effect of the physical problem as a sign of my insecurity. My currency was my ability to dance. Without it, I was penniless—or so I thought. There is no savings account for dance. I could not pay my way forward on the value of my performance from yesterday or last week.

I could withstand pain, if that was all I had to bear, but it was the prospect of dancing with a compromised body part that was so awful. Too scared to let on that I might not be able to deliver what I was contracted—and expected, and wanted—to do, my instinct was always to hide what was wrong and tough it out. Doing so took a psychological reserve of steel nerves that turned me temporarily into a military man, impersonal, removed, and, yes, perhaps verging on masochistic. It was as if, during the many episodes like this in my career, another dancer took over, sparing me from having to make the decision to push on instead of admitting defeat, even temporarily. Again, it seems there were multiple actors within one body, taking me through the drama as I watched from the side.

Why? Why, why, why, why, why? Why now?

It was the worst possible moment, or nearly so. Certainly, the timing of a crisis can almost always be worse, somehow, but does that really matter?

It had been a sustained period of heightened pressure. Her anxiety and growing apprehension, partially self-imposed, perhaps, had turned into a foreboding sense of dread. Expectations and demands had been made very clear, and as time grew short, with the dancer's sense of what was possible—and impossible—came the very real threat of disappointment. The dancer felt an inescapable doom coming over her like a cloak.

The ingredients in this boiling stewpot:

A temperamental partner, whose egotism was a thin cover for his self-doubt and almost desperate fear of appearing imperfect. His refusal to admit fault for any mistakes that were made, and his unpredictable rage at any perceived criticism, leaving the women he danced with trepidatious, anxious, and diminished.

A terrifyingly difficult ballet: George Balanchine's *Allegro Brillante*—a masterwork, an iconic piece of dance performed the world over. The choreography challenged the body, with virtuosic technique; the lungs, with nonstop dancing that spiraled upward in speed until the very end; and the mind, with glorious music that ran along joyously, teasing the dancers as if to ask why they couldn't keep up.

An injury, a persistent Achilles tendonitis that had flared up, scarily and ferociously, in the first days of rehearsal. A repetiteur from The Balanchine Trust, who had staged this work all over the world, had arrived to cast and teach the ballet. The pressure to learn quickly, deliver the goods, appear completely in control and compare favorably to some invisible, universal standard hung in the corners of the studio. The dancer's Achilles pain and instability caused feelings of unworthiness that had taken root from the very beginning and now refused to leave.

All of these strains compounded, becoming more and more intertwined until they were snarled in one big, snarly wasp's nest. Each made the others worse, and none stood a chance of cooling off, not until this was all over.

In the middle of a bitterly cold winter, the company had traveled by bus to a theater in a neighboring city. The dancers arrived with little time before the opening performance. The imposing snowdrifts outside the stage door were like a mean "Keep Out" sign on a nasty neighbor's cyclone fence. The familiar ritual of a warm-up class was small comfort— the freeze outside seemed to have penetrated into their bones and their minds. Each dancer's own burdens were magnified by the uncertain surroundings, preventing anyone from standing up straight and strong.

Three ballets were to be premiered that night, each notable and important in some particular way. The dancers felt the weight of their responsibility and shouldered it stoically, though some carried a greater share than others. That was expected and accepted—no matter how large or small your role, you deal with your own task. The unspoken rule is that no one tosses their troubles to anybody else. You learn and perfect your choreography, take care of your body, keep your demeanor in check (don't rub your dark mood off on your dressing room mates), because exuding it only makes others resentful. Wear your strong shell, even if you feel yourself struggling under its weight.

With no time for a blocking or technical rehearsal, dress rehearsal was first on the agenda immediately after the warm-up class. Rushed, unsettled, and still feeling the subzero temperatures clinging to her muscles, the dancer erased everyone, everything, out of her mind. She concentrated on getting through this rehearsal—just making it to the end without wasting one precious bit of energy, without irritating her ankle, without provoking her equally unsettled partner. The ballet began, continued, finished. The stage floor was unforgivingly hard, with no resilience, and just sucked the juice right out of her muscles. Afterward, there were corrections, comments, queries from the director and ballet masters as to why she'd done this step this way or hadn't done another one as coached. There were suggestions to try it one more time, differently, even though the performance was now only two hours away—this is akin to changing your route without a map in the middle of a nighttime snowstorm. Her partner disappeared, without a word, leaving her alone.

And then, while she was bending over to pick up her leg warmers in the wings, it happened. Vertigo.

It took several seconds for the spinning to stop, and once it did, any slight movement of her head set it off again. In the privacy of a corner backstage, she experimented, first cautiously, then defiantly, then with a growing sense of panic. There was no change. Twisting, pivoting, standing up, sitting down, certainly when bending over or back, any movement caused her eyes and head to whirl like a rhythmic gymnast's ribbon.

Everyone's attention had turned to the next rehearsal, now in progress onstage, so she told no one. She walked tentatively to her dressing room, praying for this to be temporary, telling herself it was a momentary blip or maybe a bad dream.

Holding on to the wall, she got out of her costume, pulled on sweatpants and a sweatshirt, and slowly lowered herself to the floor to take off her pointe shoes. Maybe if she proceeded as if everything was normal, if she pretended hard enough, it would be. She vowed never to be gloomy or depressed again, if only this would stop. Promised to be thankful for every moment her Achilles did not hurt, and even for the moments when it did, if only this would stop. She would be compassionate and gracious even when her partner was icy and demeaning.

Maybe if she lay down, carefully, and rested for a while it would go away. But how long could she rest? Time was flying. Normally, she'd be glad of it—she didn't like having too much time to stiffen up and become anxious—but now, with every passing minute, the knot of panic in her stomach tightened.

Clinging to the wall again, she pulled herself up and waited for the swirling to stop. She knew she had to tell someone, to find help. In a daze, she ventured back to the darkness of the backstage area, where the artistic director happened, for a rare moment, to be sitting alone. She told him she was unwell, and somehow even just forcing out the words, sharing her fear, was a small relief. He seemed nonchalant—not uncaring, but almost a bit dismissive. His suggestion—his avoidance of the unpleasant fact that he would have to rearrange the already tight casting if she couldn't perform that night—was to go rest again until the performance. He probably also prescribed deep breathing.

Her little-girl hope for someone to magically appear and make everything better evaporated. She felt frozen with disbelief—she was going to have to dance like this. There was no way out.

Having no other choice, she did retreat to her dressing room to lie down again and wait. Dress rehearsal was almost over. Curtain was in an hour. Her dressing room mate came puffing through the door, still sweating and red-faced and buzzing, her normalcy somehow comforting. She was unaware—and remained so—of the possibly threatening situation: they understudied each other in their respective ballets. If one was out, the other was in.

From then on, she was in a daze. Mechanically, she sat down at her dressing table and started to put on makeup, twist her hair in a smooth and tight updo, and pin the small, flowered headpiece in place. There was nothing else to do but get back into pointe shoes and try warming up again. Desperately, she held on to the sliver of possibility that somehow this wasn't really happening. . . . There was a knock at the door, which cracked open just far enough for the ballet master's face to poke through. The dancer caught her breath, expecting a sneer and a sigh of irritation for the trouble she was causing, for surely the director had relayed the news of her condition. But, instead: *I heard—I'm so sorry you're sick!— don't worry, just get through the show tonight, do whatever you have to do, change what you need to change, it will be okay—you poor thing . . .*

This uncharacteristic show of sympathy was a jolt—the situation seemed real again but not hopeless anymore. She knew that the ballet master was a mother, but her usual demeanor when conducting class or rehearsals (sternly demanding, harsh, and quick to judge) made that a fact easy to forget and, often, hard to believe. The dancer was struck by such a show of warm, genuine maternal concern and was momentarily distracted from her own problem by an image of this older woman caring for her like her own mother would have, tending to her in bed while she was sick with the flu. The dancer breathed again and felt life returning to her body. She was comforted and bolstered—this sickness was not a shortcoming, a mistake, a flaw in her nature, or a deliberate act. It was not a failure. *She* was not a failure. What a relief to be told that. She hadn't believed it herself. There was, in fact, an exit.

Knowing, now, that all that was expected of her was a valiant effort, that she didn't have to perform as if everything were normal, and that this cursed dizziness in her head was everyone's enemy and not just her own, she carried on—she warmed up at a barre backstage, carefully and without bending over; she got into costume, taped her feet and put on her pointe shoes. Her partner had been told that she was sick, dizzy, yet was going to dance. When they met in the wings, his encouraging expression and reassuring words startled her. They didn't practice any steps in the last few minutes before curtain—she was afraid, and he probably was, too. As they danced, he spoke to her throughout—*beautiful! Excellent! You can do it! Yes!* It was excessive, of course, and transparently self-serving, and he eagerly assumed the role of chivalrous hero to an ailing damsel, downgrading his own performance to safeguard her from her own demise. But she appreciated it nonetheless, wistfully imagining that this warmth might last.

The performance ended. Without tragedy. She stayed upright, he supported her, she modified some of the steps, and they finished. What are the forces that arise when the curtain goes up and the music starts? They protect the dancer—or any performer—and shield her from true harm. Perhaps they shield the dancer from herself.

Arrangements were made for the remaining performances, and a very young up-and-coming dancer got her chance to step out from being the fourth-cast understudy into the spotlight. She became the *real* hero, adding this crushingly difficult ballet on top of her other corps de ballet roles without showing a sign of fatigue. Her energy and talent and zeal outshone the now-grumpy partner's annoyance at dancing with a neophyte.

A photograph was taken during that first performance, capturing the dancer in a pristine, purely held arabesque, a crystallized moment of serenity and stillness. It was sold to a stock agency sometime later and now appears on posters, ads, CD covers, billboards, and websites, used to depict the world's generic definition of "ballerina": on pointe, pink, and perfectly poised. Only she, coming across her image years later, unexpectedly and in unlikely places, knew what turmoil was spinning inside that vision of calm and control.

—

I went on to perform *Allegro Brillante* many times after that unhappy debut. But as beautiful a ballet as it is, and as uplifting and glorious its score (Tchaikovsky's *Piano Concerto No. 3*), it remained slightly cursed for me.

Most times I performed it, and in most rehearsals, too, I would hit the wall three-quarters through. The fatigue, by then, would have built up to the point where I came out of "the zone"—conscious thoughts and awarenesses broke through the higher plane of superconsciousness on which a performance usually took place. A jolt of information from my legs and feet that they were out of juice forced me to try (with limited success) to actively operate them, since they had not enough resources to function on muscle memory. Perhaps it is like shifting from auto-play to manual drive. It is definitely like trying to type after walking outside without mittens on the coldest winter's day.

Allegro is notoriously hard, despite being short in duration. Balanchine was quoted as saying it "contains everything I know about the classical ballet in thirteen minutes," and I believe it does. The female lead's choreography has brilliant allegro (of course), sumptuous, grand adagio, and a solo that blatantly lays bare her turning ability, as she takes center stage and performs multiple pirouettes in several different directions with no extraneous steps to cover up any mishaps, accompanied only by a solo piano cadenza. All other movement and sound pause, hovering breathlessly, while the two artists suspend time together, tempting and daring each other to go further, higher, longer. The steps are almost a classroom exercise but done in the spotlight and with more stretch and risk than anyone can (or should) calculate in advance. It seems to me a rare example of Balanchine wanting to show off pure virtuosic technique expressly for that reason—to show off. The entrance with those pirouettes comes midway through the ballet, after allegro and adagio sections (and then come more of each). I would be in the wings, taking measured, deep breaths to regulate my lung capacity, before running out to center-center stage as the corps cleared and the orchestra quieted. I felt that the pianist and I were all that mattered, in our own little world in front of an audience of expectant eyes and ears. Even my partner stepped aside, waiting patiently and proudly as his ballerina displayed her skill, yet I always felt his presence there.

The strength of the piano cadenza took over when my legs would otherwise have collapsed. The power of Tchaikovsky was the only thing holding me up and urging me to go on, the notes adding a power surge to my leaden feet. The pianist and I were a team (even when I performed to recorded music), a partnership in which I always felt like the lesser half, but the music's brilliance kept me from letting her down. I couldn't falter—the music simply would not let me. It would have been an injustice to let slip an opportunity to embody Tchaikovsky and Balanchine's perfect creation.

My body goes numb, feet absolutely unresponsive, no more connection between brain and legs, but I can't (am not allowed to) stop dancing, stop trying to do the steps; my brain is doing the steps, but I don't think my body is. There are three pirouettes, sauté arabesque, grand jeté, and exit into the wings for a blessed, but painful, fifteen seconds. The last pirouette should be a double, which I never manage to do—but this time, somehow, I stay on pointe twice around—am I too tired to throw myself off balance? The stage manager, at her station downstage right, is practically onstage with me, she's so close to the edge of the wing. I scream with glory as I grand jeté offstage, inches from her victoriously raised arms, her face brilliantly lit with her own joy, sharing my triumph—we slap hands in a huge high five as I run past her to take place for my next entrance, twelve seconds away.

30

The Rib-Cracking Episode

I was lucky enough to sustain only two fractures during my career, but oddly, both were to my ribs.

Patrick had very large hands and a very, very strong grip. With one hand positioned on my rib cage, the other on my thigh in arabesque, he bent his knees into a deep plié, inhaled, and delivered me to the height of the lift. I braced my stomach muscles so I would stay sturdy, pressed down with my leg so I wouldn't flop out of position and, barely breathing, pointed my bottom foot (now off the floor and easy to forget about) as hard as I could, as if to distract myself from the pressure on the rest of my body. It worked perfectly. Holding me aloft, directly over his head and with completely straight arms, Patrick took the choreographed four or five steps diagonally across the floor as the music hit its crescendo, and I gazed intently at the high corner of the studio, waiting to be gently lowered to the floor at the end of the phrase.

Being lifted overhead is really cool. Even though it's the man doing the lifting, when the two of you are coordinated and your takeoff is timed right, the woman feels as though she's propelled herself up there. Like a perfect balance, if the dancers have worked out their positions and grips just so, a lift can be, mostly, easeful and strain-free. The lifter has got to be strong, yes, but also has to know, not approximately but precisely, where his partner's center of balance is. He has to "listen" through his hands for the split-second timing of her push. And she, in turn, can't rush into it before she can tell he's ready.

Once she's successfully aloft, both dancers feel powerful. He's the pedestal, sturdy and valiant, and she's the icon, proud and free. Until, and unless, communication breaks down.

This time, that is just what happened. My signals went unnoticed or ignored. I was waiting to be brought back to earth on time with the music, but Patrick was happy. He was proud of having nailed the lift and didn't want to end it when he was supposed to. Perhaps he wanted to show off a bit. He kept me up there—I knew we were late, and being held in arabesque with two hands pressing like kickstands into my ribs and leg is not comfortable. I fought to keep my position strong, though I wanted desperately to feel the floor beneath my feet. But moving at all would compromise the safety of both of us.

Patrick held his grip and tightened it with his fingers as he finally, slowly—too slowly, unnecessarily so—brought me down. As he released his hands from my ribs, something felt funny. I didn't hear a crack, but I felt it, sort of. A muscle spasm? There was a feeling of tightness, suddenly, in my side.

Rehearsal was over. I walked downstairs to the dressing room, gingerly peeled off my dance clothes, and stepped into a pair of sweatpants for my short drive home. Carrying my dance bag in both arms like a sack of groceries instead of hanging it on my shoulder, I went out to the parking lot, opened my car door, and gasped as I hinged at the waist to get into the driver's seat. Shooting pain stabbed me in the side.

Patrick had fractured my rib with his bare hands.

31

"You Were the Music"

There are dancers, and there are ballerinas.

Just like there are cooks, and then there are chefs.

The first time a dancer, a woman, is called a ballerina may or may not be a defining moment. It depends on who has done the calling. It may be flattering or give a tickle of excitement or an ego boost, but the dancer herself knows already if she is a ballerina or not. She may not think that she knows, but she does. And if she thinks she can become one, if she feels that there is something greater inside her that has not yet flourished, being prematurely called "ballerina" can be a little empty. The word's honor will have lost some luster.

The dancer herself knows whose words she can trust. The person who has seen it all, or seen a lot, seen the best, been in the presence of sincerely, seriously transcendent artistry: that is someone to trust. The person who knows the dancer and has seen, step-by-step, her body and mind evolve from caterpillar to butterfly, has seen her go further than necessary, push herself harder than necessary. She will have had much help along the way, from teachers and mentors, and much inspiration, but her motivation will have come as much—or more—from within as from without. Knowing that her place in the field of astounding dance talent is just a single tulip among acres of blooms, each more imposing in its beauty than the next, will only have stoked her resolve. She will take in everything she sees, intuiting what is useful to her and what is not. Eventually, she will go the final mile by herself, because she knows exactly what to do and has, in her DNA, the means to do it.

Dance watchers love to say they can pinpoint the defining moment when a dancer crosses over into ballerina territory. But in truth, there is no one moment when that happens. Ballerinas are born with a blueprint, but then they are made. The process of the ballerina's construction may never be complete, but there comes a time when the title is justified. Who decides when that is or what lifts the dancer into that arena? There's no official scorekeeper or judge. The bestower of the ballerina crown is self-designated. She herself decides when to accept it.

After a dancer is born, she begins to grow. Dancers are cultivated, and if they are lucky, they are nourished and tended by gardeners who know how to fertilize them, how much sun they need, how much shade and water, or how much benign neglect. The gardeners have to know which dancers will flourish under duress, which will wither, and which will need gentle daily pruning. They'll probably have some of all types in their garden and will need to use multiple tactics and techniques to grow them all successfully. And then, after the gardeners have done everything possible, season after season, and the dancer is nearing full maturity, they have to know whether to snip her from the vine or not. There will be some dancer-flowers that stagnate on the vine, and others will die if they aren't cut off from it.

The ballerinas are the ones that are cut off—or that leap off, at the gardener's tiniest tug. They don't die or stagnate, far from it. They are really only at the beginning of their lives.

The ballerina flower has an inborn understanding of music, of relationship, of humanity, such that when she is onstage, a single person in an audience of one thousand feels they are being directly spoken to. The ballerina's gardener may continue to monitor her growth, but the ballerina is going in her own direction now. And her instincts are right.

Offstage, she's self-confident yet humble. When she walks into the studio to take a class, or into the wings to prepare for a performance, or down the street to get groceries, people around her feel something— they're not sure what, but it's intriguing—that draws them in but also keeps them at a respectful distance. She's proudly carrying ballet along with her but isn't flaunting it like a prize.

The ballerina is not egoless—she is aware enough of her own gifts to see how important it is to protect them and do them justice. She feels self-respect because she's working, and dancing, in service to something that belongs to everyone on earth. Ballet isn't hers alone to enjoy. Sure, she craves doing it, but that thought does not drive her every day.

A dancer may dance because she loves to move expansively to music and has a beautiful physique, a natural facility, a knack for doing a lot of tricky steps—and the adventurousness to try them. But the ballerina dances because she has all of that, plus more. She can communicate, through the choreography, with all those who've come before her, all those who are watching her now, and by leaving her perfume on the steps she dances, with all those who come after. Where others find the freedom and exposure of the stage paralyzing, she is emboldened. She's not afraid.

When she performs, she sheds her offstage persona and, almost literally, becomes the steps she is dancing. The audience forgets that they are watching a human being, because the ballerina is inseparable from the music. She is inside the notes, and they are wrapped around her. The music is her costume, and she is its instrument. Her deep, inborn awe and respect for ballet doesn't weigh her down or strike her with fear but empowers her. She knows that she can—and must—let go of her ego to get past the dangerous, scary zone of purely technical dancing and rise to the next level, to where it doesn't matter what her name is. Where she can stop being a competent artisan. Where she surrenders to the invisible forces of music and movement just enough to make the audience gasp while keeping a firm toehold on her hard-won technique.

She is, after all, like all dancers, a craftsperson first. But she doesn't stop once she's honed her craft to the finest point her body allows, which may be short of the ideal. Even then, she digs below the lovely shapes that are just superficial (though in breathtakingly clear evidence). She is a stickler for precision in her technique and lets no step, however small or brief, be unconsidered. She knows that, like the fur lining inside the collar of a coat, even what's unseen is visible, if not to the audience in the back row, then to her—and since she is responsible for the steps she is doing, if she lets one of them slide, she has lost a small fraction of her power to create an artwork.

I am in my dressing room, moments after dancing the *Romeo and Juliet* bedroom pas de deux. I have a fractured rib but don't know it yet. I just know that while onstage, something crunched—popped—in my side as my partner positioned his hands on my body to lift me. It was a pain so shocking that my breath, already heavy from dancing, disappeared for a second. For the rest of the pas de deux, all I could think of was how to survive: my brain raced to stay ahead of the music and choreography, frantically calculating how to negotiate each upcoming step to protect my side. Miraculously, we finished. Our final pose: a serpentine embrace on the floor, the climax of two lovers' desperately, passionately painful last night together. We were both panting and slimy with each other's sweat. The panicked clarity of my adrenaline-fueled thinking during the few minutes of emergency self-preservation disappeared. Everything was a blur from then on—I moved robotically as we bowed and I received the traditional opening night bouquet of flowers, pulling out a single stem to give to my Romeo. We waited for the curtain to fall and exchanged a quick "thank you" hug and kiss. I might have murmured something about the pain, but he was already distracted—the next ballet was only a few minutes away and he had to rush to change into another costume. He dashed off, leaving me alone amid the sudden bustle of stagehands efficiently changing the scenery and sweeping the floor. I walked stiffly to the wings and squatted down to pick up my leg warmers from where I'd tossed them on the floor.

I somehow made it down the hall to my dressing room and awkwardly sat down in the folding chair in front of the makeup table, grimacing, the pain getting worse as my muscles began cooling and tightening. I could barely stand to wriggle out of my costume. Any movement or touch was excruciating. My dressing room mate, preparing to go onstage herself, was warmly sympathetic and calm, offering validation and support, reassurance that all would be well. But she, too, was preoccupied with her own imminent performance and disappeared quickly when the stage manager called "Onstage!" over the intercom. Then there was a knock at the door. Alone now, and half-dressed, I hobbled over and peeked out: *Yes?*

It was the ballet master. The same woman who had taught, rehearsed, coached, and driven me so hard so many times that I thought I would crack.

That was it, she said. *You WERE the music.*

You are a ballerina, girl. You be a ballerina.

—

A chef may still prefer to call himself a cook. Maybe he doesn't like fancy titles. Maybe he resents or disagrees with the associations that come along with the word "chef." He wants to stay close to the ground, to his roots, to his compadres on the line. He'll protest that what he does with ingredients is just a thoughtful exploration and celebration of food and that his creativity with flavors and textures simply reflects a love of creating good meals that make people happy.

A ballerina, also, may stiffen at being called a ballerina. If the word is tossed off too easily, it conjures up an airy image of a spindly, tutu-clad, light-headed music box figurine—an insulting disservice to the bone-crunching work she does every day. Such a flippant use propagates misinformation and stereotyping.

Or maybe she flinches at hearing the term alongside her name because she doesn't believe it herself. To believe that you stand beside the *real* ballerinas you have thought of as untouchable—does that mean that your ideal is no longer perfect? Because then you know that those idols, the epitome of ballet, are as fallible and flawed as you.

But perhaps that is part of what makes her a ballerina, after all. She never feels she has arrived at the destination. And, in fact, she never wants to arrive, because then the journey is over, the jig is up, and the music will end.

32

Boo Hoo, Jeremy Denk

My time in Canada was relatively short. The ballets, roles, and coaching I got there, along with the surprisingly frequent visits from important choreographers, were hugely valuable—and they were thanks to the man who had hired me, our artistic director, Mikko Nissinen. He had come from a major career of his own and used his connections and reputation to build not only this out-of-the-way company but also his own credentials. It worked, for all of us. But when he found the next stepping-stone on his path upward, I feared being left behind. He went on to take over a much larger company, so I immediately started planning my exit, too. A repeat of my audition process from years earlier ended almost the same way—but without the job offer at the end. So I moved back to New York, back in with my parents, and with some excitement at my new autonomy, I began a year of life as a freelance dancer in the big city. It felt real: hardscrabble but valid and prideworthy to be one of the free-floating gang of dancers making their living gig by gig, through contacts and good words and friends recommending friends for jobs. Scouring ad listings for "Dancers Wanted" was fun at first, and while some jobs turned out to be rewarding, they all had negative trade-offs. I paid for everything myself—pointe shoes, classes, costumes, transportation, which would normally be covered in a professional company—and suffered through endless rehearsals for cringingly bad choreography that I could not believe I was doing. I traveled

two hours to the far reaches of Staten Island to teach a young children's
ballet class, but the painstakingly prepared exercises I planned to give
them were wasted when I arrived to find they knew not even the most
basic steps. I auditioned for a Broadway show and was cut as soon as
they asked for a reverse grand jeté, a trick I had never seen or heard
of (my attempt must have been even worse than my desperate try at a
pirouette, way back in the Greek Teacher's class). I substitute taught
an adult ballet class in Soho, but when it turned out that my pay was
determined by how many students there were—and that the accom-
panist's fee was taken out first—my mother forbade me to do it again
(my check was for three dollars). But mostly, thankfully, I danced.

Years later, as I read an essay by famous pianist Jeremy Denk mus-
ing on a particularly vapid musical job he had taken, I was struck by
how we—all of us artists, high and low, famous and not—make sacri-
fices and compromises along the way, but some are on a vastly different
plane than others.

⏜

(A response to "Piano Man," published in
The New Yorker on October 14, 2013)

So sorry to hear, Jeremy, that you only grossed $10k for your gig play-
ing Mendelssohn and Piazzolla for those Japanese "Four Seasons" DVDs.
And while you were still a struggling Juilliard student, no less! I know, it's
belittling and degrading to be in the background, creating art that's to be
used as fodder for sappy commercialism, but at least the limo ride to and
from location must have been nice.

I can empathize, although my own first taste of the rat race wasn't until after I'd been out of school for ten years and was fully established as
a professional dancer. Up until that point, I'd had—blessedly—no personal experience with dancing for the money as opposed to for the "fun"
of it. I'd been with a very well-respected, mid-sized company on the West
coast but quit after several years in the corps de ballet in pursuit of greater
opportunities to shine. I landed in a smaller, regional Canadian company
where I did find that opportunity. There was less money—lots less—but

far greater career development. I became a principal dancer almost over-night and was coached and nurtured by astute and generous directors and choreographers.

But then I quit that job, too, when those mentors left for greener pas-tures themselves. And for the first time, I was without work—it was un-employment by choice but still unemployment. So I joined the ranks of freelance dancers in New York City.

It's a pretty solid, tight-knit community, this "freelancer's union," de-spite being cutthroat, because really everyone's competing for the same thing. But at the same time, people look out for each other and help each other find work. For example, during *Nutcracker* season (everyone's cash cow) established freelancers often find themselves with more offers than they can fit into one short month. So we shared, referring friends for jobs we couldn't (or didn't want to) take.

And that's how I found myself, for the first time ever, creating my own performance schedule, and it was fun! It felt important to book myself for various weekends in various towns around the country, work out the logistics of finding partners and costumes and travel arrangements. But that feeling, like the tinsel-glitter-glee of holidays in the city, wore off well before January 1 rolled around.

The first gig I did was in suburban Houston, Texas. I can't honestly remember the name of the school that hired me to be their Sugarplum Fairy, but the director promised me that my Cavalier (whom I didn't know and had never heard of) was a marvelous partner, very experi-enced, and that he had performed with them for years. Every Sugarplum she'd ever hired just loved him. The director was making a new Sugar-plum tutu that year, so it would be fitted just for me and I wouldn't have to worry about bringing my own (lesson 1: don't agree to a blind date with a tutu). She would get me a room at a hotel near the theater (the latter, I soon found out, was the local high school auditorium). The hotel was next to a mall with restaurants and a Walmart and Starbucks (a born and bred Manhattanite, I'd never been inside a Walmart). And, of course, my flights to and from Houston would be taken care of.

Somewhat ready for anything, I got on an early morning flight from LaGuardia one December day and arrived in Houston around noon. No one was at baggage claim to pick me up as promised, so I called the director's cell phone. She apologized profusely and asked me to take a taxi to the ballet studio, where she was waiting and would pay the fare. Fine. I hopped in a cab and two hours later arrived in the burbs of Houston. The meter said sixty dollars, which she did indeed pay.

Rehearsals started straight away that afternoon at the school's studio, a storefront in a strip mall. I would come to understand that many, many, many dance schools in the United States live in strip malls, but this was the first time I'd seen or been in one. The studio floor was slipperier and harder than any I'd ever felt. Pointe shoes (my own, unreimbursed) felt like ice skates—I had to bang the tips with a hammer and douse them with rubbing alcohol to gain any traction. This meant I ended up using many more pairs than anticipated, and at eighty dollars a pair, that was cutting way into my fee. I saw cash leaking out with every bang of my hammer.

The director's assistant flash-taught me the pas de deux, variation, and coda on my own and the finale with the rest of the cast that first afternoon. My partner arrived that night. As promised, he was indeed wonderful, strong, and funny. A tall, gregarious fellow from Bulgaria.

After rehearsal was my costume fitting. The aforementioned Sugarplum tutu was indeed new—so new that its layers of tulle did not fan out from my hips in a gentle, elegant downward slope but splayed upward, aiming toward my ears and completely exposing my legs and rear end. It was puffy and short like a child's Halloween costume—not the intended effect of a classical tutu. And it was a purple, dark grape color, with sequined sugarplums sewn (or maybe pasted) all over the bodice. I might have loved it when I was five.

But I was approaching thirty and was supposed to be at the apex of my artistic and physical powers, nearly the climax of my career, and here I was, wearing a tacky costume on a treacherous floor somewhere in the sprawl of Texas, trying to maintain a sense of pride and praying not to get hurt.

Dress rehearsal was the next day. I walked from my hotel to the theater by myself and found the rest of the cast (all students from the school) filling the hallways, already prepping hair and makeup and acting like the hyper, overexcited kids and teenagers they were—who just happened to be wearing ballet shoes. I didn't know where I should go to change and get prepared myself and couldn't find any dressing rooms. The director was darting throughout the theater, frantically trying to oversee the fleet of parent volunteers who were masquerading as stagehands, costumers, lighting designers, doormen, stage managers, babysitters. . . . So a nice woman, someone's mom, proudly showed me where my private dressing room was. I'd passed right by it on my way in and not even noticed. It was the handicapped restroom, marked with a big gold "STAR" sign right under the wheelchair logo on the door.

And if you must ask, Jeremy, I got $1500 in all—$375 per show, and no per diem.

33

Suzanne

A very plum gig during my freelance period was an engagement to join the Suzanne Farrell Ballet for its performances at the Kennedy Center in Washington, DC. The company was not a full-time organization; it was a pickup group that formed with a rotating roster of dancers, recruited by Suzanne Farrell herself, for several weeks each year. The length of the company's season varied, but that year it was a six-week contract: five weeks of rehearsal and one week of performances. Some dancers returned year after year, but given the irregular nature of the company's work, it was impossible to retain the same group in its entirety, and Suzanne had to find at least a few new members every time the company reformed.

A friend of mine from my ballet school days had done her time as a freelancer in New York already. When I returned home and started into the complicated and very confusing business of hustling for work, she and I reconnected and met for lunch. A true go-getter if there ever was one, she grilled me on everything I was doing and laid down the basics of how to succeed in this new world: where to take class, who to talk to afterward, what choreographers to send my resume to. I was overwhelmed—I had no idea I needed to be so proactive. "What about Suzanne? You should call her," was the one tip she offered that really threw me for a loop. I'd heard of Suzanne's company, of course, but assumed it was a closed-circuit enterprise that I had no way of penetrating. I suffered from a lack of assertiveness, which is a crucial element

of getting anywhere as a self-employed anything. The Suzanne Farrell
Ballet? Don't you have to BE someone? I had not even thought about
how, in order to get work, I would have to grab for it. Work would not
come knocking at my door.

Tara, my stalwart friend, gave me the name and number of Su-
zanne's manager and coached me on what to say. I summoned up a
huge amount of courage—though at the same time, knowing I had
absolutely nothing to lose made me calmer—phoned, and was asked
to send my resume. A few days later, the manager called back. Could
I please send a video of a performance? Luckily, I had already made a
demo reel of performance clips for just this purpose (along with what
I thought were snazzy headshots). Slightly elevated, I sent it off and
waited, but also sort of forgot about it—as before, my timing was off
and it was already late summer; the season was due to start shortly
and it was unlikely she needed anybody. But: The phone rang one hot,
humid afternoon after I'd returned home from class. It was Suzanne
Farrell herself. "I would love to hire you for my season, if you are
interested and available. Your video is lovely and I think you would be
a beautiful addition to my company." I was frozen and could barely
speak, but fumbled out a "yes." "There's one more thing, though," she
continued. "I am afraid I don't have any more principal contracts and
can only offer you a soloist one. Is that all right?" Floored, absolutely
floored, at the concept of Suzanne Farrell, the legendary ballerina
closer to George Balanchine than anyone else alive, considering me
principal-dancer quality—I managed, I hope, to sound gracious and
confident as I gratefully expressed my eagerness to dance for her. One
notch down the hierarchical ladder from the top-rung principal status
was more than fine with me.

Then I hung up the phone and screamed.

———————

Suzanne was very, very quiet in the studio. She spoke in such soft tones,
and often with her face angled downward or away from us, that most of
her words—of which there were few—evaporated before they could
be caught. Particularly in class, she said very little and explained almost
nothing.

I had flashes of feelings from my very first ballet classes decades earlier: struggling to figure out what was going on and what was expected of me, floundering, at sea, frantically trying to keep up, to decipher instructions that seemed to be in code, or at least in a language I didn't understand.

Yet now, I wasn't alone. We all—the members of her company—grasped at the few words we could make out, desperately trying to interpret what she wanted. Some of our group, having danced with Suzanne in previous seasons, knew her methods better than the rest, knew her ways, her habits, and could guess at what she meant or wanted even if her words were unclear. I, along with the other neophytes, looked to the veterans and followed them closely. I learned to stand at the barre positioned so as to have a view of Shannon or Chan or Meredith, all of whom were reliable leaders and acted, at least, confident. To me, this type of class-taking was crazy hard, but these veterans knew that most of her tricks weren't new. The combinations she gave were fast, complicated, and arranged in patterns as cryptic as a word puzzle or number game, which in fact many of them were. Suzanne would not share the pattern, though, leaving it as a test to see whose brain could work fastest to figure it out and then—ha!—actually execute it. Sometimes I gave up and just did the step without the musical pattern, hoping she wasn't looking my way.

Suzanne Farrell had been Balanchine's muse, though not his only one. Many of my teachers had also worked directly with Balanchine, some very closely, and all of the Balanchine repertoire that I knew had been taught to me by someone who had personally danced for him. Some roles I'd learned from the very dancer on whom Balanchine had choreographed them.

But learning from Suzanne was different. Being in her presence felt like a direct conduit to Balanchine, something I'd never felt before.

I bristled at what struck me as an irresponsible way to teach, or to expect us to take, daily technique class. The extremes were great: faster, shorter, higher. The progression of class did nearly nothing to warm me up. Despite arriving early every morning to prepare my body on my own, I soon ended up with bursitis in my hip. It wasn't bad at first, but by week three I was choking with pain. I turned everywhere for help—other dancers, the company manager, my parents' medicine cabinet—but not, definitely not, to Suzanne herself.

The old fear of showing injury seemed magnified by ten. The season was short, I was almost at the end of it, and I was not going to drop out. Through my agony, I felt something special was happening. I did not want to have any regrets.

Fatigue lay on top of my hip pain. The schedule of rehearsals intensified as we neared the performance dates. In the Balanchine tradition, according to legend (and Suzanne was legend personified), everyone should dance their fullest at all times. Never save, never conserve, dance as if this moment is all that counts. In strictly practical terms, this is nuts. Pushing your muscles, joints, and tendons to their maximum and draining all energy during a full day of rehearsals makes a dancer feel desperate by the time the evening's performance approaches. Yes, adrenaline comes in, surging to pull you up and make your body operate as you command, but it is miserable.

My roommate on this tour to the Kennedy Center was just like me— shocked and outraged at the injustice of being worked so hard, and incredulous that everyone else seemed to take it in stride, but hanging in there and focused on mere survival. We counted the steps from our hotel room to the stage door to minimize the demands on our feet. We added protein powder to packets of instant oatmeal for breakfast in our hotel room before going to class. We needed much more sleep than the schedule allowed—rehearsal finished too late at night and we were called too early in the morning. Every ounce of energy and strength was preserved for rehearsals and the performances at the end of the week. If I was alone in the elevator, I knelt on the floor to give my legs another chance to rest. I sat on the edge of the bathtub when brushing my teeth.

But when Suzanne walked into the studio, everyone was on their feet. She was not mean, not demanding, not harsh. Just quiet and expectant.

She never spoke of herself. Her story, her life and legacy, was perhaps the most pivotal of anyone's to that of George Balanchine and New York City Ballet, yet she did not carry that in front of her. She only spoke of the work. The ballets, the steps, the energy, the intent.

There was no ego in the room. Just the ballets and us.

I felt, and almost could see, the ballets as entities, or maybe as people. We—all of us, Suzanne and each dancer—shared the room with these works of art. She was there to unwrap them for us, and we were there to get inside them. Working together, we'd polish the steps, build the formations with our bodies, and weave them into the fabric of the music. Eventually, a ballet would emerge, first in the studio, like a working model, and then into a final draft. Onstage, the velvet curtain would be pulled up and the nugget of the finished piece would show itself, clear and lit and costumed—and a slight bit of a surprise to everyone involved. None of us, no matter how many times we'd danced or seen a ballet before, really ever knew exactly what it would look or feel like in the moment of live performance.

If Suzanne had no ego, then I could not, either. My own pain and tiredness mattered, but they would go away. Time would pass and I would forget how hard it was. But now, now, now matters more.

On opening night, we had an afternoon dress rehearsal for *Chaconne* and the two other ballets on the program. The night before, we'd run the three ballets we'd perform later in the weekend after an afternoon tech rehearsal. In between each, there were notes and a working rehearsal upstairs in the theater's studio. I was spent and genuinely fearful my legs would not hold me up. I knew the feeling of my body crumpling underneath me and felt I was dangerously close.

When Suzanne hired me, she asked me to learn and understudy the principal ballerina role in *Chaconne*. I was a soloist in her company, the fact of which alone humbled me—I did not feel worthy. She began teaching me the role in *Chaconne* but never finished. It was a role she was famous for, and I'd watched videos of her dancing it many times. *Chaconne* remains one of my favorite ballets, with music of the heavens and choreography to match. But teaching and coaching the first cast principal dancers took precedence over my learning the part, and I concentrated on my demi-soloist role.

That afternoon, dress rehearsal ended. We had two hours before the curtain would go up on opening night. I walked offstage to get the leg warmers I'd left on the backstage floor, already thinking of how to maximize my rest time, when and what to eat, where I could lie down, how long I could stay horizontal with my feet against the wall before having to warm up again. My dressing room, mercifully, was carpeted and had enough floor space for a rest, but the theater's cafeteria was a long walk away. As I calculated the energy expenditure and wondered how quickly I could get there and back, Suzanne silently appeared in the shadowy privacy of the wing where I hesitated. She stood there, so close that I finally saw how beautiful her translucent alabaster skin was, which Balanchine is said to have loved. Powdery eye shadow, thin brown hair, and I could almost feel her heart beating. A real person.

Is there anything you want to ask me? Her voice was low and quiet. Immediately I cried. There was so much, it was all so much, too much, for one person to handle. I was fighting so hard to take care of myself and take care of the ballets and justify the two. And here in front of me, giving me everything, was the person who had done it all. I should have had a million questions to ask, but all I could do was shake my head and try to hide my tears. But when I looked up, there were tears in Suzanne's eyes, too.

Just a few days after my last performance with Suzanne's company, still limping with pain in my hip (though, miraculously, after being diagnosed with bursitis and resting for a very short amount of time, it healed as if its sudden and severe onset was mirrored by an equally swift and complete departure), I was making my way down Broadway when I saw a vaguely familiar figure coming toward me. I knew his face and physique, but not well, and I idly wondered from where my memory of him came. But his recollection, apparently, was better than mine—and once our eyes met, he swerved toward me, waving and clearly about to stop and talk. Now my brain went into that panicked mode one feels when cornered without a clue what to do. Thankfully, as soon as he said my name, I knew—he was Christopher Stowell, the son of my former directors at Pacific Northwest Ballet, and we'd met a few times over the many years I danced for his parents.

I was surprised, though, at how eager he was to stop and talk. I was a nobody in his parents' company, and we'd probably exchanged fewer than a dozen words over seven years.

It became clear. After a "Hi, how are you?" he asked what I was doing. As in, with my life. The ballet world, like every industry, is so interconnected that your moves are likely known much more than you might imagine. Through the threads of his own web, Christopher knew I'd been in Alberta Ballet, had left, and then had disappeared from the ranks of any regular company. But I, not into gossip nor caring enough to keep track of anyone but myself, hadn't heard that the longtime director of Oregon Ballet Theatre (OBT) had resigned. Or that Christopher would be taking over. Our short conversation in the middle of a busy sidewalk that day led to phone calls, e-mails, letters, and more phone calls, as he told me he was looking for new dancers to bring in as he started a new era at OBT, redesigning the company to his own taste. Although it was only about four months into my freelance adventure, I'd already figured out that it was not as glamorous as in the movies, I couldn't afford it financially or otherwise, and I wanted to be in a company again. I did hesitate to take Christopher up on his invitation (thinking his parents likely still held a grudge against me for having left them so suddenly and that that negativity might be passed along), but when I came clean to him about my worry, he professed to have never heard about it nor to care. I grew more and more excited at the thought of dancing for this energetic, exciting, incredibly smart and visionary man—the plans he told me about for his new OBT were things I'd dreamed of doing, and now maybe I had the chance.

In January, I signed the contract, and in July I moved to Portland to start the last chapter of my professional ballet dancer life, which proved to be the richest.

34

Places

"Places please, places for the top of *Sleeping Beauty!* Places, we're at places!"

Everyone around me was abuzz with activity, but I was completely engrossed. In my head and with my body, I was fine-tuning, rechecking, and re-fine-tuning every single detail, repeating carefully each step I was about to take. I had to feel that I had each one down before the curtain went up, even though I'd already spent dozens upon dozens of hours rehearsing them in the studio and had known that sense of perfect execution. I needed to know, NOW, at the moment of truth, that each movement was at my fingertips, hovering, ready to answer my commands right on cue. I needed proof for my suddenly doubtful mind that I was ready, because there was no time left.

The other dancers kept a distance from me, giving me an invisible circle of space, a sort of buffer zone with an electric fence no one would cross. At the stage manager's "Places" call, my brain said to do the first step of my variation one more time: from tendu arabesque, I stepped into sous-sous, perfectly balanced from absolute tip to toe. Plié in fifth position, relevé passé, and—SNAP—

The beaded armband of my costume, a gloriously embellished white tutu fit for a princess (I was about to dance Princess Aurora in act 3 of *Sleeping Beauty*) had torn apart as I lifted my arms overhead. Dozens of tiny, round, clear plastic beads that had been strung on the elastic band around my upper arm scattered, rolling all over the stage.

Oh. What . . . With my needle-sharp focus broken, my body froze and I stared blankly at the floor, momentarily unable to think. Milliseconds passed before I looked up and around for someone to tell me what to do, since I felt incapable of switching gears into crisis management. The stage manager—uncannily aware of everything happening on her stage and able to react with trigger-like speed—leapt into action.

Three broom-wielding stagehands magically appeared, swiftly and efficiently corralling every last bead into dustbins. Even one lone invisible rolling object under the dancers' feet would be dangerous, potentially disastrous.

"HOLDING, we're holding for three minutes, curtain holding for three . . ." the stage manager commanded into her headset. "Dancers, CLEAR THE STAGE! Clear!"

All I could do was step aside. Get out of the way and forget about it. . . . Wardrobe seamstresses (also appearing instantly, seemingly out of thin air) were snipping the remaining threads from my tutu and cutting off the other armband so my classical costume would not be asymmetrical. They murmured reassuring coos in their motherly way as they fussed about me, re-creating the bubble of self-focus that had just been shattered by a tiny thread.

There was no time, now, to finish my final preparations. The audience was already antsy at this unexplained delay. The shuffling and rumbling of two thousand bodies shifting in their seats and flipping through their programs, usually muted with reverent anticipation, was getting loud.

The conductor had already gone down to the orchestra pit. I, along with the dozens of other dancers in the cast, had crowded into the wings while the stagehands worked—I prayed they'd found every bead. Even squished into the tight quarters of the upstage right wingspace, the circumference of my stiff, regal tutu kept the others at arm's length. Its edges formed the border of my small world. The other dancers' chatter and movement in the wings were dull to my senses.

The overture punctured the hum backstage, pushing me into countdown mode as measured as a NASA takeoff, though without the option to abort mission. I realized that in the chaos, my partner and I had separated to our entrance-wings on opposite sides of the stage without wishing each other good luck.

As if to make up for the speed of the pre-curtain frenzy, the conductor drew out Tchaikovsky's sublime music in slow motion. During our first entrance, a polonaise in which the guests and entertainers at our wedding present themselves to the King and Queen and my Prince and I arrive with great fanfare, we nearly stumbled with the shock and effort of moving so slowly through the steps of the simple processional. Waiting in the wings after that first entrance, I listened to the other divertissements, trying to gauge what to expect from the conductor when it came time for our grand pas de deux, the climax of the ballet. The uncertainty didn't rattle me. Our preparations, hours of rehearsals in the studio, were not rigid. We would just breathe a little deeper, hold and stretch and extend a little farther, to fulfill the possibility of the empty space inside, and within, the notes.

Arriving center stage to begin, it was clear from the first hushed, spare phrases of music that this would be the slowest we had ever danced the pas de deux. It was not easy to sustain the développés (already precarious with only one-handed support), but we silently coordinated our timing to pace ourselves through each moment. Without a word, we agreed on how to take a hair longer to prepare for the pirouettes and fish dives, moderating the speed at which we'd move from place to place on the stage and broadening the simplest gestures—the offering of his hand, my acceptance of his support.

We milked it for all it was worth and drank in every note.

We had only one performance—did the conductor know that? Was he slowing it down for us, to make it last, let us savor each delicious drop? My arms felt freer than ever before, thanks to the release of those scratchy armbands. After the pas de deux, we each danced a solo variation, and I triumphantly concluded mine with the glee befitting a princess who had slept for years before her prince arrived to kiss her awake: arms thrown overhead, slightly open, fingers reaching to the sky.

35

Quivering

A professional dancer spends as much time observing as actually danc-ing. (Similarly ironic is that, as with every performing art, many, many more hours are spent in the rehearsal studio than onstage. Behind every two- or three-minute solo are dozens of hours of rehearsal.) And as you advance upward through the ranks, you will dance less and less than your colleagues in the corps de ballet, who are cast in more ballets simply because there are more ensemble roles to be filled and fewer principal roles to go around. Watching performances from the wings, with a restricted side-angle, but very, very up close, view, affords a com-pletely and totally different impression of the dance and dancers, one that we in the business are much more accustomed to seeing than the audience's wide-angle, across-the-footlights panorama. The threads of tension on which a dancer suspends her technique disappear from afar, but perhaps the best seat in the house is within arm's reach.

From the audience, she looks rock-solid, balancing on pointe in ara-besque after a series of precariously difficult one-armed promenades with her partner. But from the wings, just a few feet away, we see the edges of her tutu quivering.

The effect of vulnerability is both true and misleading, since her strength is real but the intensity of her effort is, too. Every single fiber of every muscle in her body is engaged—not stiffly rigid but called into play with calculated, modulated precision. Up close, a nearby watcher can see the constant recalibration required to maintain her arabesque and even lift it higher and higher when human nature would tell it to droop. The determination reverberates to the edges of tulle spanning out from the basque of her tutu.

Her effort has been overtaken by some power she did not have when she woke up that morning. Yes, the physicality of her poses and movements is human. They are HER legs, arms, torso, neck, fingertips. But the surge that fuels them comes from somewhere else. She's calculating every split-second maneuver, but there is also an unseen manipulator—an internal god, maybe?—who guides and powers her to the end.

It's electrifying for both dancer and audience. When the promenade is at its ultimate climax, as the ballerina releases her partner's hand for an impossibly long balance alone, on one pointe, leg at a full 90 degree arabesque, some man from the back of the house ROARS, and the rest of the crowd erupts in turn. She is jolted, startled, shocked, and stunned with the realization: *There are people out there! And they like what I just did?*

But it's not over—there is a lift, a pirouette, a toss in the air, and a fish dive to finish, the audience's thunder nearly drowning out the music. As her partner lifts her with compassionate strength (he's on fire from the response as well), gently placing her on pointe in a piqué arabesque and sweeping her into their agreed-upon pose for their bow, she gives him a secret "oh my God" look. The sturdy fabric of their costumes makes noise, too, but the friction between his tunic and her tutu is far from audible, and he barely registers that the harsh tulle of her tutu is scratching his face. Recovering from the lift brings them into a momentary embrace, their faces inches apart, giving them a second of privacy in front of one thousand people. They move to center stage with a shared glee, disbelief, and gratitude. They bow for each other more than for the audience.

And then, as she exits stage left, he walks upstage alone, takes a deep, deep breath—and then another—to begin his coda. It's not over.

36

I Think I Was Perfect, Once

There was one time when I was completely satisfied. One.

Many times I was happy about how I'd danced, more or less proud of what I'd done. Often I felt a sense of worthy accomplishment, no different from any other mid-career professional wrapping up a productive day's work. Those dancing experiences—whether they were performances, rehearsals, or even just an exercise in class—were like a collage of textures and shades, Impressionist paintings where dark spots weave in with bright ones, highs with lows, but positivity wins overall. The good stuff (or, at least, the not-so-bad) outweighed the "darn it" moments. As a dancer—and as a person—you accept that nothing is going to be perfect in life. But a dancer suspends that truth every day. She has to. Because we relentlessly hear that our personal best can—and should—be improved upon, further achievement is obviously just a matter of working harder, and more. If you always do your best, your best will become better. We dancers concoct images or definitions of our own version of the ideal, and usually that ideal is based on what we've seen in another dancer, since other dancers' bodies or interpretations are our only frames of reference. Someone else—whose foot, pirouette, arabesque, legs, or portrayal of Juliet I admire—is who I hold in my mind as inspiration. Is the fact that I cannot become or dance like that idolized dancer a way of buffering the reality that I can't be "perfect"? Since I was born with this pair of feet, once I realize they're not the greatest in the world, how can I feel valid enough to keep going to class every day in pursuit of . . . what? Something that is, truthfully, unattainable?

We dancers bonk up against the insanity of pining after someone else's pair of legs day after day, but with age and maturity and years of fixating on our bodies—our instruments—we come to grips with what we have and what we can do with it. We even start to feel pleased with it, a little bit, sometimes, but not in a vain way. Our view of ourselves is almost impersonal. I scrutinize my physique in the same way a painter stands back to examine her canvas. It's my creation, made for a purpose. We keep trying to mold ourselves to be a little longer, a little archier, a little looser and stronger, but the work becomes less self-deprecating, more accepting, with every adjustment and, simply, with time and maturity. Complacency is the enemy, but the changes that we ARE able to create, over the years of stubborn refusal to believe we're stuck with marginal turnout, mediocre extensions, or stiff arms, feel like prized possessions. We grow up enough to stop being ridiculous and start being realistic. People *will* approve of—even applaud for!—my dancing even though I may have been frustrated with the way I executed my fouetté turns or bobbled out of the chaînés. Someone will compliment my performance without even seeming to have noticed—or care—that the dancer next to me onstage has more beautifully arched feet than I do. But the ultimate validation is what may come from another dancer. For only a comrade understands the struggle, the journey, the path.

Among my colleagues, I was known to be a perfectionist, which is silly to say because every dancer is, in some way, obsessed. We all get crazy over something having to do with technique: maybe it's speed, height, pure brute strength, "tricks" (the flashy, bravura steps that make audiences go wild), or the subtleties of partnering. My personal craziness was a fixation on detail and precision. I calculated the placement of each millimeter of my body and every nanosecond of my movements. Finger positioning and the exact curve of my neck, shoulders, and arms were my hallmarks. Turnout (which I was not born with) was not limited to my legs—I wanted to emanate outward rotation from the middle of my soul.

An effect of my anatomical self-scrutiny was that I craved the satisfaction of perfect balance. And by perfect, I mean holding a position on my own terms: every part of my body obeying my commands, arranged exactly just so. When everything is accurately lined up, you are completely at ease, there is no struggle, just the continual outward stretch of each muscle away from your center. It's a stasis that keeps the energy moving and the shape alive. It's a feeling like no other. You're a body of water that appears still, though the current flows swiftly beneath its skin. And then, when you are ready, you decide to bring yourself out of that balanced position and on to the next. You don't fall out of it because you've lost control, you *take* yourself out of it.

We think of those balances as being most impressive when they're held on pointe or demi-pointe, but performing an adagio, with its sequence of slow extensions and smooth transitions, is just as balance-challenging as a static pose, if not more so. Your center of balance keeps shifting. There isn't time to look for it—you have to have it in hand while you're moving and be balanced before you even arrive. Most dancers dislike adagio because of its slowness, but I loved it, for perfecting an adagio meant having utter control. The majesty of long, weighted movement, seamless flow from one second to the next, leaves time for pure beauty. Purity of shape and movement. Pristine cleanliness. Glory. Bliss. Peace.

Usually, in class, an adagio exercise is done at the barre and then again in center. At the barre, of course, the goal is less about balance and more about strength (holding a leg as high as possible with correct alignment, for as long as the music dictates). In center, that strength challenge quadruples. Your core muscles are what hold up your leg, with no assist from your hand on the barre. Through my obsessive explorations, I learned that perfect balance is achieved when the strength at the middle of one's body is equal to the dynamic energy being stretched out to its extremities—the fingertips, toes, and the top of the head. Push from the center, pull outward from the edges.

Once my body figured that out, adagio was fun—not easy, but the kind of physical puzzle my detail-centric mind found satisfyingly hard. I could, in any given adagio exercise, usually perform some portion of it with the kind of ease I knew was ideal. A sixteen- or thirty-two-bar exercise, though, is a long time to be so pinpoint correct. But I never stopped trying.

In class, I liked to stand toward the back and side of the studio, in a spot where I could see myself in the mirror but not be directly under the eyes of whoever was teaching class. I didn't hide—I stayed far enough forward to be noticed—but I wanted some cloak of privacy as well. The day of my perfect adagio, I was standing fairly near the center of the group of dancers but toward the back. The dancers waiting along the periphery of the studio for their turn to do the combination were closer to me than the teacher was.

I don't recall the adagio combination exactly, but I do remember the feeling of doing it. I didn't once need to shift my foot on the floor to stabilize myself. I didn't have to struggle and fix my balance during any extension midair. My hips were square in développé front and my shoulders open just enough in arabesque. My back felt broad, my chest lifted, eyes focused clearly and brightly, and each transition was easeful, seamless, and wedded to the music. It wasn't effortless, but the effort I exerted was just the right amount, in just the right places and at just the right moments. I started and finished, and I realized I hadn't had to make a single adjustment. I was perfectly balanced through the entire thing.

The accompanist let the notes fade away, but I didn't move from the final fifth position until I was positive I couldn't hear any last strains. I didn't want to ruin what I'd just done by breaking away before the music and I were completely across the finish line. Finally, I was there. The dancers around me dispersed, and the next group moved in to take their places, mine included. I turned to the back of the studio, still inside the private little world I'd just created. My friend Paul was standing in my path. He'd been watching. He, too, was a perfectionist. All he said as he squeezed my hand, sharing my satisfaction, was his pet name for me. "Gavina."

37

Henry's Living Room

The conflict between dancer and self is constant. Where does the person end and the commodity begin? The dancer is the objet d'art, but she is also just a person like any other. Selling my art means selling myself. Even when the buyer has pure, innocent intentions—simply wanting to consider the dancing in front of them, appreciate it and move on—it is often hard to not feel like a thing.

Henry and his wife are avid art collectors. Their home, a modernist, U-shaped house arranged around a central patio, is full of very expensive original pieces. There are many paintings on the walls, but the couple's true passion is sculpture. Outside, large, striking works are displayed around the property like those in a museum's garden. The real gems, though, are indoors. At every turn, along the hallways, perched on pedestals, shelves, in corners low and high, are examples of their high-end acquisitions.

Henry and his wife are also politically active. They donate large sums to support their candidates of choice, and one autumn, not long before the November elections, they decided to host a fundraiser for a candidate needing a boost in her quest to become Secretary of State.

It would be an intimate gathering, by invitation only of course, limited to carefully selected guests who were likely to be generous. Also, while the home is quite luxe, it is not terribly large. The rooms are many but relatively small—the better to showcase the art collection, perhaps.

A fundraiser in an art museum-gallery-home would already be a draw, and most likely the invitees would mark the invitation "high priority," but Henry always wanted to emboss his things with a touch of exclusivity, some detail that elevated what was already prestigious to something truly remarkable and enviable. How to make an ordinary party stand out on the calendars of busy socialites, in the middle of election season? Add some ballet, of course.

The candidate for Secretary of State was known to be a fan of dance and had perhaps even studied it herself, more seriously than most, as a child. And Henry, as it happened, was on the board of a ballet company and was proud of his personal friendships with some of the dancers.

A small performance by two ballet dancers at his fundraiser would be just the ticket to up the level of intrigue and help entice potential donors—they might feel they were getting something in return for their donation, something immediate, like a party favor, but a priceless one. And since Henry expected his ideas to materialize regardless of obstacles or inconveniences, there was no reason why two ballet dancers could not perform in his living room, on a "stage" set with priceless artwork.

Henry asked two of the ballet company's leading dancers to perform. And they agreed—why not? A performance is a performance, and these dancers in particular loved doing unusual gigs that made for a good story. Perhaps they were flattered to be asked to aid a cause that dancers can't usually support through their craft. And Henry is not a person to say no to, either. They prepared a short excerpt from a contemporary ballet. The choreography had a minimum of jumps or fast movements, though there were some lifts and expansive partnering maneuvers. Knowing the floor would be slippery parquet, they altered the choreography a bit and planned to dance very cautiously. They rehearsed in a real dance studio, though—staying within a taped-off area the size of Harold's living room.

What they did not plan for, however, was the art.

The dancers arrived at the house on the afternoon of the soiree and were warmly greeted at the front door by a caterer, who interrupted her work setting up a cocktail bar in the foyer to let them in. The male dancer had been to the house before, but his partner hadn't, so she was given a short tour and shown the living room where they would dance. They were both surprised to see that the dimensions within which they'd rehearsed, which accurately reflected the square footage of the room, hadn't taken into account a dozen sculptures, objets d'art, and busts, as well as mobiles hanging from the ceiling. They both now assumed, however, that the area would be cleared and the pieces moved to safer quarters before they danced. Henry arrived, quietly jovial as always, warm, smiling, welcoming, relaxed. (His face, even at rest, wore a slight grin, giving him an air of confident serenity.) Apparently unaware of the potential obstacles his art collection posed to the dancers—and vice versa—Henry had the caterer's assistant move the couch, chairs, rug, and coffee table to the perimeter of the room. Henry and the dancers stood back to assess the space. The setting was indeed lovely, if nervous-making for those two who would be moving through the obstacle course of art that remained. They murmured words of admiration, and slight apprehension, about dancing a hair's breadth away from things of such incalculable value, but Henry seemed unconcerned about any possible risk and excused himself to attend to other preparations. The dancers began to mark through their duet, strategizing where to hold back, what steps to modify or eliminate—the lifts couldn't go anywhere close to full height, and leg extensions had to be curtailed—their stomachs in knots for fear of breathing too close to the handblown glass Chihuly piece, the translucent stone urn, or the delicate figurines perched on a pedestal.

The guests began to arrive, and the male dancer mingled while the woman (who was more concerned with staying warm and limber and less comfortable making small talk, particularly just before performing) hid in a guest bedroom while cocktails were served. The guest room was luxuriously cozy, and the dancer's anxiety about what was to come made her wish to pull on sweatpants, curl up under the fluffy comforter on the bed, and read a book. The thick, plush carpet was perfect for stretching out on, though the silky-soft pile made it difficult to do any of her usual pre-show warm-up. So, figuring also that the guests would be happy just to see movement and music in an unexpected place, she mostly just rolled around on that carpet and did abdominal exercises. The sounds of distant chatter and clinking glassware made her stomach fluttery.

After what seemed like eons (were they having so much fun out there they'd forgotten about the performance?), her partner came to say it was time. Time to go to the living room and do what they'd come here to do. It was odd to walk through the house in costume (for this contemporary piece, she wore a leotard, Lycra shorts, and ballet shoes). She wasn't sure whether to make eye contact with the guests as she and her partner squeezed through the crowd or pretend to be invisible until after she was no longer "entertainment" and could join the party as a real person. She stayed close to her partner, who was very tall and easy to hide behind.

Having wound their way through the throngs of chattering guests, the dancers took their starting positions in the living room while people were alerted that the show was about to start. The crowd moved away from the hors d'oeuvres table, wine glasses in hand. Someone pushed play on the iPod and put the volume on max, but it was still very, very quiet. They began the duet, pretending it was a dance in silence since they could barely hear the music. Late afternoon sun streamed in from the floor-to-ceiling windows on two sides, adding a bit of theatrical effect, and as the guests quieted down, the caterers' dish-clearing could be more clearly heard. They danced, amid the art, swept away by the novelty of it and the elements of risk. Harold's grin deepened. He was satisfied with his newest acquisition.

Their dance was short, touching, and received with enthusiasm. Only the dancers knew, between themselves, what they'd just squeaked through. They secretly shared their smugness at having pulled this off. And now, with the candidate beaming her appreciation (more genuine, and more sincere, than the guests'), the dancers relaxed. The woman scurried back to the guest room to put on her civilian clothes, now feeling celebratory and relieved, no longer drawn to the feathery bed but eager to talk and drink wine. Returning to the living room, the "stage" now occupied by high-heeled guests and littered with crumbs and cocktail napkins, she was startled to see how quickly Henry's latest piece of art had disappeared.

A universally sleepy, lazy, take-it-easy Sunday morning. I'm driving to work on deserted streets, past cafés with lines of bleary-eyed customers outside, waiting for brunch. I feel a self-pitying envy. It feels wrong to go into the cold, echoey, concrete-walled theater: it's still asleep, too. It's a matinee day, so my performance makeup has to be done before class starts at noon. Dancers trickle into the dressing room one by one, cradling travel mugs of coffee, reluctantly shedding their outerwear and getting settled at their spots at the makeup table lining the wall of bulb-framed mirrors. Starting with foundation, concealer, and powder, pale faces are transformed by fake eyelashes, eye shadow, eyeliner, brow liner, blush, and mascara into prom-worthy glamour. Can't we just stay here all day and play with makeup? Reality looms: suiting up, warming up, summoning up energy of body and mind to performance-level verve. Slowly, some quiet chitchat starts, then a little laughter, and then someone puts on a playlist. After half an hour, the room has a warm hum and the dancers are feeling the possibility of the job ahead.

38

The Fourth Wall

I've fallen onstage many times. Every dancer has—it's nothing to be ashamed of, or proud of. It's just something that happens.

Nobody *tries* to fall, but you can't dance—not really—if you're concentrating on *not* falling. There are times when a dancer has to be careful, of course. If they have an injury, or are recovering from one, each step has to be done with deliberate thought, even the ones practiced so many millions of times that muscles execute them almost before the brain says to. The simplest, most basic tendus and pliés have to be reconsidered and reevaluated. They have to be done tentatively at first, and the muscles that perform them may have to have their hardwired memories erased. Pain is very effective at encouraging—or forcing—new ways of doing things, but it doesn't always choose the best ways. Pain just boosts the brain to craftily devise ways to cope. So when a dancer is in pain, she subconsciously scrambles to override both the pain signals and her muscles' automatic responses.

A slippery floor, or a slanted one, or one that's mined with ridges or dips, sudden drop-offs, loose boards, or trapdoors hidden beneath its surface layer are all reasons for caution, too. Without the security of good traction beneath her feet, a dancer can't help but tighten up—stiffen, brace, keep her energy close. Every step she takes will be measured—she'll calculate exactly how much or how little pressure to use against the floor before, during, and after every jump, turn, relevé, even the smallest gesture or step. Imagine standing on an ice rink without skates. Walking and running on an unpredictable floor can be more dangerous than a grand jeté, if a dancer forgets about the treacherous surface, even for a second.

But the point of great dancing—or music, painting, or acting—*is* to stop thinking. The instrument, the fiercely trained and disciplined body, begs to be allowed to run on its own, to take charge of the mechanics of dance so that the artist inside has complete freedom. The dancer's subconscious instincts for phrasing, characterization, shading, and nuance are unleashed—without concern for technique—because her fingers and legs and eyes, every fiber of her being, in fact, are in perfect coordination. They react spontaneously, and gleefully, with millisecond-perfect precision.

I've fallen onstage for almost every possible reason. Slippery floors have been the most common culprit, but I've also had unexpected trips and slips that had no apparent cause. Even when I've rehashed those moments afterward, I can't figure them out. It's startling, and very disconcerting, to have let go enough to dance with freedom and confidence but then suddenly, in the blink of an eye, be in a heap on the floor, as completely out of control as humanly possible—and as ungraceful. Your carefully created world, however theatrical, crumbles.

There's only one way to recover from a fall, and that is to keep going. Stand up, gather your wits, and pick up right where you left off—or find your place in the music, and catch up to where you should be. Pretend like nothing happened. I've crashed down so badly that getting up off the floor took real effort—ungainly, unladylike effort—as well as several bars of music. But those on the other side of the footlights didn't know they'd missed seeing three phrases of choreography.

Minimize the amount of time the audience sees you as one of them— a fallible, mortal, clumsy human—and most of all, don't acknowledge that it happened.

I have broken this rule only once.

The program that we'd been performing comprised a series of excerpts from several different ballets. I had roles in a few of them, but in this night's performance I was cast to dance in only one piece, the very last on the program: Christopher Stowell's *Eyes on You.* I wouldn't take a step onstage until more than two hours after the evening began.

So I waited. I warmed up, put on my makeup while the performance got under way, did my hair, watched from the wings while my friends danced, got into costume, and warmed up again. By the time intermission finally came and went, my energy had peaked and was starting to slide. My role was short and small, though, and the ballet was a fun piece, always a crowd-pleaser. A balletic version of a musical revue, it was built around catchy, familiar Cole Porter show tunes (the audience always got revved up), and the glamorous costumes, glittery set, and bright red dance floor turned the normally bland auditorium into a Broadway theater in the heart of Times Square. The audience's enthusiasm was audible through the curtain the moment the conductor kicked up that overture. It got me excited, too. It felt like a party, and I was ready to have fun.

My first entrance was a grand one. My partner, Adrian, and I were to run out from the upstage right wing, straight to center, and all the way down to the very front of the stage—a real "Here we are, folks!" moment—where he'd give me a swift little twirl before we launched into a couple of fast, spiraling lifts, another quick little soutenu and a running exit. Even our costumes, matching in white satin, were straight out of my childhood dreams. He was absolutely debonair in tuxedo tails and cummerbund, and I adored my slinky, floor-length, Ginger Rogers–style ball gown.

We waited in the semidarkness of the upstage wing for our cue, watching the corps de ballet spin through their choreography, the bright lights reflecting off their silvery dresses and gleeful faces. Irrepressible grins proved that everyone was reveling in the pure joy of the moment—we all adored dancing this ballet. Caught up in the spectacular fantasy world of an MGM movie, I couldn't wait to join them. I felt the audience's electricity—they seemed ready to jump out of their seats and rush onstage to dance with the swirling couples in white. Adrian and I counted the last three bars of music until our entrance, he took my hand, gave it a squeeze, and off we went—

After hours of being kept in check, my uncontainable energy bubbled over. Adrian had me firmly in his grip as we charged downstage to meet the audience, just inches away from the orchestra pit, almost giggling with exhilaration at the song's irresistible melody. We swerved into place for the first step I'd danced all night—and somehow, for some reason, out of absolutely nowhere, I was flat on the floor. I was a pile of white satin, on my rear, legs splayed, feet flying, while my tall, gracious partner looked down in confusion at his fallen starlet-turned-klutz. He never let go of my hand—my feet must have just slipped out from under me in the zealous speed of our entrance—and yanked me back up in a flash, before I even had time to think.

Startled but not frazzled, we sped through the few steps we had to do, still squarely on our front-and-center mark. The hilarity of it all, and the irony of screwing up the tiniest role I'd ever danced, overrode any potential embarrassment. In all of twenty seconds, I'd run onstage, collapsed as floppy as a rag doll, been pulled to my feet, spun and lifted overhead—and the audience, as surprised and confused as I was, gasped. As we rounded our last turn, I looked straight out to the audience, shrugged my shoulders—"Oh, well!"—and we dashed offstage, laughing as hard as the audience was.

39

Big Hair

"Do you have a fear of big hair?"

Yes. Yes, I do.

The question wasn't being asked out of concern or with the intention of helping me overcome my fear. It was sort of a curious inquiry, an investigation into why I seemed to become very uncomfortable when my hair wasn't somehow contained. It was an issue of control: as with the rest of my body, I needed to be in charge of what my hair did. I needed to be the decision-maker of every movement of my legs, feet, fingers, and even the locks of my thick, wavy, mid-back-length, dark blonde hair. Unpredictability made me very uneasy. I became tense and stiff, as if the straighter I held my body, the less my hair would fly around.

I'd never been directly asked about this before. People would comment that I should wear my hair down more often, but no one ever asked why I always had it pulled back—ponytail, barrette, or braid—and sprayed down. They didn't realize that without hair spray, the slightest breeze turned me into Medusa. This particular query came from Christopher himself, on the morning after dress rehearsal for a ballet in which I—horror!—had to dance with my hair not in a bun or some other classical style but down and loose. All the way down, without even one tiny unobtrusive clip to keep the front locks off my face. I was at the mercy of my hair, and that was almost the most difficult thing about the ballet. I dealt with it by rinsing my hair and keeping it in a tight braid until moments before the curtain rose, hoping the wetness would keep it tame long enough after I started dancing that I could think about what I was doing with my body, not what my hair was doing in front of my face or how to get it out of my mouth or what sort of rat's nest was developing around my head.

Answering his question was a relief, almost, an admission that I had a phobia that I'd been ashamed of. Other people went around with loose hair all the time, so why couldn't I? What was wrong with me? I remembered a photo shoot I'd done a couple of years before . . .

———

Preparations for the photo shoot began the day before I got in front of the camera. There was an ad campaign being waged. The hook was to intrigue the public by dropping hints about various dancers' nondancing lives, to highlight their real-world skills, hobbies, habits, or quirks. These little, almost-gossipy tidbits would be referenced in posters to be plastered all over the city. A catchy tagline would accompany a full-body photograph of the dancer in some location and pose that juxtaposed his or her civilian and dancer traits.

The photographer began by interviewing each dancer, trying to dig up nuggets of interesting facts that might be hidden deep down within the nooks and crannies of their public dancer-persona. One woman revealed her urban-farmer alter ego: every morning, she gathered her chickens' eggs before ballet class and milked her goats when she got home from rehearsal in the evening. For the poster, she was photographed in her backyard, wearing pointe shoes and a chic, designer version of a checkered "farm girl" dress, egg basket in hand, goats milling around behind (think Dorothy as a ballerina). Another fellow, known to have raced cars in a previous life (the ballet company contract restricted such high risk activity now), was shot on location at the local racetrack, reclining on the hood of a snazzy sportscar, in jazz pants and with perfectly pointed feet. The tall Russian cavalier of the company was too shy or modest to admit to any hidden talents, but his colleagues attested to his special taste for vodka. It was decided to photograph him at the Eastern European restaurant and dance club where he'd hosted his birthday party, decked out in a debonair suit, shot glass in hand, his long legs stretched as if about to send him leaping over the bar.

And I, after the photographer's probing questions about hobbies ("But what do you do for *fun?*") revealed only my enjoyment of farmer's markets and the *New York Times* crossword puzzle, finally mentioned that my parents had taught my sister and me how to play poker around the dining room table when we were kids. And that I'd learned from my grandmother to shuffle a deck of cards like a casino pro. Lately, I'd tried to corral friends to come over for poker nights at my apartment. That was all the photographer needed to know—her questions ended.

The hairstylist had never met me. I was sent to his salon the afternoon before the shoot for a "style assessment" right after I'd finished dancing in the Sunday matinee. I arrived with my hair (still damp from sweat and stiff with hair spray) yanked back into a ponytail. Its natural waves were nowhere to be seen, and once the stylist pulled off the ponytail elastic and started combing through, looking for my hair's real "personality" (much like the photographer's investigative interview), he saw only fine, flat, limp, dark blonde lengths. Unaware of the wildly unruly curls that were only waiting for a good shampooing, he got out his flat iron and completed my transformation to Marcia Brady. He warned me not to wash my hair, or even to let water touch it before the next day's photo shoot, and sent me home feeling like a different girl. I'd always envied the shiny, straight, obedient hairdos of childhood friends, and now I had one!

No water touched that hair, and every glance in the mirror until the next day threw me off: "Who IS that?" I quickly realized I looked ridiculous, and certainly unlike myself. Luckily, both the photographer and the fashion stylist for the ad campaign hated it as much as I did. Early, early, early the next morning, we—the photographer, the hairstylist, the clothing designer, the makeup artist, the marketing director, and myself—met on location: a billiards club/restaurant/bar, the closest thing to a card room that could be found. We were getting to use it for free (donated by the club's owner, since one of the other company dancers worked there as a bartender on her off nights), and it was empty on a Sunday morning.

Why, or how, the poster's final image came to be constructed remains a bit of a mystery. I was turned into a card shark, gloating in victory, sporting vibrant bronze curls piled on top of my head and cascading down my back, sneering at the camera with disdain for the losers. This creation was the result of five cooks tweaking, primping, pruning, fussing. The subject of the ad—me—was completely sidelined, as voiceless as a piece of meat being transformed into a gourmet entrée. But it did make me think it would be fun to have a poker night again soon.

There were several changes of clothes as I rotated through the skirts, tops, pants, and accessories the designer had brought along, modeling each ensemble for the judges and waiting for their verdict. The hour or so of makeup application turned out to be the easiest, least controversial part of the process. The hairstylist immediately saw that straight hair didn't evoke the fiery, hard-nosed spirit of a gambler and set about watering down the flat locks he'd made the day before, producing strand after strand of ringlets and pinning them painstakingly one at a time to produce the carelessly stunning effect he wanted: The Hairdo. As the curls reappeared, he got more and more excited about the potential volume that could be achieved. Gel, pins, and more gel swept it higher and higher, but I had no idea what was happening on top of my head—this was being done in the billiards room, not in front of my dressing room mirror.

It was decided that my pose would be most powerful from on high, so up on top of the pool table I went. I felt unable to speak, but my ally, the marketing director, stood by quietly. He handed me my prop—the winning hand of poker cards, a royal flush, in spades.

The photographer urged a sneery "HA!" attitude and an uncharacteristic (and somewhat provocative) stance. I was told to hold the folds of my skirt (a flared, orange velvet number) with my free hand, shoving my fanned-out cards toward the camera and showing off as much leg as possible. I struggled to hold my balance since the plush surface was scarily slippery under my pointe shoes. But I was too weary to protest—we'd been there for hours already—and I knew that the sooner the photographer got her shot the better, since happy hour was drawing near and the bar would soon open for business. So I channeled my obedient dancer-training to give her the image she wanted.

After several hours, as patrons started trickling in for early evening cocktails and rounds of pool, we finally wrapped it up. I hastily, and with huge relief, slid out of the orange velvet skirt and drapy black top and back into my comforting track pants and fleece sweatshirt. Such happiness to get out of pointe shoes, which shouldn't ever be worn on a day off. Not wanting to take the time to wash off all that makeup or remove a million tiny hairpins, I just zipped up my parka, pulled up the hood, and walked outside. I headed down the street with my friend, the marketing director, who'd thought to add the one detail that really *was* me. It wasn't the aggressive pose, the big hair, the sexy outfit showing a lot of leg, or the sneer on my face. It was the satisfaction of being dealt, for one day, perfection: the winning hand.

40

Theaters Are Mysterious Places

Theaters are mysterious places. Their architects and builders aim to create a sense of grandeur, an atmosphere of reverence and importance for what goes on inside those walls. But who really knows for sure what *does* happen? We know that a company of actors, or musicians, or dancers comes together, practicing a craft that then becomes art, a crew of stagehands and managers and electricians and carpenters creates sets and backdrops and lighting designs, front-of-house staff sells tickets and checks coats, cleaning crews vacuum, dust, and polish, security guards lock and unlock doors. As a performance approaches, legions of people do a job of some very specific sort, steadily focused on a result for their work: shinier doorknobs, more tickets sold, smoother-running set pieces, subtler lighting cues, more resonant music, tidier costumes, or a visit from the muse of dance.

A performance's "magic" is often spoken of, and it's true—something magical does seem to occur when expectant onlookers settle into rows and rows of precisely ordered seats to be transformed from pedestrians into an audience. When an orchestra fills the pit or occupies the stage, when dancers and actors fine-tune their steps or their lines until the stage manager calls "Places," when the crew members man their stations on the rail, there is an invisible yet perceptible change in the air. No one thinks very much, if at all, about the other team players in this game—it's taken for granted it *is* a team sport, but all are preoccupied with their individual mission. The musicians know their music stands will be in place, the ushers know the audience members will come, the dancers know their costumes will be ready, the stagehands know the performers will act, or sing, or dance. And everyone knows the curtain will go up. It just will. It has to.

And once it does, there is no stopping. Dancers won't stop dancing to tell a stagehand that the floor is too slippery, and if a costume rips on-stage, there's nothing the wardrobe master can do—at least not until the show's over. The conductor can't tell the cellist she is off pitch, the carpenter can't fix a broken set piece, the light board operator can only call his cues, and the box office won't sell any more tickets. Latecomers are out of luck. And no one can tell the actors, or singers, or musicians, or dancers to stop, to go back, to do their choreography or say their lines again because they didn't sing well enough, or play well enough, or dance well enough. Finally, for once, and at long last, the performer has the stage.

Or do they? Does the performer really "have" the stage, even when the curtain is up and paying customers sit in the dark, awaiting a masterful display of talent and finesse, expecting and needing to be transported into another world, to have their own lives taken away for a little while, and then returned with broader edges or with a perfume of beauty and grace?

Who, or what, really does *control*—if such a word can be used—what transpires on the boards? The dancer knows that even at her most tired, injured, aching, or unhappy, she gets *some* sort of help, from somewhere, when a performance begins. The musician knows *something* inhabits his fingers when the spotlight is on. The actor knows she slips out of her own skin and into a character, no matter how much she might want to stay inside.

Even the stagehands (the "crew"), the working men and women who know every technicality and quirk of the theater's bones, who care for it like their own child, who are the final word on illusions and effects—the magic that's visible—even they admit that their manipulations are only the framework for something else. Something that surrounds the dancers, the actors, and the players, too. The crew outwardly controls the machinations of the performance's effect by pulling the ropes, shoving the sets, hauling the props, mopping the stage floor, and they only bring in the curtain when the magic has run its natural course and it's time to say good night.

But who is saying good night? Who, or what, decides when the show's over? Is it ever really over, even when the applause peters out, the house-lights come up, and the performers shed their costumes and become civilian again?

Embedded in the plush of the theater seats, the fibers of the carpets, the glass of the light fixtures, the wood of the floors, are fragments—pieces of every performance and rehearsal, every actor, dancer, and musician who has performed underneath that theater's flies, disappearing into darkness so many stories above. And with every passing day, week, month, or year, the theater itself performs, too.

41

Into the Night

By the time I get home tonight after the show, it will be late, my legs will be tired, and I will need protein and sleep as quickly as possible. Waiting for dinner to cook will only make me grumpy, so at four o'clock in the afternoon, I preheat the oven to 400 degrees and pop in a frozen ricotta-spinach-stuffed chicken breast from Trader Joe's. I'll cook it now and reheat it later, or just eat it cold. It smells good, savory and cheesy. I'm pre-chopping some vegetables, too, since who wants to come down from a performance-high by slicing carrots? My dinner-making ritual is comforting, familiar, and automatic. I duck in and out of the fridge for ingredients, and my hand reaches for the bottle of wine before I realize what time and day it is. That glass will be much more welcome six hours from now, when I get home and am seeing the performance from the other side.

I lock the apartment door and hover on the landing for a second doing a mental checklist: I've got pointe shoes in my bag, a clean leotard to warm up in, sewing kit, trail mix and Clif Bar, water bottle, and my tea mug. An umbrella's in the car for the walk from parking garage to stage door, and my makeup case is still at the theater after last night's dress rehearsal. A wisp of thought about the performance tonight flickers up from my stomach and echoes in my head.

I live on the second floor of a duplex, an old Victorian house divided in half. Walking down the wide staircase with its ornate, dark wood bannister and dated but fancy-looking chandelier, I feel like a 1920s starlet, making her entrance in a ball gown and fur stole. The ground floor vestibule is dim, since the afternoon sun has gotten low but it's too early for the lights to come on. The walls are the same dark wood as the staircase. There's a giant framed mirror over an elegant but tired side table, and a frayed Oriental rug. The porch looks squiggly through the front door's beveled glass windows. When this house was a single-family residence, paneled pocket doors led into a formal dining room, which is now the ground floor apartment. I can picture a white-gloved butler parting those doors to welcome dinner guests.

My downstairs neighbor has a piano, but she rarely plays. She confessed to me once that she's ashamed of not having practiced enough over the years, of having let her technique slip, and didn't want to become sad at her lost ability if she were to try playing again. But she had been a musician once, and a singer, and toured with a band.

As I get to the bottom of the stairs, the faint tinkle of music I'd heard from the second floor landing becomes stronger, and although I'm nervous about the time, I stop—is it a recording, or is someone playing the piano on the other side of that door? I can't tell, quite. It sounds old-fashioned, almost like a Victrola record player but not scratchy. Am I imagining the hesitancy between the notes? The melody has life and breath, but it isn't polished, either. It sounds frail, delicate, a little tentative, but doesn't pause as someone practicing might. It makes me think of a sweet old lady, and lace doilies, and a parlor on a quiet Sunday afternoon. I stand there listening, expecting the music to stop, but it goes on. I have to leave—I'm already late—but this moment seems timeless.

The music is Chopin, the very same étude to which I will dance tonight.

42

A Prayer

Before going into the theater or the studio, I must say a prayer. I am not religious. I may not even believe in a God as organized religions see it, but I pray, and the way it sounds in my head is how I have heard prayers recited in church.

Please dear lord, let this go well. Help me do well and feel strong.

I say this silently to myself while fixing my eyes on a spot in the sky. I have to hold my visual focus steady. If my eyes flit away from the spot I initially latched onto, the prayer won't work. It needs to be repeated, maybe several times, but at least two or three.

The last thing I look at, before going through the door and into the dance world, has to be the sky.

I'm resolute and steadfast about this. It might be awkward if I'm with someone else, or if it's raining, but I make it happen.

Then, I can go in, and go on—not necessarily more assured or overly confident, but ready to face the unknown. My hope for the next few hours is articulated. I don't know what will happen or whether I will indeed do well or feel strong, but I have asked for it out loud (even though only I could hear it), which means that my intentions, in the eyes of the universe, are good.

What matters not at all is that my prayer has no effect on what I do in the studio or theater. I have had horrible performances that were embarrassingly bad and ones that left me feeling triumphant. Before each, my prayer was said.

As soon as I've repeated my prayer, gazed intently on a star or a cloud or just a clear expanse of sky, and gone through the door, it's all forgotten. I've created, and crossed, a bridge from the solidity of the now to the mysterious forces of the next.

43

Curtain In

I keep my eye on the tassels of the main curtain's vaguely dingy gold fringe as it slowly lowers, getting closer, closer . . . a huge mouth closing down over the gaping hole that exposed us to the audience. It's almost there, almost touching the stage floor . . . ah! The *split second* it hits the deck we let go of our final pose and scurry/shuffle/half jog to the nearest wing before it goes up again on the corps de ballet, who have rearranged themselves—dragged themselves—into fairly neat lines for the bows. I've got a few seconds, thank God, in the front wing with my partner, to exchange a quick thank-you kiss, blot a tissue on my forehead, and now, finally, have a sip of water. The day's work is done, and what a day, what work, it has been.

That this morning's ballet class took place on this very stage, several hours earlier, hardly seems possible. It was a lifetime ago, and this space, this theater, was a completely different world then. The climax of the day—this performance that we just finished—loomed in the distance this morning but was far enough away to look manageable, completely doable. With every passing hour, it grew, its size and weight inching closer, as it gradually, almost imperceptibly, began to take over the theater. As we went through the afternoon's rehearsals, got notes and corrections from last night's dress rehearsal, worked through problem spots, and did a second cast run-through, it was noticeably closing in, but there was still a buffer zone between us and it. There was a couple of hours' lull while we dancers scattered for food and rest and the union stagehand crew took their mandated break time, settling into the improvised living room they've carved out of the backstage area—a curtained off area upstage right, crammed with well-worn Goodwill furniture, a kitchenette stocked with economy-sized cans of instant coffee, bags of Doritos, and Red Vines, a few beat-up easy chairs circled around a card table, and an old TV tuned to the sports game or local news. Any prep work that was still needed for tonight's show happened quietly, off in various corners of the theater. The lighting designer kept tinkering with cues on his computer, sitting alone at a temporary workstation set up for tech rehearsals in the middle of the orchestra section. He calmly gave updates via his headset to the fellow manning the light board at the back of the house. Upstairs, it was crunch time for the wardrobe staff, and they, too, were calmly industrious and steady. They were still fixing and altering newly designed costumes for tonight's premiere, but there was also laundry to be done, clean tights to be sorted and dropped off in dressing rooms, and dancers wandering in to ask if it was too late to have another set of hooks put on their slightly too-tight bodice or new elastic to replace a sagging shoulder strap. A quietly persistent bustle of activity hummed as the clock hands advanced and the performance's presence became palpable.

Even so, when I returned to the stage an hour and a half before curtain time to warm up, the expectancy in the air felt easy and light, even a little sleepy, like the handful of dancers still napping in the green room. I was almost alone, one of the few dancers needing a full hour to get my body ready to dance again. As others trickled in, we joked about the smell of the sloppy joes the stagehands were making for dinner wafting onstage. We felt relaxed enough to carry on conversation about things unrelated to what we faced tonight—last night's episode of *The Bachelorette*, who's vacationing in Mexico on our next layoff, whether the long lines at the popular brunch spot were worth it, what bar has the most substantial late-night happy hour food. For some, it was a way to cope with any anxiety or apprehension about what we were about to do, since hyper-focusing too early on the main event has a backlash effect—it becomes overwhelming and paralyzing. So instead, we bantered and laughed with the stage manager, who liked to come and haul her leg onto the barre to "warm up" with us. We were onstage, but the curtain was up and the house was empty, not yet filled with strangers ready to sink into a velvet seat and await their money's worth. Even the orchestra pit was still empty, aside from one or two early bird musicians already in place to loosen up their instruments. It's my one chance to see who's down there in the pit, and theirs to see us up above. I'm friends with one musician, the pianist, and she waved up at me when I peered down into the shadows at the sound of her scales. But soon, I was ready to let go of all this buildup and anticipation, ready to walk quickly toward the starting line—curtain time. The others' energy switched from a welcome distraction to an interference. It was time for me to focus inward and listen to my internal rhythm. I moved away from the other dancers and blocked out their easiness.

Too soon, tiny human figures appeared, one by one, in the far-off reaches of the back of the auditorium: ushers, ready to man their stations, stack programs, and tidy up the house for the public who'd soon start trickling in. In a few seconds, the stage manager would call "Curtain In!" and the crew guys on that detail would put down their books or leave their poker games to pull the thick, heavy ropes that control the curtain's smooth ride up and down. Once the stage was safely hidden from view, the house would be officially opened, and kids would gleefully scamper down the steeply sloping aisles as adults peered at each numbered row, searching for their seats, feeling slightly jarred by the stark contrast of the regal theater with the traffic, dirt, and concrete outside. The faint hum of the front-of-house staff penetrated through the pass doors. The Performance had taken over its rightful territory. This is what this place is built for, what is meant to happen here, what brings all these hundreds upon hundreds of people together: Showtime. The stage manager pulled her leg off the barre and made her announcement over the backstage intercom: "Half hour call, please, half hour to the top of the show. Clear the stage, please. Crew, sweep and mop. Half hour!" And it was here. It had arrived.

Then, real-world time didn't matter anymore. It was all theater-time. At the half-hour call, I take off my watch, lay it to the side of my dressing table, and don't look at it again until the performance is over.

And now, miraculously, it is. Gratefully, it is.

The corps de ballet has come forward in their formation, bowed, and backed up a few feet; the other soloists have run out gracefully to do the same, and my little moment of privacy in the darkness of the first wing is over—my partner takes me by hand and waist to lead me to center stage, not slowly, but not with the prancing energy of the corps. We take our own pace. For now, there's no music to follow. He gives me a small, gentle turn into our pre-discussed pose (even the bows are choreographed), I curtsy slowly, he graciously steps back. I gesture to him and we bow to each other, with sincere gratitude. A few steps toward the audience we go one more time, then we back up and join the lines of the full company. The conductor—"Maestro"—steps out from the downstage right wing, and I respectfully meet him halfway and lead him to center, where he takes his moment in the spotlight and acknowledges the orchestra. We're all together for one last full-company bow, and then we're really ready for that curtain to fall again. And when, slowly, it does, we're suddenly back where we started nearly twelve hours ago. The stage gels are cut, and we're just a group of tired, sweaty, adrenaline-flushed people standing under fluorescent work light. The stage floor is hot from the intensity of the performance lights, soft and worn, scuffed, although moments ago it looked slick and polished. Its size looks comfortable again, almost cozy. The intimidation is gone. It's not a mountain anymore, just a space full of sympathetic cohorts. A few of us, stubbornly, refuse to let go of a step or two that we flubbed in the show—and inevitably, that devilish pirouette that I fell out of in the moment of truth goes perfectly now that the curtain's in. Why is it different now? Oh, well, damn it.

The audience, meanwhile, has turned their backs on us and shuffled their way up the aisles. And on my side of the curtain, I can already sense the theater itself sweeping tonight's performance out the door, right on their heels.

44

Helena

The role of Helena in A Midsummer Night's Dream *was created on me during my years at Oregon Ballet Theatre. Its comedic melodrama suited me perfectly, and it immediately became one of my favorite parts of all time. Every time I danced it, I discovered more ways to give nuance to the character, make it deeper, funnier, more poignant. The ballet itself already held a permanent place of honor and joy in my heart, which it assumed from my very first exposure to it when I was a tiny bug at the School of American Ballet. Over the course of my career, I danced six different parts—from a ladybug to a butterfly and on up to Helena and Titania—in three choreographers' versions of the ballet, beginning at age eleven and culminating three months before my retirement at thirty-five.*

Everyone should dance. Everyone should let their soul sing.

You are in an embrace, so tightly wound that your two bodies' weights have become one. But the outline of your shape is unusual, and oddly discordant, disrupting the impression of tenderness. This is how the pas de deux begins.

He walks forward, looking out over your head, far beyond at something in the distance; you've snaked your arms around his waist, laid your cheek on his chest, eyes half-closed as if praying but actually watching the floor. He strides ahead, carelessly oblivious to your heaviness hanging from his body. You're clinging to him, trying to resist his steps, but with each one, he shoves you as carelessly as a shopping cart.

The music, if it were visible, would be the deepest, darkest blood red, warning of what lies ahead, streaked with a mournful pity for you both. You love him, but he is preoccupied with greater, loftier thoughts and cannot notice you.

By the time you arrive on the center mark, having lurched there together from upstage left, the buzz of motion in the studio is quieting. A dozen dancers who've just finished the powerful, driving, pyrotechnic Scherzo are finding their water bottles and pulling on sweatpants as their heart rates slowly descend and they begin to breathe normally again. Some stay standing, stretching, but others don't hesitate to slide to the floor. They squeeze into spots around the room, in the corners, under the barres along the walls, even beneath the grand piano in an alcove near the front. The only chairs in the room are placed front and center, facing you as the audience will. There, two people sit, one with notepad and pencil, watching, waiting, silently recording every observation or critique.

Now, you start pleading with him, grasping for his hands, wrapping his arms around you, but he shakes you off. He's irritated but not angry—to him, you're a fly and need to be swatted away.

But. He *is* supporting you. As you pull on him, leaning away in an arabesque, he reacts—retracting you toward his body, he flips you around, his palms securely on your hip bones, his long legs planted in a deep lunge. You are reclining against him now—uncomfortably—your back flush against his chest, reaching your arms blindly behind you to find and cradle his head. Your leg, unfolded in a long développé front, aims upward to the studio's corner, completing the diagonal line running from his back leg, braced into the floor and supporting you both, through your bodies, and out beyond your pointed foot. The tip of your pointe shoe is an arrow, urging you onward, together.

And you do go on, just not in that direction. Throughout the pas de deux, tension keeps you close. He's reluctant to acknowledge you, but he won't, or can't, quite leave you. He responds with elasticity to every move you make—he throws you away but with a natural rebound that recoils you back.

Finally, one throw does separate you—it is strong and harsh; now, he *is* getting angry at this irritating insect that won't go away. He broods in one corner. You, overwhelmed, tired, and self-pitying, dance a few quiet steps alone, summoning up your courage and resolve. You meet again on center, face-to-face; he fiercely grabs your upper arms, threatening violence. Being so close and seeing such genuine intensity in his eyes does scare you—into a moment of doubt. He whips you around, on pointe, using your shoulders as levers, trying to physically wear you down. You look for an escape, but with each leap you take away from him, he throws you down and slaps you into dizziness. Again and again . . . you're trapped, now.

This is the climax. The studio is dead silent.

The pianist's heart is in every note of Mendelssohn's rich, soulful melody; in fact, she is dancing, too. She loves you both and grows teary-eyed to witness such anger, such pain, such drama. She plays *with* you—not for you—and you can feel it. You imagine her fingers massaging the piano's keys with warmth, tenderness, and hope. Her music envelops you, guiding and leading your way.

Warm sunlight beams into the studio. You're very near the end of this pas de deux, your efforts as Helena to awaken Demetrius to the inevitability of your love. You've both quieted your emotions—his anger has faded to disgust and dismissal, turning your momentary fear into resignation. With little hope, you make one last attempt to entice him. You repeat the opening steps, at a slower tempo, and the crowded room's silence intensifies. The presence of penetrating eyes, framing you on three sides, somehow makes you feel even more alone.

You've come to the end. He's leaving you, wandering offstage in a distracted reverie, and you're left standing there, reaching out as if trying to call his name but unable to make a sound. In truth, you've been talking to each other since you entered, five minutes earlier, but words were really never needed. The amount of tension, resistance, pressure, and impetus each of you exerts, the exact degree of each lean, the inches and centimeters of distance between you at every moment, the split-second coordination of your preparation before he lifts you off your legs—these are your words. You and he have a secret—a language of your own, made up of those words and thousands of others. You can't translate it, but you both understand it innately and speak it fluently.

The last notes, they're fading away, and you wish they wouldn't end. The usual smattering of supportive applause breaks out from your colleagues lining the room like wallpaper. The air's pressure normalizes, and the notepad is set aside.

Excellent. That was excellent.

You've only heard that once before, and it was a long time ago.

45

"I've Never Heard You Make a Noise Like That"

It was later, well after I'd recovered and quieted, that Kathi, my fellow dancer, friend, and dressing room mate, made her comment about my "noise." *I didn't realize how hard it was,* she said.

I hadn't, either.

I'd been warned, though. *Lambarena* is legendary among dancers. Val Caniparoli, inspired by a seamlessly swirled-together score of J. S. Bach and traditional African music, choreographed it to see what would happen when two seemingly diametrically opposite forms—classical ballet and traditional West African dance—were fused together. The result was glorious: an artwork evoking the landscape, colors, and drum-driven pulse of West Africa, highlighted by the uplift and precision of pointe shoes, crafted with thoughtful attention to and respect for the details underpinning each.

The choreography doesn't simply present African dance movements and ballet steps side by side; they were truly melded together while—incredibly—remaining distinct. Long arabesques fold into tilted hip sequences, grand jetés came from a contracted crouch. It is a thrilling, daunting hybrid for a ballet dancer to take on.

The legend of *Lambarena* surrounds both the joys and challenges of dancing it. The music, so powerful in even its quietest moments as to feel almost literally heart-lifting, shows the spiritual impetus shared by two visually contrasting continents and cultures. The European violins and African lutes play perfectly well, as if they don't know they come from different places. They build together, grow contemplative together, explore and exist and, ultimately, in the ballet's final movement, share in the exaltation of community.

But for a ballet dancer like me, learning how to move as an African dancer while wearing pointe shoes and without losing my classical technique is a real test of physical and mental flexibility. The African dance motifs in *Lambarena* are deceptively hard to master—coordinating the movement of my hips and ribcage in opposite directions was especially foreign to me—since even the arm movements and finger positioning are as specific as in ballet technique but in completely different ways. The African dance experts who came to give us a crash course in their style made it look so relaxed, so easy, which is how it should be but also why it was so hard. It was immensely frustrating to be unable to grasp coordinations that required a sort of letting go of my ballet structure, a more organic approach. The strength to move like they did—where did it come from? After an hour's work on a sidestepping pattern incorporating those oppositional hips and ribs, I had to think superhard on where exactly each part of my body was supposed to go—and my thighs and back were burning. It was like learning a new language, but not being anywhere near fluent, and trying to have an intelligent conversation. I felt and immediately wanted to exude the joy of the music, but it turned out that that reward would be waiting much further along the journey.

Lambarena is also renowned for being aerobically hard, stamina-wise, so much so that there were tales of dancers throwing up from exertion after their first run-through (or subsequent ones, or in the wings during a performance). Though each section varies in tone and texture, it's all nonstop movement, whether pure power or tenuous legato or bright, sunny jumping. My muscles had years of knowledge about how to perform classical steps, but they were a lot less efficient at doing the African movements, even the smallest transitional ones, or arm and hand gestures that should have erased the seams between the two styles. My body had to *think* every second, as it had only half as much muscle memory to rely on. The music, so big, so grand and magnificent in scope it is impossible not to want to try to equal it, dared to be matched—even the softer, quieter sequences wanted a feeling of suspension, a tensile quality that emanates from deep in your core. After high-octane jumping and thrusting one moment, the next had me tiptoeing across a high wire, evoking mystery and possibility.

On the video that I'd watched of another company performing *Lambarena*, I'd seen how heavily the dancer doing my role was breathing. It did worry me, but there was no way to avoid it.

The only thing to do was try, and try, and work my way up to doing it full-out—maybe it would be easier for me. Maybe I could find a trick no one else had discovered, or maybe I had better lung capacity.

The first few times, it was hard but not to the point of absurdity. The whole ballet was hard; everyone in the cast was heaving. I was in good company. The stage rehearsals felt noticeably different, though—the air of the theater was colder, there were more nerves, more space to cover from stage right to left. It was like running uphill when the incline suddenly increases. Dress rehearsal got even tougher, but on opening night, adrenaline pushed me through.

But then. Fatigue, built up over days of intense rehearsals and the pressure of opening night, was embedded deep into my muscles. By the second performance, I already felt worn down at the start of the ballet. My first entrance was a long, languid series of piqué arabesque balances—so precarious that the smallest wobble was impossible to mask and, in my opinion, ruined everything—in near-silence, accompanied by the faintest, most delicate strains of a stringed instrument. Immediately came another entrance just like the first, and then the restraints were pulled off—for the next two minutes of choreography, all engines were firing, every muscle pushed to its max, every step punched and staccato. For that short time, my partner and I were shot out of a cannon to the pulsing drumbeat.

The duet ended on a dime, abruptly, smack-dab on the final drumbeat. The lights snapped into blackout. In the pitch-darkness, Javier, my partner, put me down from the curled-up shape he'd caught me in as I took a running jump past him but was caught by his arm, as if he'd reached out to stop me from leaping off a cliff.

I squeezed his hand in a silent "thank you" before he scurried offstage, and I, still in blackness, found the glowing fluorescent tape that marked my starting spot for the next section. Two other women had entered from the wings in the blackout to take their places, and as the lights went up, we were posed neatly in a triangle as if we'd been waiting there forever.

In those few seconds, I tried to steady my breathing. As we began dancing the trio, I tried to relax any muscle that wasn't needed, just braced my center and used every bit of stillness in between steps as a vacation.

It wasn't long, this trio, but that didn't matter. It was long enough. The steps were sweeping and full but had to be accurate and controlled as well. Our trio's formations were a key part of the choreography. We shifted from one tight geometrical arrangement on the stage to another while executing complicated movement, and since most of the dance was in canon, we also had to stay exactly on our individual musical counts or the whole effect would be muddy. (Maiqui Mañosa, the *répétiteur* who taught us the ballet, had spent hours explaining the exactitude of the spacing and educating us in the subtleties of various types of triangles.) I hung on, but as we drew closer and closer to the end, I stopped caring whether I was doing anything well and just counted down the seconds until I could get offstage. And then, safely out of view of the audience, despite my mental relief, the physical pain got worse.

The moments just after extreme exertion are more painful than what's felt during it. The body knows better than the brain how to survive and thinks the performance experience is life-or-death—as do I. There is no exit, no "time out." The concentration required to dance overshadows the physical feeling of tiredness, and the music acts as a vehicle carrying you forward—a surfboard helping you ride the waves. You don't feel how hard it is because you're so focused on the steps you're trying to do. The mind and spirit unite to protect the body.

But as soon as there was no more dancing to focus on, everything hurt—my lungs, my face, my burning legs—and my body doubled over, trying to get oxygen. Unable to breathe fast enough or deep enough, my gasps for air turned into semi-muffled shrieks. Even though they were involuntary, I still worried over the rule about talking too loudly backstage. I let myself fall onto my hands and knees, instinctively feeling that was a better position to get more air, and my gasps began to slow. Relief began to arrive.

I didn't realize that a visitor had been watching the performance from the wings, a perk given to a certain level of donors. From my pathetic crouch on the floor, I noticed an elegantly dressed pair of legs and high-heeled shoes in my blurry field of vision. They seemed out of place on the rough, splintery wooden boards that line the backstage floor, but my preservation-focused mind didn't waste time wondering why they were there. I had to get up and make my way to the other side of the stage for my last entrance in the ballet, now only a minute away. As I ungracefully pulled myself upright, the woman's legs backed away, almost in fear, and I didn't have time to smile. Later, I heard that she'd had to leave—disturbed to tears at the sight she'd just seen.

I've never heard you make a noise like that.

46

The Human Monolith

Some people sweat a lot more than others, and even those who are not heavy sweaters begin to pour and drip as soon as extreme exertion is finished and they are slowly, stealthily, creeping and crawling and oozing their way across the stage to become part of a huge, undulating, slimy mass of dancers twister-ing themselves into the towering pile of limbs we called the Human Monolith.

This is *The Rite of Spring,* and the moment of the Human Monolith is perhaps the apex of the ballet in more than a literal sense. Two dozen dancers of all ages, sexes, and ranks turn themselves, for these few minutes, into primordial slime. We are instructed to "ooze" ourselves from upright stances into prehistoric, one-celled organisms, snaking our way through and on top of and in between each other until we reach an approximate place upon the stage, when certain designated dancers get lifted, some evolve into two-legged creatures, some make it only halfway to standing, and the rest of us remain as a muddy base. No two people may be in the same position. Limbs stick out of the structure we're making, always undulating, never becoming motionless, and (*important*) always remaining in contact with another body in the pile. We are all connected, breathing with life and sweat, heaving. There is a lot of bare skin. The women are in leotards, no tights, and the men are in briefs, no shirts. The puddles of sweat on the stage become treacherous. Like slugs, dancers leave paths of slime behind them.

And there are the giggles. How can you not? Training in the epitome of structure and classicism for decades, pushing oneself to conform to classical shape and line, cramming feet into pointe shoes, and now to achieve freedom by oozing from mud? The strength of the bond between dancers has never been stronger than when our hierarchy is made meaningless and we hold on to each other in the monolith, scheming how to make a creepier creation, with one person's foot in another's face and one's leg on another's rear, holding on to her ankle and breathing into his stomach while she rests her elbow on my back and the guy I danced *Sleeping Beauty* with lies writhing just under my rib cage.

Somehow it doesn't feel wrong, though. This is just another part of it, the life upon the stage. Another human experience, and one of the most grounding, real ones I've ever had.

On cue, the monolith tumbles down and we emerge from our prehumanity, evolving into upright creatures as we walk offstage to dance again.

47

A Conversation with My Feet

Hello, feet.

I haven't seen you in a while, not since a few hours ago when I taped you up and stuffed you into pointe shoes. You—we—have been working hard since then. I couldn't see you, of course, but I imagine it's like a little factory down in those shoes, pistons firing and engines gunning. I sometimes expect to see little puffs of smoke and steam escaping through the seams of my shoes after we've been going at it hard for a while. Like today, during that three-hour-long rehearsal: by the last hour you were screaming at me to quit hammering you with those hops on pointe, and then all that running (which hurts even more), but I'm sorry, I just couldn't—the choreographer is not sympathetic about sore toes, especially when he's putting the finishing touches on his newest creation, shaping and sculpting his ballet from a hunk of raw clay into a masterpiece or, at least, a success. I must seem like a tyrannical dictator, commanding orders to you at a rapid-fire pace while you scramble to obey. But I know—really, I do—that all my dancing relies on you.

Now that I've taken you out of those pointe shoes and cut away the layers of toe tape and corn cushions, I see that I was not wrong about the burning-hot engine room scene I imagined. You're red, sweaty, and oddly puffy, even though my toes are still squashed together into a single unit. Your skin is soft from the moisture and lack of air, and you're very slowly morphing back into a normal foot shape after being corseted for so many hours in rigid pointe shoeboxes. Pulling my toes apart from each other is painful—the corns that had dulled to numbness scream "PAIN!" when they're disturbed—but what a relief to carefully, carefully, start to wiggle them around, playing with them like a little kid. I can almost laugh at how ridiculous they look, and how fun it is.

I ask you to do so much, feet. And you do so much for me. I complain that YOU complain and that you aren't perfect. I wish for short, stubby toes instead of the long, bony ones whose bursae get inflamed and that breed those corns, but I also love how long and elegant they are and how much more arch they give the rest of my feet. And although I wish that that arch was higher and stronger, I appreciate that you naturally glide into a smooth line at the end of my arabesque. I know I'm lucky.

Lying here on my back, lifting you straight up overhead to let the fluid start to drain away, I know you're as grateful as I am. Now, I'm your bene-factor, and you're my innocent, earnest, diligent little darlings. Now, at last, I can treat you as you deserve, pamper you, elevate you to a place of honor up in the air. I won't make any more merciless demands of you to-day. Your redness is starting to fade and a tingle is setting in as the blood drains out. I'll roll my ankles in circles a few times, up there over my head, just easily, lazily, not caring whether my toes point or not. The workday is done.

Looking back at rehearsal's end, I can't believe what I've asked you to do, nor how hard you work to give me what I want. You articulate every tendu, making each one fine-pointed and clean. You lift me onto pointe, and you cushion and control my descent, no matter how fast, slow, or sophisticated I want that descent to be. You propel me into the air when I take off for jumps, and you decelerate my landings, letting me smoothly transition from one step to the next, shifting directions with barely a nanosecond's notice. You're the foundation of all the technique and strength we've built together, over these many years, but that's why I keep asking for more. You give me artistry and power. We can't be done, not yet.

Most amazingly, you heal. As much work as I put you through, hour after hour, day after dancing day, you rebound. Not instantly, and not completely, but enough, so that what seems inconceivable tonight, after eight hours of jumping, turning, twisting, squeezing, standing, running, waiting, and then doing it all again, will become moderately achievable in time for tomorrow morning's class. I do my best to take care of you. After I ease you down off the wall you're resting against now, I'll reluctantly stand on you again, as it seems wrong to ask you to serve such a pedestrian need as being plain old human feet. (I should have a spare pair of "regular feet" for everyday, human uses.) In the ice room, I'll fill a garbage can with cold water and a couple bags of ice. I'll lug it all downstairs (walking barefoot, since even socks are too harsh for you right now and you need to breathe deeply, just as I do), where I'll get situated on a chair in the dressing room, cover up in a warm sweatshirt, and gently slide you into your ice bath. You'll both love and hate it at first, but after a minute, it's all bliss. When the cold penetrates deeper through my skin, it relieves more than just the ache in my toes and the swelling from my tendonitis. It seems to dull, even temporarily erase, any disappointments over the day's dancing: dissatisfaction, shortcomings, failures. Whatever beat me down—dauntingly hard steps, lung-busting choreography, a temperamental partner, disappointing casting, anxiety about injury—fades in importance as it gets frozen in time, iced into today, not to be carried over to tomorrow. It's a cleanse, a reset button. My comrades and friends in the dressing room, many soaking their feet in ice as I am soaking you, might ask "Brown or clear?" as we fill our shot glasses and toast the end of the day.

It doesn't take long—ten minutes or so—until you're completely numb in your ice bath. As hard as it is to stand up again, I'll have to pull you out, one by one, and gently dab you dry with paper towels. I somewhat enjoy how funnily clod-like and stiff you are now, after hours of being so supremely supple. I'll delay putting on shoes as long as possible, but when I do clomp out to the car in my gloriously roomy and sensible Swedish clogs, the hard wooden support under my arches will be utter heaven. Just having made it through the day will feel like a triumph, however small, and the cold freeze will linger like a badge of honor.

48

My Little Toe

I dislocated my little toe on the living room carpet. Got home after dress rehearsal for *La Valse* (I'd just done the pas de deux with Artur) and did my usual ice-bucket foot soak while eating dinner and checking my email. Afterward, feeling rigor mortis setting into my legs as they cooled and stiffened, I stretched out one last time on the living room floor before going to bed and managed, while moving a leg from one position to another, to catch my little toe on the carpet. It was so numb from the ice water that I barely felt it, but a small alarm bell chimed. I didn't think I'd ever seen my toe bend 90 degrees outward from my foot before. The toe was frozen cold but not frozen in place, obviously. I curiously tried moving it out to the side like the rug had done—and there it went again. I thought that wasn't right at all, but it still didn't hurt, and there was nothing to be done in any case. I was more concerned about getting enough sleep for tomorrow's rehearsal and performance. So I went to bed with a touch of worry, pushing aside more dire thoughts of what the morning could reveal.

Sure enough, the next day, it was swollen, red, and not happy. Walking barefoot, I had to adjust my steps to avoid bending it. The usual feeling of deep dread and entrapment accompanying any serious pain didn't quite appear, though. Somehow, I felt humorous about it—it was the smallest appendage on my body, and such a silly thing, to injure oneself by stubbing a toe rather than doing a fancy leap or turn. My story seemed to prove the ungraceful truth of how clumsy dancers are in real life. At the theater for class, I experimented with padding it, but there is so little room inside the box of a pointe shoe that anything thicker than a Band-Aid makes it too tight and more painful than leaving any wound exposed. Luckily, other foot injuries had long ago driven me to abandon wearing soft ballet slippers for the beginning of class as most dancers do. Encasing my foot in pointe shoes, effectively putting my toe in a cast, gave me the most relief. Since my toe was significantly swollen, squeezing them on was the worst part, but once that was done I didn't want to take them off, knowing how painful it would be to repeat. I did, though, to tape my little toe to its neighbor so it couldn't even be jostled in the cocoon of my pointe shoe.

Even though I would have preferred to wear softer pointe shoes for *La Valse* that night, I chose a nearly new pair. I loved this pas de deux. I had been an alternate cast but, through the complexities of casting all the different ballets on the program, had gotten bumped to perform opening night. I felt so lucky, like I'd been given the most beautiful present for no occasion at all. When Yuri Possokhov choreographed *La Valse,* I wasn't even in the ballet, but now that we were reviving it, there was my name on the bulletin board. The choreography made me think of a series of spirals all spinning around each other in constant motion, a stream of steps so smoothly blended that you couldn't see or feel where one ended or began. It was lush and flowing and felt perfectly matched to my natural movement quality. I wanted, as I so loved to do, to move as seamlessly and noiselessly as possible.

During the performance that night, Artur and I were perfectly connected. I thought of the two of us not as human beings but as the choreography itself—we actually were the steps. Our physical bodies carried each other through and above the waves of the music. It was a pas de trois, two dancers and Ravel's voice, swimming patterns around the stage.

I only hit land once, wincing when Artur and I accidentally knocked ankles during an arabesque slide.

A few days later, the company gathered in the studio's lobby for a meeting with staff and board to hear announcements and news of the weekend's ticket sales. I found myself standing next to one of the board members, Donald, a generous donor who'd always struck me as an unlikely patron of the arts. He was always cordial but businesslike to the point of seeming more interested in the financial workings of the ballet company than its product. I couldn't quite imagine he had a significant degree of emotional investment and wondered why he chose the ballet to patronize.

After news was shared, the group began breaking up into a hubbub of mingling voices. Donald turned to me. I could see he had tears in his eyes. *La Valse the other night,* he said. *That was the most beautiful thing I have ever seen.*

49

The Millionth Nutcracker

Ballet dancers are supposed to be tough and steely, to have superhu-
man senses of drive and determination and passion that compel them
to push forward every day through mental and physical pain. But in
reality, we just try to get through each day without slipping backward
or falling behind. Just hang on tight, pull your body through another
class, another rehearsal, and rally in time for the performance. I
learned, eventually, that feeling my physical and mental best for every
show, night after night, was a myth, and although it had happened a
few times when I was very young, it would never happen again. The
chances of feeling strong, rested, energized, healthy, calm, focused, and
centered all at the same time were nil. So, as all dancers do, I created
my own standard of reality, my own baseline from which I could gauge
how I was faring at any given moment during any given day. Ankle
pain, brittleness? Hamstring ache? Overall muscle fatigue from last
night? Self-confidence, optimism, energy level? Usually all of these
would be middling, neither great nor terrifyingly bad. Developing my
own personal standard was an emotional escape hatch. It was the only
way of convincing myself that it was all going to be okay, that I could
go home at the end of the day and just be me, even with all my aches
and faults and missteps.

Here they come—it must be almost time. The kids . . . so excited and
so carefree . . . God, I remember that. How amazing and thrilling it

was. There was absolutely nothing, not one thing, about a performance that wasn't fun and exciting. There was no anxiety, no fear or uncertainty . . . and certainly no subsequent dread, arising from insecurity. There was no stress or frustration with pointe shoes, no worries about an injury or about satisfying the director. No fatigue to push through to warm up, yet again, an overworked body, no inner-dialogue pep talks to summon up the courage . . . the courage to tell myself I know what I'm doing, that I can do this. No need to pretend that everything is fine.

I wish I could just be that happy about performing again, but I'm not sure it's possible. I set standards for myself, you see, and then build them higher and higher, and now I feel immense pressure to deliver the goods as expected—not just for myself but for everyone watching. I don't think they know how unpredictable it is.

It feels like chance, now, or just a fluke, when a show goes well and every piece of it happens just like I want it to. But people think that I *made* it happen, that I had deliberate control and knew what I was doing. I say "thanks" to people who compliment me on a good show, but I can't really accept their words—the truth is, I was totally surprised that I'd hit my turns spot-on, and I have no idea if I can do it again. It was probably just a good pair of pointe shoes.

The cruel thing is that once your body does something *right*, you should, by the principles of physics, be able to do it again, exactly the same way, whenever you want to. You've proven (or your body has proven to you) that you are physically capable of executing that step in that manner. So then, why doesn't it happen that way? What goes wrong? It's because of all the other factors that don't have anything to do with physical mechanics. And my brain knows that. It takes only one failed attempt after a successful one for self-doubt to be planted. And then I become my own enemy-friend-enemy, taunting myself: "Can you or can't you? Will you or won't you? You're not really that good. You're a fraud."

Don't think too much, people advise, just "do it." Your body knows what to do better than you do, so just let it do its thing and go along for the ride. But it's not that easy, because in fact, my body ISN'T the same every day, or every hour. It's got some cracks now, deepening all the time, and I never really know for sure how well I've patched them up.

That's really my fear: physical failure. I can push through fatigue, no problem; that's just brute strength of will. Mind over matter. Be a military man. But when my tendons, muscles, bones, ligaments, are ready to give out, I can't control them. My body, ultimately, is only interested in survival. It has a plan for its own preservation that it hasn't consulted me about.

And that's the scariest feeling in the world.

Seeing these kids giddy in the wings. . . . They're staring at me—at all of us—with these wide-open eyes, having no idea how much of a struggle we're going through. Because we all play it cool, and these kids are like another audience. We play to them as much as we play to the people out front. We don't admit it, but we're putting on a little show backstage for them, knowing that they're watching every single move, listening covertly to our words, absorbing every gesture and attitude we strike. So I play the calm, confident, gracious, secure Sugarplum Fairy, with all the poise I can muster, just like I remember seeing those gorgeous women do back when I was a Polichinelle.

But they have no idea, nor should they, that two hours ago I was a crumpled mess of tears in my dressing room. I had totally cracked. There are these pirouettes in my variation that I have trouble with even on the best of days, but when I'd practiced them after class today, they were so much further off-balance than I'd ever experienced that it literally felt like I was trying to turn on a ski slope. I had no idea what was going on—my body felt senseless and numb. My instincts to adjust my arms or lift my knee or step in a slightly different place to straighten things out weren't working. Each time I tried again, the turn got worse, until I was turning on a 45 degree angle—and I panicked. Truly, truly panicked. The stage manager called half hour, so I had to stop trying to solve this emergency problem and clear the stage. It was the ultimate in powerlessness—all signs said I was about to fail miserably onstage, but the only thing I knew to do to avoid disaster was snatched away. Desperately, I wanted to troubleshoot until I was reassured I still had the ability to do that pirouette, but I had to leave it and just hope and pray that something miraculously would change between then and now—*now*, when I'm about to go onstage and dance.

Cleared from the stage at half-hour, I had no choice but to go upstairs to my dressing room. There, unable to hold in my emotions any longer, I totally broke down. Months, maybe even years, of pressure and fear overwhelmed me. For one of the first times in my life as a dancer, I caved in. The step was bigger than I was, and I couldn't find the tools to tame it. I sobbed and sobbed, until I was breathless, almost wailing. There was nothing on earth that I wanted to do less at that moment than put on fake eyelashes, makeup, a rhinestone tiara, and a regal pink tutu. Nothing felt less possible. Like a baby, a child, all I wanted was to cry and wail and have someone hold me and say, "It's okay, we don't have to play this game anymore. It was all just a bad dream, and now it's over."

But, the awfulness . . . the sick feeling in my gut was the hard fact that I had no way out. I had a job to do. I was a professional, after all, and ballet is a real-life business.

My friend and dressing room mate, Kathi, talked me down from the edge, God bless her. She seems to have a sort of perspective on dancing that allows her to, enviably, treat it like just another thing in life, as natural and inevitable as walking, working, eating, and sleeping. Maybe she looked at it as *more* like a job than I did, something to simply be done as well as one could when required, and enjoyed, but not be allowed to overwhelm.

Or perhaps it's just how it appears to me, when I feel like I'm about to crumple from strain. Kathi can make me laugh, and she shook me out of my spiral of panic. So what if I flubbed those turns? I wasn't going to get fired, the audience wouldn't boo, the whole rest of the solo and pas de deux would go fine—or better than fine—and within two hours it would be over and I could go home.

Then, I could breathe, and the fog lifted. The situation just seemed hilarious. I sat there in front of the dressing room mirror, looking like the ugliest troll on earth, but I was about to transform myself into the image of maternal goodness and joy? We laughed pretty hard at what the audience, settling into their seats downstairs—or those little child performers—would think if they could have seen me at that moment. Their idea of the perfectly poised, flawless, polished, and happy ballerina would be demolished if they saw the sad picture I made at that moment. But I turned to the magic powers of foundation, powder, concealer, and blush, hastily swabbed on now that the overture had started and the countdown to showtime had ended.

And now, here I am. My makeup is on, my hair's done, headpiece pinned on. I chose my pointe shoes (two pairs, one for the solo and another for the pas de deux) and put on my costume. Got my feet taped up and my warmers layered over my tutu and tights. I did my warm-up at the barre backstage, tuning my inner radio dial to block out all interference. I felt calm, but in an unfamiliar way—it was a sense of surrender. Act 1 was under way, and as I did my tendus in the dim light of backstage, I stared at the scenery for act 2, where I was soon to hold court with polish and bravado.

Intermission's over now, the littlest children are in their formation onstage for the start of act 2, and I just heard the "Places" call. During intermission, I did try, with some trepidation but without pushing too hard, the pirouettes I'd struggled with before the show started. But who knows what will happen when, in a matter of minutes, the curtain rises and I'm onstage in front of two thousand people? Everything's different then, everything changes. We never know why. My partner and I, as always, ran through our checklist, almost out of superstition: we practice the same few steps from our pas de deux, just as I always tried to nail my solo's pirouettes. The overture starts, and I take my leg warmers off at the same exact point in the music that I do every show, put them in the same place, take one tiny sip of water, go to the wing where I'll make my first entrance. I do one last balance in fifth position on pointe, totally pulled up, pulled in, perfectly secured on my legs, deep breath in, deep breath out. I'm balancing the uncertainty of the stage with an unshakeable routine backstage. The whims of the gods tempered by the pagan ritual. I watch the little girls gliding around under the stage lights and count the seconds before I join them. I feel the slightly older kids watching me from the shadows, farther back in the wings. My anxiety is gone. My fear is gone. Onstage, I am not afraid of anything.

And, now—it's time—four more counts—three, two, one . . . and GO.

50

No Tights

One minute you're a superstar, the next, just a cog in the wheel. It's wondered why dancers teeter between puffed-up pride and scathing self-criticism. Humans can't separate body from mind, but dancers must try—they need to be clinically removed from the technique of their craft, but then reinfuse what has been produced with their soul, their spirit, their DNA. With the exactitude of a nurse's syringe, life is carefully, delicately, injected into one's dancing in the tiniest of increments. The fear of overdose—of investing too much and losing it all— is real.

The Rite of Spring is minimally costumed. We are a horde, a cast of dozens, wearing mostly skin and feeling conflicted about it. Normally, in the studio, we carefully construct outfits that are sleek enough to look professional, warm enough to protect the joints, comfy enough to give moral support, and stylish enough to boost morale. This exposure of bare skin feels childlike—little kids running around in their underwear, splashing in the kiddie pool.

The women are in red leotards. That's it. Sleeveless, high-cut, low-backed, as tight as sausage casing, blood-red leotards. The men wear briefs as red and as tight as our leos.

It's a premiere, this production of *Rite*. An in-studio run-through is scheduled a week before opening night. Choreographer, lighting, and costume and set designers all want to see the work fully, and up-close, before it's set onstage. A note is made on the rehearsal schedule: *Wednesday 3:00–5:30: Rite of Spring, Complete, in costume.*

No one wants to admit their insecurity. Nor do they want to admit their relish.

We put on our red leotards downstairs in the costume shop, but then layer on sweatpants, shirts, leg warmers, and track jackets, and head upstairs as if dressed for any other rehearsal. We warm up, stretch out, choose which pointe shoes to wear, practice a few steps, tug and pull at the tightness of the leg seams and fuss with the low necklines. And then it's time to strip down. Unceremoniously, outwardly cool, inwardly shy, secretly feeling a tickle of thrill . . . pretending not to size each other up, to compare, pretending not to stare at ourselves in the mirror. Startled at how cold the air is on bare legs, how strangely vulnerable—how *wrong*— to be so naked in such a public place. The box office is in the lobby just outside the studio, and those fully clothed people waiting in line for tickets look overdressed. But then, after a few minutes . . . how free it is to have no encumbrances at all. Those mysteriously concealing tights were a barrier much thicker than the minuscule weave of their mesh fabric. There's a little pride in seeing muscles, usually veiled, now in full, bare, exposure. I feel eyes looking me up and down. My legs are very defined.

Are we children or adults? Professionals, but what kind?

My pride is confused. It's bolstered, then squished, while my brain fires on all cylinders to propel this red leotard-clad race car through the choreographic obstacle course of *The Rite of Spring*—by the finish, I think *I* am the sacrificial maiden. And then, immediately, I am reduced to a costumer's faceless mannequin as we line up under fluorescent lights to be scrutinized, every inch criticized, commented upon—from the neck down.

By the time rehearsal is over, after two hours in a single layer of stretch fabric, fatigue and resignation have overcome any lingering self-consciousness.

There's another layer, though, beneath that leotard, or perhaps on top of it. Usually, I see just the outline of my dancing, the shapes and positions I carve in space. In motion, I know only what I *feel*, and I must try to imagine what it looks like. But now, exposed like this, the hood of the race car lifted while the engine is running, the machinery that produces my dancing is (with shy pride) visible. *Hello, legs.*

Onstage, no one cares anymore about what they have, or do not have, on. There is too much else to worry about, and the viewers are too far away, and the mirror is gone. We're used to each other in red now. My partner glances at me, as we line up in the wings for an entrance. *Nice stems.*

And a comment, overheard from out front: *Who's the gymnast?*

Onstage, no one cares anymore.

51

The Highest Note

Everyone should dance. Everyone should let their soul sing. We all deserve to feel our spirits expanding past the boundaries of our skin, to be powerful without needing to hold power over anyone else. Dancing takes the most beautiful, extraordinary, and universal instrument—the human body—to its fullest, highest, most complete capacity. Physical body, intellectual mind, emotional spirit, interpretive artistry all unite in even the simplest classroom exercise. When I dance, I feel like I am sharing a gleeful, knowing chuckle with our creator: I've found the key to sublime paradise on earth, which he has masterfully "hidden" by putting it in the most obvious place—our muscles, tendons, bones, and, indeed, every cell of our bodies. When dancing, one need not go to church to seek out the divine. I've found my spiritual salvation in the dance studio. And I'm not alone.

Everyone should dance.

The orchestra builds, builds, builds, to one perfectly simple and completely transcendent high note. Artur and I have been building up to this moment, too, throughout the entire pas de deux—it is the peak of our eight minutes onstage. It is also the high point, quite literally: from our pose, bodies nested together in tendu, matched in breath and impulse, we take an energy-generating step forward and I am launched into flight, lifted well over his head into a soaring grand jeté. The arc and length of the lift match the peak and roll of Tchaikovsky's music, ascending and descending scales that have grown in intensity until right now, when I think my soul might burst with joy.

The pas de deux began with our serene, noble entrance, calm but commanding, from upstage left. The conductor watched for us to appear from the wing, baton poised, signaling his musicians' first notes when we'd taken a few steps onstage. The music is so pure, so delicate, so quiet and beautiful just as it is. It seems perfectly unadulterated. I almost wish the melody would stay away.

The first steps of this, the Sugarplum Fairy and Cavalier's pas de deux in George Balanchine's choreography of *The Nutcracker*, are spare and deceptively simple, too. I pose facing away from Artur and swiftly turn toward him, fit my hand into his and simultaneously begin to rotate into a promenade while extending my right leg into a grand rond de jambe—essentially a slow and controlled fan kick—with only his forearm for balance. He walks a circle around my supporting leg while my rond de jambe lifts higher and higher from front, to side, to back, turning my body to display all angles of us to the audience. We're ballerina and prince figurines on the rotating pedestal of a music box. Once he's fully around, he lunges deeply forward and I lean with him, my extended leg now in a full penché behind my head, toes pointed straight over my body. He's nearly horizontal to the floor; I am nearly upside down.

This promenade is the first paragraph of the story: it sets the stage for the entire pas de deux. It establishes us as two independent figures embarking on an adventure together. We make tensile plasticity with our arms and legs and torsos. We use each other just enough—neither of us dominates—to be reliant on, but separable from, each other. We are having a dialogue between ourselves and, through their music and choreography, with Tchaikovsky and Balanchine.

I run away and step up into fourth position on pointe; Artur follows close behind but only to offer to help me turn toward him, a suggestion I take. We repeat that exchange, then decide to pirouette together for the first time. But this is no typical supported pirouette: Artur, standing attentively several feet away when I carefully reach my right leg into a single piqué en dehors, is ready to reach me in an instant. I go for only one revolution, as pulled up as an intake of breath, and at the exact moment my leg opens to arabesque—I could never stay there by myself, on pointe—Artur is there, grasping each wrist to stop my, albeit slow, momentum. He barely holds on, maybe not even using all his fingers, making the pose feel as light and stretched as a length of thread.

The music is still quiet here, though the tone of the orchestra's string section seems to be deepening. There's just a hint, now, of urgency and anticipation. After our threadlike suspension, Artur and I swiftly separate in opposite directions to pose, momentarily, facing each other across the expanse of the stage, connected through timing and energy if not our eyes. We run full throttle toward each other, but just before we might smack faces, he deftly steps behind me to catch my waist as I dive into a no-holds-barred piqué penché, picks me up from my nose-to-knee full split on pointe with so much speed my leg almost automatically swings into a grand battement front, nearly kicking my nose again, and passionately sweeps me into a layout backbend over his arm. He lunges so low into his right leg that the rhinestones on the top of my tiara graze the floor.

He brings me up from this luxurious lean, but I help myself, too, using the arm I have wrapped around his shoulder and, of course, my abs, which have never let go even when my back was so extremely arched.

One hand on my waist, Artur offers his other to me for support. I accept, and we promenade again, this time our bodies slightly facing each other. My right leg is lifted in between us, bent in an *attitude* position. I feel I'm presenting my lower leg and foot for us to share in a moment of appreciation. But then, I reach my leg to the floor, close my feet together into a fifth position, and on pointe, begin to move away. He steps aside to watch.

My solo is short—tiny steps on pointe, a piqué arabesque, and two pirouettes—and as soon as I land my second one, Artur comes forward again, mirroring my position. Now the push-pull of our dancing becomes even stronger: we're within sight of the climax. I run to the farthest corner of the stage, pose momentarily toward the audience but abruptly turn to face Artur, who's waiting at center stage. I run—fast—directly at him and take a leap, turning my body 180 degrees in midair while he swoops down underneath my jump so that I land sitting squarely on his shoulder. Once is not enough for that trick—he sets me down and I immediately race to the downstage left corner of the stage to do it again. The farther away from Artur I take off for my leap, the more likely it is that I'll land successfully, and securely, on his shoulder. If I wait a fraction of a second too long or take one extra step before launching myself into the air, I won't have enough time to turn in the air before our bodies meet. The audience often gasps at the distance between us, but it feels safer to me.

Safe is an illusion, though I never feel vulnerable in Artur's hands. His palms are wide, his fingers long (his six-foot-four-inch height makes me feel tiny in comparison, my head barely reaching his shoulder), so I often wonder if this is the feeling of being a bird cupped in the hands of a gentle giant. When we pirouette, I barely feel him, but his support is so strong in the deep backbend afterward that we can immediately recover our shared centerline and go for more turns. Each pirouette into the backbend is its own mini-climax, stepping stones toward the inevitable purpose of the pas de deux. I gradually lift my arms while we're pirouetting (dangerously close to his face with my elbows) into a first arabesque, and then we're there: a quick, small *sauté* jump takes me to our upstage spot. Artur takes the long route—he hangs back until I've arrived, so I can watch his exuberant, enormous solo grand jeté, aimed right to where I'm waiting for him to join me. He lands and steps right beside me, matching my pose, and as we do our huge port de bras in unison—arms circling up, forward, and down—in the last four notes of the scale's ascension, our two bodies are one.

Artur's hand at my waist is warm, his grip firm and encouraging. And then, suddenly I'm aloft, unfolding my legs into a full split, arms overhead, reaching my feet and stretching my limbs for eternity, every cell driven by the power of the orchestra raging under us like the waves of an ocean.

Ever since I walked onstage at the start of the pas de deux, my thoughts have been a fast-moving, shifting stream of second-by-second calculations and adjustments. I hadn't consciously told myself what step came next; my body knew the choreography on its own. Sensations like the heat of the stage lights, a glimpse of someone in the wings, and the roughness of the fabric of Artur's tunic against my skin registered distantly, well below the current.

But suddenly, at the height of the lift and on that one magnificent note, everything was crystal clear: this is the apex of life. This is the happiest a person on earth can be. This is perfection.

I may never be this happy again. And that's okay.

The performance is over. The theater is quiet. A shower has washed off the sweat and makeup, the evidence of my having danced, hard, under bright lights. The route from my dressing room to the stage door and then to the outside world, homeward, means crossing from stage left to stage right, in the shadows behind the backdrops. Look up—up to the flies, so many stories above—is there even a ceiling in here? The walls of the theater are endless, powerful, and silent. They are so big, and I am so small. And tonight, this one, tiny, minuscule person, all by herself, filled this enormous acreage.

52

Vertigo, Part 2

Vertigo was a recurrent shadow lurking over my shoulder. A brief, scary first episode in my early twenties I chalked up to a fluke—although it coincided with my initial push to leave the company, the solid bedrock I'd thought was going to be my permanent home, and upon reflection, it could have signaled my emotional turmoil. Over the years, occasional recurrences sidelined me for a day or two here or there, and one summer I had low-level dizziness for weeks. A small number of flare-ups were strong enough to be debilitating, but, except for two occasions— my debut in Allegro Brillante *being one of them—they only threatened disaster.*

Telling the story of this chapter in my life now, from a level, stable perch, I see that the vertiginous state of my inner ears spoke as a deep, unsettling, harbinger of change that I had been trying to ignore. To cope with my fear of that looming, yet unidentifiable, reality, I separated my mind from my body—the most un-dancerly thing a dancer could do. I watched myself go through the motions.

She lay very still in bed, wondering what to do. This time, it had started in the middle of the night, with a turn of her head as she rolled onto her side. Even in the darkness, the room spun wildly and didn't stop no matter how hard she clung to her pillow. She did fall back asleep, praying that

in the morning this would prove to have been a bad dream or a temporary middle-of-the-night weirdness. But now the alarm had gone off and
reaching for it turned the bed into a seesaw.

What she was wondering about was not *what* to do, exactly, but how
to do what had to be done. There were no rehearsals (it was Sunday), but
she had a photo shoot later that day to capture images for a poster adver-
tising an upcoming performance. Rescheduling was inconceivable—the
thought of calling in to say she couldn't do it didn't even enter her mind.
The location of the photo shoot was a city-owned site, and an entire
street was going to be closed to traffic. A photographer, two assistants, a
makeup artist, the marketing director, artistic staff, and the other dancer
to be featured in the shoot had all been booked for weeks. If she couldn't
do this—the thought of how much inconvenience she would cause was
unbearable.

The photos were to be taken on the sidewalk outside the downtown
performing arts complex. She and her partner would pose, Fred-and-
Ginger style, casual and suave, with an old-timey lamppost and a classic
theater marquee in the background. The scene called for dusky twilight,
just enough so the marquee's bulbs would sparkle behind them. The
window of time between sunset and darkness was narrow, since it was
January, and dry days like this one were rare. An outdoor photo shoot in
January, at night, in pointe shoes, tights, and a short, sleeveless, low-cut
flouncy red costume: that was what she was facing. With vertigo.

But evening was hours away—she held on to the hope of a sudden,
miraculous cure. Maybe just acting as calm and normal as possible,
which was easy so long as she sat perfectly still, would make it all better. It didn't. She tried willing her inner ears to quit their games, testing
them constantly, tipping or turning herself and challenging her brain to
get steady. She thought she could force it to stop, overpower it with scorn
and disgust. Faint waves of nausea came and went.

In the late afternoon, she packed her bag with a shiny pair of pointe
shoes, an extra pair of less-shiny ones, and plenty of fleece warm-ups. She
put on makeup, did her hair, and, even though it was a winter evening,
put on sunglasses to hide her false eyelashes. As she drove her way downtown, she blasted the car's heater as high as it would go.

At the site, the photographer's crew was already setting up. She'd told no one what was wrong, that it took all her concentration just to walk in a straight line, that every few minutes she had to grip her stomach and focus on planting her feet into the ground to keep from reeling. There was no access to the theater's dressing rooms, so in the lobby bathroom she pulled on her pink tights, stepped into the red sequined costume, and stood staring at her image in the mirror. The makeup and sparkles and glamour almost hid the greenish tinge of her face. She zipped up her parka over the costume and smiled—all that was visible below the hem of her coat were pink legs and pointe shoes.

Out on the street, the light was nearing its golden hour luminance. The photographer taped out the area on the sidewalk where the two dancers would be perfectly framed by the theater marquee. They tried out various poses, including, unfortunately, a dip and a backbend, while the production assistant—a godsend—hovered nearby with the dancers' coats, dashing in to drape them over their shoulders in between takes. It was cold out there, January-cold, but the light was perfect and the sky was clear. There were other blessings, too: this could only go on for a short time before it would become too dark to shoot; they were on concrete so they couldn't be asked to actually dance—only to hold static poses. And her partner was tall, strong, and sturdy. Even when her head spun, she felt secure in his arms. She was, unbelievably, able to enjoy it, a little—she was glad, now, that she'd kept her insecurity to herself. The cold air on her bare arms and back was so bracing it wiped out the stress that had been building all day. By the time the sky lost its last touch of dark blue, the realization that this was nearly over made her almost giddy.

A stiff breeze signaled the end of twilight. Everyone was ready to wrap, and within minutes the cameras, lights, and gear had been folded up and packed away. The street was reopened to traffic, and cars sped by, oblivious to the scene they'd just missed.

Indoors, in warmth again, she put her costume back on its hanger, chucked her tights and pointe shoes in her bag, laced up her sneakers, and speed-walked to her car, feeling steadier now, or maybe just braver for knowing what she'd pulled off despite the spinning in her head. The vertigo clung on, but by the next morning, the world spun at a slower and slower pace, until it finally came to a stop.

The image from that night that was chosen for the poster was a good one—the two dancers look debonair and cool, snazzy, joyous, classy, and carefree. The bright theater lights behind them, the lamppost, her saucy grin in his chivalrous arms all evoke an evening when two sophisticates swirled around town, dancing through the streets, leaving a wake of perfume and glitter.

53

Scarred

The passage of time, a philosophical wonder for all humans, is especially difficult for dancers to grasp. Time never seems to move at a normal or logical pace in the studio, onstage, in rehearsal, or simply as one grows older. It stands still only when you least want it to, during the most tedious rehearsals with the most boring choreographer and you're the fourth-cast understudy in the back of the room. It speeds up when you need more of it, either in the last seconds before the curtain goes up or when your body starts to wear down but you still have work to do. Fatigue creeps up slowly and then surprises you with a sudden declaration that it has won the game and it is pointless to resist. As the years pass, you begin to see the dark cloud of spiritual fatigue stealthily creeping across the sky, like an ominous tornado miles away that will overtake you within moments. Why can't the race be fair? Why can't the dancer's body and mind run in tandem instead of in relay?

There are moments when time does seem to cooperate, though, as if the universe is offering a small gift of crystalline moments to hold close forever or perhaps place on a shelf to gaze on over and over.

In that moment of utter uncertainty, all of the sounds and activity around me became muted and fuzzy, as if there were cotton in my ears, but my brain's dialogue was crystal clear. For that one frozen minute, I knew with absolute, unemotional frankness that I had just danced my last step. I saw the future, the past, and the present all at the same time as I hovered there on one leg, looking down at my foot raised slightly in the air (for once not even trying to hold my balance, just miraculously stable). These were the strongest words in my head: "You are finished now."

Then the terror came. Not panic—I was levelheaded throughout—but a deep fright and loneliness, as when you are alone in a time of crisis. The moment of this injury had come in the middle of company class, the most familiar of daily rituals. Dancers in class perform exercises in large groups, loosely spacing themselves in no particular formation, like a scattering of trees in the forest. We move in unconscious unison, absorbed in concentration, so when I stopped moving in the middle of the forest, it took a moment for the others to notice that something was wrong. But it was just a short moment—the pop from my ankle was loud enough to have been heard over the music (strangely, I seem to have been the only one who didn't hear it). It felt as if someone had shot a BB gun into my ankle. I looked down, thinking that the elastic on my pointe shoe had ripped off (and felt a surge of shame that I may not have sewn it securely enough), but the sewing was still intact. As I hesitated there, logically deducing that whatever had snapped was inside my body and not outside, some kind of words or sounds came stuttering out of my mouth, asking for help.

There was a rush of activity then, but to me it all seemed slow. Surrounded by people, one of the other dancers picked me up like a baby (that I can't remember for sure which one is testament to how much was rushing through my brain). I clung to his neck and whispered, "Please don't leave me alone, please don't leave me . . ." as he carried me offstage and toward the Green Room. The fuzziness of my hearing was broken by the sound of shoes hitting the hollow wooden floor as the director of the company, who'd been sitting in the audience, came running backstage to see what had happened.

The usual injury protocol was followed—I was given an ice pack (another clear moment that broke the fog: a feeling of tenderness, watching my director try to tie a plastic bag of ice around my ankle with a leg warmer) and fed a few Advil to beat the swelling, and doctors were called. The clarity of my inner dialogue had dissipated, but my initial conclusion spread more broadly and deeply into my brain, and resulted in slow tears of calm despair. Not pain, just sadness.

The word "dancing" implies playfulness, a carefree spirit. The paradox of classical ballet is that in order to display that quality to her audience, the dancer has to move within a strict set of physical rules that are anything but casual. Only after thousands of hours of training can she forget the rules and soar. When there is no more need for cautious movement, the artist truly appears. We balance ourselves on the brink of disaster and taunt the rules of physics because that is the only way to truly dance. Our only safety nets are our bodies, training, and courage.

I had surgery a week later to repair a torn retinaculum, the band of tissue from ankle bone to heel that holds all the tendons in their grooves. Mine had detached from its anchor-place on my ankle and was flopping around, allowing all the tendons to do the same. Three tiny nails were used to pin the tissue back into the bone, and everything was secured back into the proper places. The three-inch-long incision left a beautiful, arcing scar that gradually receded from angry red worm to the subtle pink zipper that it is today.

My ankle healed well, considering. The surgeon did a masterful job, and I will be forever grateful for his sensitivity to my need to regain every degree of flexibility and strength. After four weeks in a plaster cast, my calf looked like a concentration camp victim's—as small as my forearm, with wrinkly dry skin hanging off the bone. The sight of such decrepitude brought feelings of weakness, frailness, and vulnerability, leaving another scar, this one on my brain.

Slowly, I did dance again. I rebuilt the strength of my muscles and tendons and reestablished the coordination of my ballet technique, from the simplest movements to the most complex. I worked hard to override the instinct to guard my healing ankle, even though its fragility had to be in the forefront of my mind. I had to push just hard enough to make improvements but not one tiny bit too much—the slightest slip caught me off guard, and the startling pain eroded any new confidence I'd built up. For me, the mental and physical rehabilitation never kept pace with each other. One was always running ahead of the other, then falling behind, in a maddening game of leapfrog.

Ultimately, my mind and body came to an uneasy truce as I developed new tricks and strategies to compensate for the deficits I was never able to fill. I figured out how to land from jumps without maxing out my ankle's flexion, how to pivot and pirouette without tweaking the repaired tendon, how to use my hamstrings to reduce strain on my lower leg in penché. But the hacks weren't fail-safe. I had to calculate every movement, even the most basic ones that I'd been doing automatically for decades. I was constantly in overdrive. It was exhausting.

Every day in the studio and every night onstage, the toll of my mental and physical input grew. It became greater than the artistry I could achieve. The scar on my brain just would not heal, and, though the one on my skin faded steadily, I could not massage out the tissue enough to find my precious balance between the safe and the sublime.

And that's what a scar is, I suppose—a tough, thick shell of a reminder that your safety net once failed you.

54

A Boyfriend and a Cat

All my previous injuries had been short-lived and minor. This time, the torn tissues in my ankle gave me no choice: it would not heal on its own, and after surgery I would not be able to dance for weeks, or even months.

I was a little freaked out by the thought of being compromised for so long, so right away I started strategizing: although I would be on crutches, unable to bear weight on my left leg, anything lying down or on all fours was possible, so I devised a rigorous routine of ab, leg, and upper body work with my TheraBands. Within a few days of the surgery, I was religiously following my plan every morning and repeating aspects of it every afternoon. I was crafty and creative and crutches were no obstacle to my getting around the apartment—I hopped on my good leg instead of crutching from room to room, used the kitchen counters and island to swing myself from refrigerator to stove, crawled from living room to bathroom (or from bed, in the middle of the night, as finding my balance in the dark felt too precarious, even for me). I followed a schedule as unwavering as my dance days had been: wake up, bath (with my booted leg wrapped in plastic bags and draped over the side of the tub), tea, exercises, breakfast, email, lunch, a trip around the block to the coffee shop to read for an hour or two, home for round two of my exercises while watching the *Ellen Degeneres Show* . . . the news, dinner, and on and on. I wasn't filling my time with such a regime only to make my ankle and body heal as fast and well as possible. Deep down, I knew I would lose the sense of purpose and self-worth ballet gave me. I was trying to fill that void before it could crack my foundation. But it wasn't the same, and it wasn't enough.

As the hours passed slowly through the afternoons (mornings seemed to go by faster, and evenings, too), I looked at myself: I was still "the dancer," just an injured one. I was working on my dancer-self every day, but not in the studio at the barre, not in pointe shoes (though I did put one on my noninjured foot from time to time, to remember what it felt like—and to make sure I still could). That fact anchored me. But the dancer-work I did in the form of rehab challenged me only physically—there was no holistic gratification. Ironically, that made motivation even harder. Getting myself up for a day of dancing was easy; the work itself distracted me from the effort I was putting in. But merely doing rote exercises, while I knew there was benefit and they were worthwhile, was pale and thin and the endorphin spike momentary.

I felt empty at the end of the days. Not bad, not worthless or depressed, not even bored, just . . . plain. Unmoved.

For the first time ever, I saw the space that ballet occupied inside my soul. I pictured it as an actual thing inside my body, a long tube from head to toe, that was usually coursing full of colorful, fluid energy but now was drained.

I didn't see the need to fill that space, really, since I was confident the weeks would pass and soon I'd slip right back into my previous existence. I was just on pause. Knowing that having this space in mind and body was temporary, I felt playful, and curious, and like taking a bit of a risk.

So I let my guard down and left my door ajar, and in came Tess and Shannon.

⁓

Loneliness had never been a problem for me, at any age. I was the kid who hated crowds, big parties, group field trips, or any sort of forced communal activity. I was the one going off to find a quiet place, who wanted to explore by herself, who had a couple of superglue-tight friendships instead of a network of pals. My instinct for self-reliance worked well with a balletic—some might say monastic—lifestyle. I clung to routine; the thought of sharing my dancer's independence and regimen with another being—all the time—rose a slight sense of panic in me. But other people did it, so why couldn't I?

Years passed, and my single-girl persona solidified.

—

Tess and I first met in a tiny visiting room at the Oregon Humane Society. It was my third trip to the shelter. Each time, I'd spent what seemed like hours peering into cages and reading each cat's "bio" on the little card hung outside: "Fluffy is a quiet lady who still likes to have fun on her own terms. Always on the prowl for a sunny windowsill, this dainty feline will warm the hearts and laps of everyone in her new forever home!" I'd never had a cat before and I was nervous.

I was alone this time, but Shannon had come with me to the shelter the day before. It was a date, and definitely the best one I had ever had—possibly the only one I had ever genuinely enjoyed. An experienced cat owner, he gave me tips on how to gauge the potential adoptees' personalities by the way they acted in their cages. Together, we held (or tried to hold) several of them, finally narrowing it down to three: a pair of sisters and a mottled fellow named Moe. Shannon told me I should put them on hold (the shelter allowed a twenty-four-hour decision period) and come back the next day, so I filled out the forms and we went for lunch. Salad rolls and Pad Thai at a picnic table under an umbrella, out front of a Thai restaurant on a quiet street in North Portland. It was hot and sunny, quiet and relaxed, and felt like vacation.

The next day, I returned to the shelter and sat with the sister cats and Moe one more time. They were all cute and furry (as cats are), prowling around the visiting room sniffing and exploring, just thrilled to be out of their cages. After a while, the staffer came in and, as if she could read my mind, said she had another cat she wanted me to meet. The sisters and Moe went back to their cages and in came Tess.

The staffer set her down on the floor. Tess was long-haired—very—and looked like a gray puffball with a tail. Unlike the others, she wasn't interested in the new sights or smells of the visiting room. She made a beeline for me and pawed at my leg, a soft, persistent claw-less padding, politely yet unmistakably telling me to pick her up. So I did and was immediately sold. Tess relaxed on my lap, purring loudly. I felt how tiny she was underneath her voluminous fur coat. Tess just wanted me, and I realized I wanted to be wanted.

I took her home that afternoon in a cardboard carrying case, ready to dive right into pet ownership. Tess had a mysterious past—she'd been brought anonymously to the shelter and was estimated to be about ten years old. She bit and hissed when a well-meaning human hand stroked her in just the wrong spot on her back, and she was the definition of scaredy-cat. The drive home in her box was torture, for both her and me. Her pitiful crying nearly broke my heart. I tried to comfort her with my voice, but it did nothing. When, finally, we arrived at my apartment and I let her out of the box, she wasted no time finding the darkest hiding place possible. For the first few days, I barely saw her—only her little green eyes glowing in the back corner of a closet or from way under my bed.

The night I brought Tess home, Shannon came over to meet her, though of course all he got was a view of her outline in the dark closet. I was hesitant to leave her alone, but Shannon said she'd probably be happier if we left so she could come out and explore. So we went out for dinner.

I'd gone through spells of dating before but always with my mind on an escape hatch—a date would be over in a couple of hours and I could go home. I assumed that no date I had would ever lead to anything more and that I'd find a way to prevent that if the poor guy sitting across from me at the restaurant table hoped otherwise. But dating was something people like me were supposed to do, so I dutifully let myself be set up by friends, agreed to give the cashier at the grocery store my number, and set up a profile on Match, which is what I'd done when I scrolled through thumbnail photos on the computer screen one night and came across Shannon.

It was all ridiculous, though. I really didn't want a boyfriend. I was perfectly happy. I was near thirty and at the peak of my career, I lived in a large beautiful apartment that made me feel like a real adult in a real house, but I was single and childless and had no responsibility for anyone or anything other than myself. I started to feel guilty. But also, pangs of doubt, and fear—could I really, for all my organization and supposed maturity, care for another being? A person OR a cat?

Without ballet competing for my attention, it turned out that I could.

Shannon swept me off my feet, which I had, by then, regained use of. I was very slowly starting back into taking class—carefully, and not in the presence of others. I was going to physical therapy by that point, too, and had a month or so left to work my way up to being able to start rehearsals. My schedule was pretty much my own and I still had a relaxed sense of summertime freedom. Shannon was funny and made me laugh without seeming to try, was droll and astute and ironic, observant and thoughtful. He was an artist, too, a cartoonist with a dry understated sense of humor that complemented mine exactly. He took the initiative, picked up on my inexperience, and was sweet and caring and sincere. I felt protected.

When Shannon and I first met, I was a dancer in name only. I was working on my dancer-self, which he found fascinating, and somewhat alluring, but the brass tacks of my real daily existence weren't in evidence. I tried to describe what it would be like when I started rehearsing again, but there was no way to express how self-involved I would become.

Shannon and I spent more and more time together, both at his house and mine, cooking, walking, drinking gin and tonics on the porch in the late afternoon heat. We didn't have to do anything in order for me to have fun with him—just the anticipation of being together on a random day lifted my heart and spirit. Everything was moving upward: my ankle was healing, my body felt stronger, dancing again felt reachable. Working alone at the barre, my thoughts kept turning to Shannon and what we'd done the night before, what we might do when I finished my class. And at home, Tess waited for me, curled up in a perfect C shape on the arm of the couch.

I adored Tess from day one—from the first minute I felt her gentle paws kneading me and pleading for my care—but a week or two later, when I came home one day and realized how eager I was to see her, pick her up, and, yes, talk to her, I had a flash of enlightenment: I was in love. With my cat.

Shannon and I dated for less than six months. Our relationship moved from summertime infatuation and excited newness to an autumn of negotiated schedules, divided attentions, and the dramatic, pressured, buildup of my return to performance. He seemed to relish his role as my supporter during that time, and I relished having one. I'd never before had someone to call when things went well or badly, or someone waiting for me at the stage door, or someone who I knew was thinking about me during the day—and who I could think about, too. Finally, I was one of the girls with a guy. But as fall turned to winter and holiday stress encroached, our communication broke down. His needs and mine clashed, and we couldn't understand each other. Going against my gut instinct, I agreed that he should come meet my family at Christmas. It was a week of mounting tensions. I felt trapped, caught in between who I was as my parents' daughter, my sister's sister, and Shannon's girlfriend. Forget about who I was as me or about that ballet dancer-person inside me. She was surrounded by people and yet desperately lonely.

An epic day with torrents of tears ended it all, and for two years afterward, I hated him, the man who had shown me how to love in a different way than I thought I was capable of. It was two more years before we had any contact.

Tess stayed with me, though. One morning, four years later, I noticed she hadn't eaten. Her bowl was barely touched for days. I left her at the vet on my way to the theater for class. We were about to open our spring series of performances. It was the day of dress rehearsal.

The voicemail from the vet said they needed to do tests and scans and have a specialist take a look the next day. I picked Tess up in between afternoon tech rehearsal and that evening's dress rehearsal. Dropped her off again the next morning, and got the bad news that afternoon: lung cancer. She'd been less energetic lately, but I'd thought it was a symptom of old age. The prognosis was bad. I was told to take her home, try to get her to eat or drink, and think about whether to have her euthanized at home or at the vet's office.

The next day, on my break in between afternoon rehearsal and the opening night performance, I ran to pick her up. It was pay day and I may as well have just signed my check over to the vet to pay the bill—the amounts were almost exactly the same—but I didn't care. Tess was my baby. Leaving her at home to go back to the theater was nearly impossible. There was nothing I wanted to do less at that moment than warm up, get into makeup and costume, and put on a performance. Performing seemed so trivial, so impersonal, so much like a job. I felt like a robot going through the motions and then like a pro for being able to pull it off with my focus so far away.

Tess hung on through the weekend. I tempted her with every treat I could think of—cream, tuna, chicken—but she wouldn't eat. Monday was my day off, at last.

I knew, at this point, that my retirement from ballet was looming. I was much, much closer to the end of this story than to the start and, anticipating the emotional turmoil the final chapter would bring, I'd sought out a counselor specializing in career transitions. That Monday, I had an appointment with her at which I tried to explain, awkwardly, what dance meant to me and what leaving it signified—but she, lacking any frame of reference, offered only platitudes, and I knew she didn't understand. I left feeling empty and alone.

Returning home with a bag full of Vietnamese takeout to comfort myself, I found Tess on the windowsill in the sun, a place she'd loved but had been too weak to reach by herself lately. My heart leapt—was she pulling out of this? Next time I checked, she had relocated again, this time to her other favorite spot on my brown velvet couch, which everyone calls magic, the most comfortable seat in the world. Cheered, I went to the kitchen to warm up my dinner.

My sister called—*how is she?* she asked. Eagerly, I went to see. But Tess was crying, trying to stand up but too weak. Her little tiny legs kept crumpling underneath her, despite her desperate instinct to get to the litter box. Her mews and cries turned to screams as she peed right there, the ultimate shameful disaster for a delicate cat like Tess. I, sobbing and frantic, phoned the animal hospital and explained as best I could through my terror and tears—*bring her over right away,* they said.

This time, the car trip was silent except for my own crying.

This animal hospital was staffed by saints, I am sure. The vet on duty did a quick assessment and heard my choked-up explanation of the previous few days. *What are your goals for Tess tonight?* she asked me, in the gentlest, gentlest voice. *We can give her something for her pain, or . . .*

There was a special room. Soft, warm lighting, a love seat and reclining easy chair, lamps and crocheted blankets. Little pictures and cards on the wall of animals and their owners, each with handwritten quotes of love.

The vet came in with Tess, wrapped in a blanket like a burrito, her tiny gray furry face peeking out. She had stopped crying. I held her in my arms, tight and close, sobbing while she purred, as steady and strong and constant a purr as she ever had, while the vet gave her the shot. I kept crying, and she kept purring, until finally, the vet slipped her stethoscope under the blanket. *She's quiet,* she said, again so very gently.

A door led directly to the parking lot so grieving people could avoid the harshly florescent-lit lobby, full of people and life. I walked out, holding my empty cat carrier, sobbing harder than I thought possible. I felt turned inside out, like my inner core had been sucked out of me.

The vacuum was back. Shannon was long gone, ballet was soon to be gone, and now Tess was gone, too. Perhaps part of me was wailing for what I knew was to come.

55

Precision, Perfection, and Mistakes

For me, the most gut-wrenching part of *Restless Creature,* the documentary film about ballerina Wendy Whelan, is the surgery scene. Whelan, the revered New York City Ballet principal dancer, the epitome of strength, of sinewy, chiseled musculature, of power and speed and expression, lies on an operating table. Eyes closed (sedated, but not under general anesthesia), she is draped and wrapped in massive layers of surgical tubes, wires, tenting. A friend gently turns her head to the side as one would a feeble invalid. The surgeon asks, "Wendy, are you comfortable?" but we don't hear a reply. He adds, "Everything is going great, Wendy," and, again, we don't know if he's speaking for her or for the camera—or for himself.

Whelan is having surgery to repair a severely torn labrum in her hip. The surgeon, renowned for his specially devised technique to repair this injury in elite athletes and dancers, narrates the procedure. We watch the scalpel break the skin of Whelan's leg. Blood trickling . . . a drill entering the side of her hip to make room for the arthroscopic camera, the robotic arms cutting away the raggedly torn labrum inside her joint, grabbing for remnants of tissue to nail to the bone, a graft being secured. We hear the metallic clash of a hammer banging against her femur, making microscopic fractures so blood will flow to the area and speed healing.

It goes on and on. Long after I expected (and wanted) the camera to pan away and bring me, mercifully, to a comfortable and calm recovery room where I could see an awakened Wendy Whelan, vibrant again, the surgery went on. It was a cold, hard, mechanical procedure, completely at odds with the qualities of the artist whose powers it was being used to restore.

Surgery seems, of course, so removed from, so different from, ballet—the settings and circumstances and motivations could not be more different. But the best surgeons have hands as sensitive and intuitive as a sculptor's. And the best ballet dancers plan their steps onstage as precisely as the choreography that unfolds in the operating room. They think of their extremities as instruments, but in both artistic and mechanical ways. Feet as sharply pointed as a scalpel can carve crystalline shapes that hang in the air as if etched on the viewer's own eyes.

The difference, maybe, is in the outcomes. Surgeries are successful or they aren't, but a balletic performance (whether in the studio or onstage, in solitude or in front of other people) can never be quantified. It can never be objectively defined. The best that we ballet dancers can want is a sense of personal satisfaction, an inner knowledge only between us and our bodies, that what we just did together was *it*. What "it" was, some in the audience might have seen or felt—or maybe not. It is an old maxim, uttered with a sigh, that when a performance feels great, the director or choreographer comes back with a slew of notes and a "meh" reaction. But when the dancer thinks they weren't at their best, felt distracted or not quite "on," the eyes from the front of the house or the studio perceive something special and rain down praise. The irony is that when it feels great, it doesn't necessarily read that way. And it can look great but not feel so: frustratingly, the way my dancing feels is not the same as how it looks.

So who's right? Who gets to determine a performance's worth? Everyone, and no one. Everyone is right because what you see, or hear, or feel on the stage is filtered through the layers of your experience and perspective before hitting the opinion-forming area of your brain. And no one is right for the same reason. So my sense, as a performer, of what I just danced is so very different from what you, the viewer, have seen. This is why the mirror is such a powerful tool and not one to be afraid of. It aids my scientific-method approach to technical improvement by proving whether I've made the right lines with my body. The mirror is not an enemy but a frankly truthful friend that might just be tactless at times.

Since there is no definition of a perfect piece of art, I try to replace that unattainable goal with precision, which *can* be controlled. Like the surgeon's hand, a slight wobble, on pointe or off, teases disaster. For me, perfect balance was my obsession. A breathlessly held piqué sous-sous without a waver, an arabesque that I could lengthen to infinity, and most of all, musical precision: wrapping myself inside the notes that in my mind's eye unfurled themselves to let me in. I never wanted to dance "to" the music, and not even "with" it, but as if we were the same thing. As a trio, my body, my brain, and the music could breathe together and dance together. To perfect my timing, I pretended that my body was creating the music, as if I was, physically, the piano itself.

While it prevented me from lagging behind or surging thoughtlessly ahead, that imagery wasn't restrictive. It didn't make for wooden, robotic dancing. Instead, it let us play together. Within each note, no matter how short, are gradations. You can be on the back edge or the front of a note, tease out the length of it, or even smudge it a little, so long as you make up for it milliseconds later. Discovering this taught me how to phrase my movements, creating wiggle room to make musical choices and deviating from surgical precision, but only enough to avoid falling off pointe.

As children, though, dance students are drilled to match their steps to cut-and-dried counts: tendu on 1, plié on 2, dégagé on 3, close fifth position on 4. To gain a sturdy, unsophisticated base of knowledge, there *is* a clear right and wrong. Letting go of that, eventually, can be scary and exciting at the same time: scary because of the risk of going overboard and being called out as "wrong," exciting because of the chance to discover life inside the music.

Experimentation takes vulnerability, though. Vulnerability and exposure to mistakes.

But what is a mistake, in ballet?

There are wrong steps, missed entrances, off-kilter pirouettes, or partnering maneuvers gone awry. Those types of things become less frequent, and more unexpected, with age, experience, practice, and the maturation of talent. And, as a dancer becomes more skilled at the art of the swift cover-up, they also become less visible. We dancers cheer each other up after a messed-up step in performance by saying, "The audience couldn't tell!" But that can feel like cold comfort. Sure, the audience didn't boo my double pirouette, but they also didn't know it was supposed to be a triple or that I barely saved myself from falling. It was the other dancers, the director, the choreographer, even the stage manager who'd watched countless rehearsals, who knew—and who knew it should have been, could have been, better.

For me, most of the time, those types of mistakes would not have been bothersome if I'd been the only judge. I didn't care if I did a double or a triple (though sailing around three or more times feels amazing). But the "industry" cared. And standards were rising.

In my last few years dancing, I had to scrounge up more and more courage every time I went onstage or even danced in front of my colleagues in the studio. They knew as well as I that my strength was not the flamboyant tricks but the quieter, subtler ones. The "trick" of timing, of underwriting steps with my own dialogue. The trick of stillness, keeping a pose alive while appearing to hover in place. And they supported me, as did the audiences, even as other dancers whipped off multiple turns.

Dancers' psyches are incredibly fragile, for our egos are tied to the physical strength we have—or do not have. Putting one's body up for scrutiny every day requires the toughest kind of inner strength. Performing—with honesty, truth, and selflessness—means relying on that core, that foundational support, to shed ego. It requires knowing that what you dance will be loved by some and not by others. That it's not about you. Remembering that the animal instinct to dance, the fire inside, never dies.

During my career, I had two ankle surgeries. The first time, I was not quite thirty and had no doubt, not even a sliver, that I'd come back, no problem. The second time was different. I was thirty-two and the accident necessitating the surgery was sudden and scary. My injury was highly unusual and the surgeon hadn't seen it before. I wasn't scared going into surgery, but after my six weeks in a cast were up, I felt different. The day the plaster cast was cut off and replaced with a removable walking boot, I stood at my bedroom window, looking out over the city lights of Portland. A dull sense of panic slowly rose from my gut. At that moment, it hit me that making my way back was now up to me and me alone.

The cast had been a protective layer, not quite an excuse, but close—an indisputable reason why I could legitimately stay on the sidelines, sit out this round of the game. And if I wasn't playing, there was no way to lose. I was still as good as my last performance.

I realized at that moment how much I had needed a break. But now, I was not sure I could come back from it. The unquestioning energy that I'd had a few years before seemed less reliable. I was terrified that I could not do it this time, that my inner strength wasn't there anymore or that it wasn't enough. I wondered if the break I'd needed was permanent.

For the first time in my dancing life, I really, truly, honestly felt what it meant to be vulnerable. Maintaining my physical strength had always been my outer shell, which I used to convince myself that I was valid. Maybe it was inevitable, but the first stones were laid in the path to my retirement that night.

In *Restless Creature,* Whelan describes a meeting with Peter Martins, then the director of NYCB, in which he tells her she is "in decline" and should stop performing certain roles that (as we presume he meant to say in not so many words) she was not able to dance well anymore. She says she was totally unprepared for his statement, although of course, as any dancer does, she was already thinking about the future and how much longer she could be a ballerina. She also says that immediately after that meeting, she began to feel pain. Injuries that had never bothered her before suddenly appeared. Foot pain, ankle, back, and then the excruciating hip pain. In essence, having her boss plant a seed of insecurity was the trigger for her actual physical decline. He told her it was so, and then it became so.

I did make it back to full dancing after my second ankle surgery. But less than six months after my comeback, I had my very own version of Whelan's meeting with Peter Martins.

Afterward, I told everyone that the decision to retire had been mine and mine alone, but that's not true. Like Whelan, I'd had thoughts of when I might stop dancing, but going into a meeting with Christopher Stowell, who'd been my artistic director for nearly seven years, in February 2009, I was not expecting him to say, "It's time to think about the future."

I'd been thinking about the future, of course, but with a bit of surreality. *Now is now,* I told myself, *it can never be a long time ago.* When my boss told me he thought the next season should be my last, I played it cool. "I know," I said.

Final Curtain

Sitting there in Christopher's small, windowless yet cozy office, his startling words hanging in the air between us, I let the sting pass by and instead focused on his compassion, his gentleness, his empathy. He understood what it felt like to see your ability slipping away. I was being let off carefully and with respect. But this was not a discussion. It was happening.

The conversation signaled my life was about to take a very sharp turn, but I really had no say in how it would look. Since the season was already set, I could not choose to perform a specific ballet, but there was a good choice on the spring program that seemed natural: I'd dance *Duo Concertant* by George Balanchine, one of the very first ballets I'd done at OBT. *Duo* is an intimate pas de deux performed to a Stravinsky score for violin and piano. The ballet opens with the dancers just listening to the music, standing by the piano, positioned downstage right along with the violinist and her music stand. The two dancers interact with the musicians throughout the ballet, often pausing their dancing to return to the piano's corner of the stage, where they pause to listen. The pas de deux feels like a meditation on the marriage of those who make music with instruments and those who do the visual equivalent with their bodies. *Duo* could be considered a quintet, actually, a conversation between the dancers, the musicians, and the music. Since my very first days at the New York School of Ballet with my old Greek teacher and that fiercely passionate accompanist, I'd learned to dance like a physical musician. To finish by dancing within arm's reach of the music makers was pure perfection to me.

I wasn't afraid to stop dancing; I was excited. My body hurt—a lot—and I didn't feel confident in my physical ability anymore. It was exciting to think about having the choice of whether to take class every day, and if I did decide to take it, which exercises to do and how hard to push myself. I could skip an uncomfortable pirouette combination and stretch on the floor instead, or only do the adagio one time through instead of twice. I imagined all the things I would do with my new life: Ride a scooter! Go to the coffee shop in the morning instead of the studio! Go hiking! Go out at night without worrying about getting enough sleep! Wear high heels!

Despite its very long runway, no one but my family, Christopher, and a few very close friends knew of my impending retirement until January 2010. I told my fellow dancers in a small company meeting one cold afternoon, after we'd discussed various issues and complaints pertaining to our jobs as dancers that would soon enough not matter to me at all: insufficient five-minute rehearsal breaks, our decreased number of work weeks, which of us should be elected to sit in on board meetings. My announcement, just before everyone rose to scurry out the door and home to hot baths and foot soaks, was met with a quiet, yet loving and touching, murmur, and as a group, everyone gathered around me for hugs and sweet, kind words.

Even then, nothing much changed. I still had a lot of work to do. Class was exactly the same every day; my body, my feet, my shoes all needed the usual attention; tendus and pliés and adagio and pirouettes still took the same effort. I rehearsed old choreography and learned some new pieces . . . rehearsal days ran on just as they had for my previous seventeen years. I tried to remind myself that the number of such days was running low, but I couldn't really make myself feel anything momentous—my routine was too ingrained. Suddenly, though, I was in the real homestretch: the last few weeks before my final performance. My cousin and her husband, generously offering to host the party that traditionally follows a farewell performance, reserved the courtyard at a restaurant near the theater for a catered affair for the entire company, staff, and friends. My parents and sister made flight reservations to come from New York, and relatives from Canada and Missouri, who'd never seen me dance before, announced they'd be coming as well. My uncle was flying in from Virginia. Friends from Seattle and California, who'd known me since I was a teenager, were going to make the trip to see me dance one last time. It was exciting. The hubbub made me feel important but also bemused. This was the kind of thing that happened to big-deal people, but I was just me, doing my usual thing. Just stretching my body, working my muscles, practicing my steps. Just inhabiting my world, but now everyone wanted to watch.

And then, in those last weeks of rehearsals, my pointe shoes started getting weird. The tips, the platform I relied on to be a perfectly flat surface for balancing and turning, felt rounded, as if I was dancing on tiny little domes. With each pair, the toe boxes were narrower, pinching my metatarsals so much I couldn't articulate my feet. I desperately pawed through the banker's box in the shoe storage room that held my entire stock, ripping each pair out of its plastic bag and praying that this strange malady wasn't an epidemic. The wardrobe master, who also had the job of ordering our shoes from London, tried in vain to find me an alternate supply—there wasn't enough time to reorder from the factory. She put out an all-points bulletin to ballet companies all over the country, pleading for them to send any extra shoes they might have in my size and approximate specs. Pointe shoes poured in from San Francisco, Seattle, Salt Lake City, New York. I spent the last month of my career dancing in other people's shoes, while I saved the very last of my own "good" shoes (the few that weren't malformed) for my final performance. It was as if my shoemaker was slipping away, had lost his edge, and was abandoning me. Knowing that if I was to continue performing, I would have to start the onerous trial-and-error process of finding a new maker all over again somehow made it easier to retire. Perhaps it was a sign. Without my shoemaker, I was helpless. Perfect time to surrender.

What I remember of my retirement day, May 2, 2010, was that I was very calm and had no nerves and none of what one might expect to feel: sadness, loss, finality. It felt like I was queen at the prom I never had. Just fun and exciting. There was none of the preperformance anxiety that had become increasingly heavy on me over the previous years. I knew that for once, I could do nothing wrong—the audience was completely on my side today and was there to give me a collective hug and cheer, even if I flubbed every step. I had forgotten what it felt like to be so light and self-assured.

Even class that morning was fun. The other dancers had surprises for me: they performed a spontaneous hip-hop dance number for me in between barre and center, and the pianist, my dear friend Irina, played all of my favorite pieces of music, including the largo from Handel's opera *Xerxes*. Doing the pirouette combination, I had a gleeful revelation: "I will never have to push, and relevé, and pirouette like this again!" When class ended, the entire company crowded around me for hugs. They knew how seriously I took class and how vigilant I was about my technique, and this final one was momentous. What I didn't know was how closely they had been watching me work over the years and that every choice I had made, every technical strategy I employed, from my pre-class stretches to the way I would continually return to the barre until I was totally satisfied with my balance, was noticed and, maybe, copied.

After the group hug, I had to hurry. In addition to dancing *Duo Concertant,* I was also in the first ballet of the afternoon (my farewell performance was a Sunday matinee) and needed to finish my makeup and hair, get into costume, stay warm, pre-set my quick costume change, and field the phone messages and texts that had come in from my family wondering about backstage access and seating arrangements. My dressing room table was already piled high with flowers, gifts, cards, and more than one bottle of alcohol. I pushed everything aside and glued on my fake eyelashes through the bouquets. I also knew that reading the cards would set off an emotional detour I wasn't ready to take.

Downstairs again, in the wings, ten minutes to curtain: I rewarmed myself, since forty-five minutes had passed since class ended and in my "old age" my muscles would tighten in mere minutes. My frequent and beloved partner, Artur, appeared out of nowhere to lift me through a few of our trickier steps. Then, suddenly, I saw my sister, a professional photographer, in the wings with her camera. How funny to see Flynn, who'd only rarely seen me dance, let alone visit me in a theater, so close by. It was immensely, immensely comforting. The Gavin my family knew had always been a separate being from the Gavin I was in my ballet world. I morphed from a sister and daughter into a ballerina figure every time I returned to the ballet company from a vacation break at home with my family. Flynn's appearance in the wings that day seemed, to me, to mean that those two personas were now blending into one.

I remember nothing at all about the actual dancing I did that day. The photographs Flynn and others took are my only proof that I danced at all. Only the curtain calls are clear in my memory. That often happened during my career—after a performance, I would be able to recall only specific moments that had, for some reason, jolted me from the single, breathless stream of consciousness that spanned from curtain up to curtain in. A mistake, a fall, a distraction of some sort was a jarring speed bump that rattled my concentration. Sometimes, lying in bed later that night, my mind would involuntarily start rehashing a show. Rewinding and playing it in stop-frame, looking for a handle on what had actually happened, since all I had were feelings. That's why photographs of performances are so fascinating to me and so treasured. They were like my brain's recordings of my dancing but in visual form: the camera caught snips of the flow, which is exactly what I felt.

On that day in May, *Duo* ended as usual, in darkness. I fled offstage in a whirlwind exit, slipping from Artur's grasp, leaving him alone, searching for me. As the intense spotlight that made us look like we were floating in outer space faded, I hovered at the edge of the wings for the curtain to lower and the stage lights to come up again. The moment they did, I scurried back onstage to join Artur. We stood in a row with Margaret, the violinist, and Carol, the pianist, who had done the ballet with me seven years earlier when I first joined OBT. We'd become friends since then. Sharing the stage with them and Artur, my first and most frequent partner, was the most I could have asked for. My partners in dance and in music, and me.

The curtain lifted, and we took a few steps forward. I could see that already the entire audience was on its feet, applauding. We bowed, and the curtain came in again—unusual, since normally once the curtain closed, bows were over and the crew started rushing to prep for the next ballet. This time, though, the stage manager, my dear friend Thyra, shouted, "Gavin alone! Curtain, go!" And to my surprise—and dismay—my friends ran into the wings. I looked around desperately as the curtain came up again, but this time, I was all by myself. I didn't feel ready—I wanted to hang on to Artur, to feel his hand around my waist, guiding and sheltering and supporting me, even though we'd stopped dancing.

I stood all alone, with only my pale blue leotard and skirt between me and my audience. I'd never felt that singular before. I was surrounded but by empty space: the orchestra pit between me and the audience, the bare stage floor between me and the wings, which were packed with my fellow dancers. Artur emerged from the downstage right wing with an enormous bouquet of roses. He knelt down to me, but I felt I should be bowing to him, so I lunged down and pulled him to his feet. A parade followed: Christopher, every single dancer in the company, my physical therapists, the designer who'd made countless costumes for me, people from my past I had no idea had been alerted to my retirement. My sister came last, her camera still around her neck, finally bringing me home. People who knew every facet of my being were there.

Rosebuds rained down from the balconies—so unexpected that at first, I didn't realize what they were. The company's passionately loyal association of volunteers had organized to pull thorns from the rose stems before throwing them to the stage, in one of the most beautiful, time-honored traditions of the theater. There were flowers everywhere, bouquets and single stems, piled and strewn across the stage. I was handed so many bouquets I had to put them down in front of me to accept the next offering. The other principal women in the company came out as a group and handed me a small satin pillow with a tiara placed on top—and gently, but firmly, slid its comb into my hair. Months before, after my final performance as Sugarplum Fairy in *The Nutcracker,* as I unpinned my sparkling headpiece for the last time, I'd jokingly told my dressing room mate, Kathi, that the saddest part of retiring was going to be not getting to wear a tiara anymore. We laughed, but she'd remembered and asked our costume shop make me one. It was more like a costume, actually, than any tiara I'd actually worn when I danced—unblemished, no missing jewels, no hair-spray residue, no stray wires or netting for hair pins. It now sits in a plastic shoe box in my closet.

The audience kept clapping, cheering, shouting—I bowed, again, and again, and again, to the audience, to my colleagues behind me, to the balcony, to everyone. I wanted to clap for them, to thank them for their love and for watching me and letting me have a reason to indulge my passion for so many years. For making me valid.

I thought it wasn't going to end, and repeatedly curtsying started to feel insufficient. But I knew that any second it would be over and that the next time the curtain came in, that would be it: the most final of curtain calls. So I stopped curtsying and just stood there, downstage center, as close to the lip of the stage as I could, and looked out. I let my eyes scan the entire house, resting on each row of seats, the tiers, the follow spot booth way up high, the sound booth way in the back. The guys in those booths had seen more of my dancing than anyone else on earth and possibly watched it more closely, too. They were my partners that never appeared but were always there.

When I was a student at the School of American Ballet, one of my teachers was, briefly, the legendary ballerina Alexandra Danilova, who had grown up with Balanchine at the Imperial School of Ballet in Russia, been one of his first loves, and eventually followed him to America. Danilova was a link to history, and I had been among the last incredibly lucky students to learn classical variations from her. She was quite elderly by the time I entered the School, barely able to stand, but somehow, through her virtually indecipherable Russian accent, we managed to learn the variations she taught us, Princess Florine and Lilac Fairy from *Sleeping Beauty*. Just being in her presence awoke something in me that was even more important than the technique of those variations, though: an awe of and curiosity for history and a proud sense of being, even though still a student, a small mark in the lineage of ballet. I felt the honor of dancers being servants to something much greater and grander than ourselves. I read Danilova's autobiography, *Choura*, around that time, and what she said about her own farewell performance never left me. "In Russia, we were taught never to touch our knees to the floor when taking a bow unless there was royalty in the house, we were to go on our knees only to royalty or to God. I notice that today ballerinas go on their knees all the time. But to my way of thinking . . . it is too much, it's like talking all the time in superlatives. At the end of my last performance, taking my final curtain calls, as a gesture of thanks for the support and devotion I had received over the course of my career, I went down on my knee to my audience."

I heard Thyra call "Curtain in—SLOWLY!" Commanding a slow descent was a touch so thoughtful and loving that finally, tears came and ran down my face. And as the curtain began its slow, final fall, I went down on my knee.

57

The Drive Home

The drive home every night is short, for which I am grateful. I'm tired, tired, tired, and hungry. It's late, and my body, wrung out like a washcloth from exertion, needs good sleep to recover for tomorrow. I have to put ice on my hip, soak my feet in a bucket of cold water, massage the knots out of my legs, and stretch my back so it won't spasm in the middle of the night.

But at the same time, I wish the drive were longer, just a little bit. Arriving home means food, blessed rest, and my forgiving, fuzzy sweatpants, but it also means a return to real life. The time that I spend en route between the theater and home is all my own, a time when I am relieved of the pressure and anxiety of tonight's performance but don't yet have to think about tomorrow's. I can sit with the satisfaction of having worked and danced hard (no matter how well or not-so-well the performance went) and just feel the effects in my muscles before I have to inevitably let it fade away. Dance is impermanent, which I find to be a tragic blessing.

I've often thought about what happens in the audience after a show is over. The performance must evaporate so quickly for them. They have no buffer between the magic world of theater they've been in for the past two hours and their own return to normalcy. The lights come up, they creakily stand, shuffle about finding scarves and programs and inch their way out of the theater in a herd to find the car, get out of the garage, maybe go out for a drink. Maybe a few passing comments are made about the piece they just watched, but what they have witnessed represents only a tiny fraction of my life's work and is designed to appear effortless.

On MY side of the curtain, things also change quickly, but since we're all performers (all of us back there, even the techies, are "show trash"), the perfume of the performance lingers. The lights come up suddenly backstage, but it's almost a relief, a reassurance—it's okay to have just bared your soul in front of all those people, don't worry, we were just pretending, it's live theater! We're all friends here, in an old-fashioned, blue-collar, union factory kind of way. Comrades. We congratulate each other on hard work well done, commiserate about the trouble spots, re-hash everything, laugh about it now that the pressure is off. The stage crew is already mopping the stage floor for tomorrow, literally sweeping us offstage. It feels good to say, "Thanks, Phil—have a good night, see you tomorrow" to the gruff prop master on my way past his station backstage left. Up in my dressing room, I slowly sink onto the metal folding chair in front of the makeup table. Got to get my costume off right away, though, so the wardrobe people can go home. I either peel myself out of a unitard or peek out into the hall for a dresser to unhook my tutu, and then, at last, I can take my pointe shoes off. Toe tape removal is frustratingly difficult and I roughly pull and tear at it. Finally my toes are free. I inspect them for new damage and wait for their normal shape to return. I carefully tug off my fake eyelashes, swipe makeup remover over my face, get wrapped up in my big towel, and head to the shower . . . but my fantasy of washing off the day in a cloud of steam evaporates when I discover that the hot water is out again in this old, persnickety theater. It doesn't really matter. I like cold water on my feet, which are now starting to burn, and it's prob-ably good for the rest of my body, too.

It's often been said that performing is like a drug, and I believe it. It's addictive, and certain personality types are more susceptible to its lure than others. It also leaves the "user" in a highly charged and somewhat vulnerable state of mind. It's best if the descent from that high place is gradual, so that the distance of the drop doesn't feel quite so drastic. An arc of emotions follows the physical transportation from stage to dress-ing room, to opening the backstage door, stepping outside, and breathing fresh air. I think that's why I cherish my drive home so much. It allows me to soften my landing, like putting out a parachute so I can ride down slowly, gradually, looking upward at the sky as my feet come closer to the ground.

Sometimes, on my drive, the descent feels glorious and jubilant, perhaps after a wildly successful premiere or a repeat performance of a familiar ballet when I finally nailed the parts that had always been troublesome. On those drives, I might blast some crazy ABBA song and open all the windows to feel like I'm on top of the world. Other times, it's a little bleak, if I'm disappointed with how I just danced and wish I could erase it and try again. And often, it's just neutral—just another show, neither particularly good nor bad, just another day on the job. There's some satisfaction at having put in a bunch of hours, but the "drug" doesn't mask much then. I just turn on NPR and listen to whatever weird late-night show is on. Strangely, an image comes into my mind of a lone security guard on the overnight shift somewhere, who perhaps is also hearing the same thing.

As I get close to home, First Avenue splits. The jog to the right would take me uphill, away from the neighborhood and around the city. Going to the left, the road curves down under Naito Parkway and snakes around to my front door. If I get caught at the red light just before this choice, I sit there thinking about the constant plainness of the activity that has gone on at this intersection while I was at the theater. Idling there, waiting for the light to change, I feel myself fitting back into the fabric of the city. The light changes, I go through it, take the road to the left, fold up my parachute, and go home.

Afterword

The Time I Taught Someone Something

I have just spent an hour and a half leading thirteen women and two men in a classical ballet class, working them through a series of dance exercises that have been practiced all over the world for centuries. As "elitist" as the art of ballet may be considered, this particular class (which I teach bright and early every Monday) is what's called a "drop-in," meaning that anyone on earth who has the urge to dance and fifteen dollars can walk in off the street and take a place at the barre. It's billed as "Ballet 1," but all that means is that you're on your own if you don't know the five basic positions and some other fundamentals but also that I won't be asking anyone to do triple fouettés.

Naturally, then, there's a wide range of ages, abilities, body types, and personal motivations for "dropping in" on a Monday morning. Some of those who come to class have dance experience from childhood and some only started dancing as adults, but for everyone, wading into ballet technique in middle age takes guts, healthy senses of humor and realism, and a willingness to set pride aside. Physical limitations like stiffness and cartilage-deficient joints are prevalent, but the natural coordination and instincts of childhood—the compulsion to spin around, jump, and be fearless—have also gone away. Coaxing adult students past inhibitions built up over the years is fun for me because of their attitude: no one comes to these classes unless they want to work, think, be brave, and get ready to fly.

Douglas, in his fifties, is tall, lean, and proud. He trained in jazz and theater dance as a kid and even danced in production shows for several years. He's in every class, standing front and center and attacking every exercise with confidence. He prides himself on being a sort of ringleader of the adult dancer community, welcoming all newcomers warmly and generally playing the role of alpha male in the room.

One of my favorites is Josh, a forty-ish, small, wiry, and muscle-bound guy with an impish grin. He thinks about ballet just as hard as he works at it (although his body is so tight it resists balletic shapes). He likes to analyze why steps are done a certain way. His questions force me to find ways to explain concepts verbally that I have always understood intuitively. Why do you press down into the floor in order to pull up out of it? If you truly stretch your arm or leg, as I'm always cuing the students to do, how do you keep it from looking stiff? I love teaching him because he's so chipper, laughing off his own wobbles and tumbles, but he doesn't trivialize the magnitude of ballet training. He understands it as an art form to be appreciated and respected, and he has a kind of fascinated awe for people who've devoted their lives to it. After all, this may be the equivalent of a recreational cooking class for non-chefs, but he and the other students are still working with sharp knives and real ingredients that shouldn't be wasted.

Today, Genevieve was in class as usual. She's a warm, lovely woman and, like Josh, tightly muscled. She quivers with effort to mold herself into the positions of ballet, straining and taking short puffs of breath although we're only five minutes into barre and just doing simple tendus. I always pass by Genevieve and give her arm a gentle shake to help her try to relax her elbows while still holding on tight to her center. She resists me, as if she's gripping a handrail for dear life. I am on an endless quest to get students to avoid over-tensing their muscles, except for that ever-necessary "tush squeeze," of course. She understands what I'm asking for, but letting go is scary. I remind her that we're just doing ballet, not brain surgery, and laughter throughout the studio brings an immediate release.

Most weeks in class, several small goals are achieved only to be washed away moments later like waves lapping up on the beach, receding, and then reaching a few inches farther to achieve more with each new surge of water. This process happens quietly inside each individual. Everyone's pace is different, as is their starting point. It feels like a beautiful miracle to see fifteen people's faces light up with understanding and then, best of all, to watch them translate that realization to their bodies. Today, as usual, we were doing a pirouette exercise. "Reach your right arm, leading with the pinky finger, resist slightly in your shoulder as if you're pushing through water, and keep your elbows lifted like you don't want to touch the tabletop in front of you," I coached them. "Make your arms perfectly round, time your relevé as methodically as a metronome." The room got hushed—that's when I know I've said something that might be sinking in—"Let's all try it together." We practice each element separately: just the arms, then just the feet, then coordinating the arms and legs but without a turn, and then we put it all together. I had been doing the step with the class, standing in front of the group with my back to them, but now I stopped and turned around to watch. I saw a mismatched assortment of people of all shapes and sizes and in outfits of every type, all reaching with their pinky fingers to the right and sailing around with the smoothness of soft butter.

Acknowledgments

This book was born about ten years ago, shortly after I retired from Oregon Ballet Theatre. One evening, leaving the studio after teaching class, I caught a glimpse of the company dancers rehearsing *The Rite of Spring*. I stopped to watch, mesmerized and awash in a flood of physical and emotional memories. I went home, sat down at my computer, and wrote the essay that became The Human Monolith (originally titled "Oozing" after the way Christopher urged us to move).

The catharsis of writing that essay sparked me to sign up for Merridawn Duckler's memoir workshop at The Attic Institute in Portland. I showed up for the first session nervous and completely unsure of what to expect. It turned out to be one of the most exciting, inspiring, and encouraging experiences I've ever had, on par with my earliest years of discovery at the New York School of Ballet. Each week, Merridawn gave us a title under which we were to write a two-page mini-memoir. From these assignments came five pieces that are included in this book: "The Drive Home," "The Time I Taught Someone Something," "Meeting My Maker," "Scarred," and "Into the Night."

I'm incredibly grateful to Merridawn for her inspired title prompts, which sparked my own creativity enough to continue writing the episodes of my dancing life, and to the other members of the workshop for their rapt interest in the glimpses of the world of ballet into which I pulled them each week. Their enthusiasm was my first indication that "real people"—aka nondancers—found ballet as interesting as I did. I also would like to pay tribute to David Biespiel, founder of The Attic, for his support, friendship, and collaboration.

As my collection of essays grew, so did the concept of this book. Several people showed interest in my writing and encouraged me to keep going, including Martha Ullman West, who connected me to Mindy Aloff, who connected me to Meredith Babb and UPF. I have enormous respect and admiration for Martha's lifelong commitment to dance criticism and appreciation, and I thank her deeply for her mentorship, advice, guidance, and friendship, which have buoyed me up so many times. Mindy's reading of an early version of this book and her subsequent feedback and direction brought it to where it is today. I can't thank her enough for her belief in this book and for showing me how much further I could take it. To Meredith and everyone at UPF, I'm sincerely grateful for your acceptance of this book and your bringing it to fruition.

Many people have contributed in a million ways to the development of *Being a Ballerina*. Dean Richardson's unconditional support, friendship, generosity, and love, not to mention his reliably sympathetic ear, have been my foundation for years, and I can only hope to be half as good a friend in return. The Helene Wurlitzer Foundation, where I spent three months working on this book in 2015, is an incredible organization whose gift of time, space, and the serenity of a casita in Taos, New Mexico, was priceless. Thank you also to the other artists in residence during my time in Taos, especially Alan Wilkinson, for listening to me read early versions of parts of this book and offering invaluable perspective and feedback. Thank you to Alan Salant for asking such thoughtful questions, which helped me clarify for myself this book's purpose and direction. Alan's enthusiasm, support, and belief in this book kept me going when I felt lost. And my deep appreciation and admiration go to Wayne Rivard for so generously using his talents to improve and immortalize my own and to both him and his wife, Kim, for their incredibly heartwarming enthusiasm, encouragement, and support.

Dancers owe lifelong debts of gratitude to all of their teachers, as I do. Two of mine were particularly influential. Richard Rapp and Susan Pilarre (aka "The Pastel Teacher"), after initially reading the chapters of this book in which they appear, asked to read the entire manuscript. Their wonderfully positive reactions excited me more than any rave review of my dancing ever could. Reconnecting with Mr. Rapp to show him what I'd written, decades after he'd been my teacher, felt like bringing my dancing life full circle. I am truly saddened that he is not here to see the completed book, but knowing that he read "The Fifteen-Year-Old and

Mr. Rapp" gives me comfort. My admiration and respect for Suzy, who spurred me to realize my potential as a dancer when I was her student, are endless. I can't thank her enough for reading this book and being my champion as much now as when I was a teenager in the throes of self-discovery. Suzy, I will always try to emulate your principles, passion, and energy.

This book, of course, would have very little content if it were not for my many, many dancing colleagues, friends, conspirators, partners, and comrades over the years. Dancers share a bond that resists erosion despite the passage of time or geographical separation. The memories of our shared experiences, laughs, tears, adventures, trials, and tribulations are part of my core, an indelible part of who I am. Thank you to everyone with whom I ever shared the stage and studio.

The ultimate thanks—although "thanks" is a woefully insufficient word—goes to my family. My sister, Flynn, and parents, Anne and Eric, mean more to me than anything in this world or beyond. Without them and their unconditional love and belief in me, this book would never have been written. My mother was convinced this book would come to life long before I was and never stopped telling me so. Her assertion that I could possibly leave a greater mark on the world through writing than through dancing is something I will always hold close. That she is not here to see the book she encouraged me to write and to share in celebrating its completion is deeply painful, but I trust she is reading it wherever she is.

My father has read more versions of this book, more times, than anyone else, including me. There simply are no words to thank him for the hundreds of hours he spent, unquestioningly, without hesitation, and at the expense of his own writing work, to help me get this book to where it is today. He has been my sounding board, idea-generator, advisor, consultant, coach, cheerleader, counselor, teacher, and editor, all while remaining my beloved Daddy. This book is as much his as it is mine.

Appendix 1

Meeting My Maker

I stood staring at the display I had laid out on the couch, trying to make sense of my inventory. Twenty-three pairs of pointe shoes, grouped into categories and subcategories: my own shoes, those that had been made for other dancers, the ones that were good enough for a rehearsal but not a performance, these ones a little too wide, those ones cut too low on the sides but with a good flat platform, a few with really hard blocks but maybe if I doused them with alcohol and hammered them they could work. They looked so uniform and pristine, shiny and lovely, one of each pink satin pair nested inside its mate, but in fact they were the bottom of the proverbial barrel. The little pile in the corner was my best hope— they were the only remaining shoes from my own stock, produced by my beloved shoemaker, "Mr. O." But Mr. O's shoes had unexpectedly started coming in with irregularities that made them unusable (Was he sick? Drinking on the job? Or just getting old?), and these were the last few that had been made correctly. I had only four pairs left.

This scene took place about two weeks before my final performance as a professional ballet dancer. This was quite a big deal. The audience would know it was my farewell and would be warm and supportive no matter what, but even so, I wanted to prove (to myself as much as anyone else) that I was going out at the peak of my powers. I needed to be thinking about things other than whether my shoes would hold me up or throw me off. This was not a time to grab any old pair of pointe shoes, put them on my feet, and go out there and dance.

A dancer and her pointe shoes—this is a supreme example of a love-hate relationship, fraught with uncertainty and ambivalence. She can't be a ballerina without them, and they seem to know it and use that power at whim, throwing her off balance with slanted pointes or edges misshapen by a margin barely visible to the naked eye. But then, teasingly, her next pair is golden. They hug her foot just right, the tip is ruler-straight, the strength of the shank is Goldilocks-perfect. Putting them on is transformative. She can suddenly defy the laws of physics, turn like a top, and balance in any position for days. They make the arch of her foot look stunningly gorgeous and don't break down after one rehearsal. And they are so comfortable she doesn't even notice she has them on.

For ballet dancers, pointe shoes represent an omnipresent dialogue that evolves but never ends. The old maxim about good art springing from hardship means that the dancer's daily efforts to live inside and manipulate this tool to her advantage produces an uncanny physical intuition, sensitivity, and control. As well as corns and funky toenails.

Professional dancers have their shoes custom-made, meaning that they are ordered from a pointe shoe manufacturer with individual specifications and measurements down to an eighth of an inch, not unlike the optional features on a car, but these aren't luxury additions. Each shoemaker at the factory has a different style, making their shoes with a signature shape, weight, strength, almost a personality. We dancers come to know and associate each maker's identifying symbol (often a letter or shape, like my Mr. O or Mr. Triangle, or an icon, like Key, Maltese Cross, or Crown), with their shoes' traits: tapered tips, high vamps, soft boxes, V- or U-cut throats, and so many more. Although one can request such exact measurements (you can even ask for a different set of measurements for each shoe within a pair—lots of people have asymmetrical feet), they aren't molded to an individual's foot like an ice skating boot. It takes years for a dancer to figure out what specifications she needs. Over the years, I'd tried dozens of variations, and every time I thought I had finally found the magic formula—and a maker who seemed to understand my body and my dancing as if we'd met, although of course we never did—"my" shoemaker retired, died, or (I speculate) had a stroke and started producing shoes with tips as round as bowling balls.

But you learn to work with what you've got, because once a batch of shoes arrives from the overseas factory, sending them back for irregularities is usually impractical (and besides, the manufacturer of my shoes would not even accept returns unless the measurements were a quarter-inch off or more, which in a pointe shoe feels like three sizes). A few years back, I was thrilled to discover that after struggling with my pirouettes for hours (and starting to feel suicidal, convinced that I'd lost every shred of technique I'd ever had), the problem was not my lack of talent but my shoes: the platform—the two-inch-wide area on the tip of the shoe, literally the "point" of the pointe shoe—was slanted. Aha. No wonder . . . I put on a different pair and miraculously could turn with ease again. I might have thrown the slanted ones across the room that day. I definitely cursed them and kissed the others.

I've named my pointe shoes with affection, stuffed worn out ones into the garbage with relish, packed them carefully in my carry-on luggage (too valuable to risk having them lost by the airline), signed my name on old pairs for little girls to hang on their bedroom walls. For all the anguish (and yes, pain) I've suffered from pointe shoes over my decades of dancing, though, I never wished I had chosen another form of dance that didn't require them. Dancing on pointe is the most sublime feeling I can imagine. It allowed me to literally extend every fiber of my body from tip to toe, to the furthest extent physically possible. Pointe shoes gave me power, finesse, and the ability to do things in dance that are impossible in soft shoes. They made me feel beautiful, feminine, and so strong. They trained my feet to be as articulate as my hands. It was fitting that my last weeks of dancing were colored by anxiety about my shoes. It kept me questioning, analyzing, and discovering what I needed and what I was capable of as a dancer.

I did end up finding a good pair for my farewell performance. Now I can't even remember how they felt, which must mean that they were perfect.

Appendix 2

How to . . .

Sew a Pointe Shoe

Swiftly. This should take no more than eight minutes, tops.

Pick a new pair from your storage basket (or bin, or shelf) and take it out of the clear plastic zip-top bag it's lived in during its overseas trip from London. Save the bag for snippets of thread and ribbon, the nails you'll pull out of the shank, and any clumps of dried glue that'll scatter when you do. This makes for easy cleanup and you don't have to be near a garbage can while you work.

(Before you get started with the sewing, though, make an assessment: Is this pair a decent representation of your shoemaker's work? Is the tip truly flat, the box shaped correctly, no noticeable abnormalities? Essentially, is it good enough to wear? If not, put it in the reject pile or save it in case of an emergency shoe shortage, to use when you have no other options.)

Put both shoes on the floor. Stand up, place your heel on each toe box, and heave all your weight onto it. Bounce up and down a couple of times to really squish it from round to flat. (Whose feet are round, anyway?)

Fold back the heel of one shoe so it looks like a flip-flop and you can get your fingers around the cloth insole liner that says "Freed of London" (or whatever the name of your brand of pointe shoes is). Pull it up to reveal the nail that's pinning down the cardboard shank. Start bending the shank, gently at first, working it back and forth, to loosen that nail. Once it's a little loose from your manipulation (this is when all those glue bits will spray around), wedge some needle-nose pliers or a strong pair of scissors under the shank to get the nail completely out, being careful to let the shank separate only halfway down. You want to be able to fold the shoe right in half—not too far down, or else the whole thing will collapse when you stand on pointe. And make sure you don't lose track of that nail; capture it as soon as it's free so it doesn't float around inside the shoe somewhere or on the floor of a ballet studio, where, when they're not in pointe shoes, everyone's walking around barefoot.

Now, tape the cloth insole back to the shank with masking tape so that the cardboard underneath gets a little protection from the dampness of your sweaty foot. Moisture is like an acid—it will drastically reduce a pointe shoe's life span. Avoid any preventable exposure.

Get out your dental floss. You'll have already threaded a needle with floss and stored it, ready to go, underneath the box's snap-top closure. Dental tape is too hard to thread through the eye of a needle, so use plain, old-fashioned, unwaxed floss. It's much stronger than thread, and it comes with such a handy storage container.

You've already got a set of ribbons and elastics measured, too, because you snipped them off an old pair of shoes. (New shoes, old ribbons— that's the rule.) The ribbon ends are singed (no fraying at the ends, please), and since you've used them before, you know the length is right and there won't be too much or too little to tie into that tight knot, fitted snugly into the notch between your ankle bone and Achilles tendon. If they look dirty in comparison to the pristine satin of the new shoes, well, you should have thrown them in the washing machine last weekend.

Eyeball where to position one ribbon and elastic (about half an inch behind the seam between the forefoot and heel). Angle them slightly so they don't impinge on your ankle tendons, stick the needle in, and start sewing. It takes only about ten good stitches and a triple knot (on the outside of the shoe where you won't feel it), and with a snip of scissors you're one-quarter finished. (All of this so far should have taken you about four minutes.)

Repeat the ribbon/elastic positioning and sewing on the other side of the first shoe, and then the whole procedure, from the beginning, on the second shoe. There's no "right" or "left" shoe until you've worn them. But it's handy to decide now, which you'll do by putting a slightly longer ribbon on the inside of each shoe so that when they're wrapped around your ankle the ends will be the same length.

Now you're very close to done! All that's left is gluing the tips to harden them. Fold the heel fabric back again and get your bottle of toxic, impenetrable, un-meltable Jet Glue (similar to Super Glue, used for crafts and model construction). Find a surface you don't care about (I have spilled or dripped glue onto many rental apartment countertops, leaving a landscape of crusty clumps and ridges), preferably near an open window for ventilation, and pour a small puddle of glue into the tip of each shoe. Watch your fingers and clothes, as this stuff will ruin both on contact (I still have a cardigan with a rigid splotch of dried glue on the front, but I did discover that I could get it off my fingers with an emery board). Swirl it around a bit so it coats much of the inside of the box, and then prop the shoes up to dry, carefully balancing them on their tips. If you've been industrious, you'll have a row of a dozen or more shiny new pointe shoes all along a windowsill, posing like a line of Rockettes.

Give them a few hours to rest, then do a quick check to make sure you weren't rushing so much (or were so distracted by the Seinfeld rerun you watched during the sewing session) that a ribbon is positioned weirdly or you broke a shank wrong. It's a drag to discover these things only when you're in class and need to break them in for that day's rehearsal. Nest them into pairs, one inside the other, as they were when you pulled them out of that fresh plastic bag. You might take a moment to appreciate their craftsmanship and sheer beauty: the perfectly pink satin, molded (lovingly, maybe?) over a wooden last in an old-fashioned London factory, every nail pounded by your shoemaker's hand. You might wonder at the construction that allows you to dance on pointe supported by nothing more than canvas, cardboard, leather and glue—and your muscles, of course. Even the shoes' smell, not unlike a brand-new book opened for the first time, still evokes a sense of excitement and adventure and possibility. Pointe shoes, prepared and ready to be used but as yet unworn, seem to represent the incredibility of ballet dancing itself.

Now that your shoemaker and your own hands have finished their parts in this creation, take a moment to reflect on the magic your feet and these shoes may, possibly, make. The unblemished satin tips and smooth, clean sole will soon be smudged and worn with the beautiful evidence of tendus, pirouettes, *Swan Lake,* and the thousands of steps in between.

Make it a short moment, though, because these aren't your first pair, they won't be your last, and you've got to get to work.

Do a Partnered Pirouette (Or: Spinning in Someone Else's Hands)

Before you do anything, you have to prepare. And before you prepare, you have to prepare to prepare.

There are many reasons for this, but a big one is that your partner must always know what you're about to do, or at least what you are trying to do. That is the only way he can help you.

Every ballet step has a preparation: to jump, you have to plié. To plié, you have to pull in your gut, lift up in your middle, and turn out your legs. To do those things, you have to have warmed up your body and stretched your muscles. The mother of all preparations—the very first one—begins, truthfully, even before you get out of bed in the morning.

Let's assume, though, that you've gotten through all the preparatory preparations and are ready to prepare to pirouette. Let's also assume that you are a woman, and your partner is a man, and the two of you have agreed on what sort of partnered pirouettes you'd like to try together: how about we take a pirouette en dehors, from fourth position, on pointe, arms in first position, multiple revolutions to the right, finishing in *passé en face?* (As complex as that may sound, it is the most basic version you could choose.)

Pirouetting with a partner is completely different from turning by yourself. As the woman (who is the one half of this partnership that will actually rotate), you will have to override a multitude of ingrained practices you normally employ when pirouetting solo. Your ongoing efforts to turn with fabulous control and ease, revolving multiple times around and finishing on a dime will, strangely and counterintuitively, have to be dialed back. With a partner, you'll have to do *less* so that together you can do *more.* Back off from the controls so he can help you fly the plane.

Your preparation stance is fourth position but not like your solo version. This fourth position, somewhat akin to a fencer's lunge but with your toes pointing side to side and shoulders and hips squared off to the front, will be smaller, even tiny, in comparison. He—your partner—is standing within arm's reach behind you, and in just a second will step in even closer, so shorten your stance and give him some room.

Next, talk to each other, but not with words (too late for that—any discussion should have happened before you had your back to him). This is your last chance to communicate with him until the pirouette is over, and—but don't panic, now—the entire thing can be ruined if you misunderstand each other at this moment, or, even worse, if one of you ignores the other.

Your dialogue: how many revolutions you're trying for, how fast you'll rotate, and, most importantly, *exactly* when you're going to start. Give him a clear signal, using your body and your breath. Overexaggerate your plié, deepen it and draw it out with deliberation so he can see it and feel your muscles engaging beneath his hands. He'll have his right hand barely touching the side of your waist as you're in fourth. That, for now, is your only point of physical contact—you're waiting for him, he's waiting for you, and a dozen tiny signals are shuttling back and forth between your body and his eyes—which should be glued to the small of your back—and hand. You have a wireless electric current.

With your deepened plié, pull a little more torque into your spine, inhale, push down in your legs, and reach forward with your arm . . . and spring, strongly and quickly, onto pointe, pushing your back foot into the floor as if you're shoving off from the swimming pool wall. Pull that leg swiftly and cleanly into passé (toes placed firmly into your left knee, right knee pointing to the side, making a letter P shape), at the exact moment you pull in your arms, tightly, overlapping your hands and wrists, hugging a beach ball into your chest. Essentially, you're creating a cylinder with your body, a tall, spiraling tower lifting up and up and up, winding tighter and tighter with each revolution.

Elbows in! (Don't jab him—he's stepped in closer now and you don't want to scare him away.) From here on, the best thing you can do is make yourself into one solid, steely block of muscle, centered right in your core. The only part of you that's loose is your neck, as you pinpoint your focus straight ahead, spotting your eyes and whipping your face back around to the front again and again as you spin. The effect is of a loose cap spiraling on top of a bottle. Brace your stomach muscles, even clench them, but relax your neck.

His job, now, is to keep you upright. To keep you balanced squarely on top of your left leg, centered all the way down through your thigh, knee, and ankle, foot, and middle toe. You'll rotate faster and faster, spiraling downward as well as up, so strong are the oppositional forces in your body that you practically make a hole in the floor with the two-inch drill bit that is your shoe's tip.

He's cupping the sides of your waist but not holding too tightly. You're a whirling top, a spindle, the needle on a record. Consider the kind of contact needed to keep the yarn spinning and the music playing. A heavy-handed grip could bring it all to a dead stop in a tangled, scratchy heap. His touch, and judgment, and adjustments to your balance are so subtle you barely notice.

All you know is that the bright red EXIT sign at the back of the theater keeps coming round and round—or your reflection in the studio mirror, which grows blurry as you strain to keep it in view, whipping around with such furious, fabulous speed. Holding your position so firmly and tightly is as wearing as jumping across the room, but keep your resolve—push your right knee, the one in passé, farther and farther to the side, turning it out more and more, never letting it drop.

He may be a "paddler"—one who slaps your right hip bone every time it comes around, generating force for more and more and more revolutions, which sacrifices the illusion of ease and makes you feel like a roulette wheel in a casino. But keep your cool and plan to negotiate later for a classier approach.

His stance is so very close to you, but, wisely, he's also keeping his distance. His feet are fairly far away, and he's bending forward at the waist to reach you with extended arms. This way, his hips are far enough back that your knee should clear his body as it comes around. Rookie mistake is standing up straight and getting whacked. But if your knee DOES hit him as it passes around, the person behind is always at fault. Just like the rules of the road when driving a car.

His eyes have stayed on your lower back, which is your center of gravity, and your hip bones, which are his handlebars. He's sensed and adjusted your balance microns to the right, left, forward, or back over the several seconds that elapsed from the moment you and he mutually agreed to start this tornado whirling. If things go south and the pirouette starts to spiral out of control, he'll go into emergency rescue mode, reach out and grab you back to safety. You may end up in an unintended, tangled embrace, but with luck neither of you will be on the floor. Whatever you do, don't give up too soon, and calmly remember what to do in case of emergency: hold your center even tighter, so you are as easy as possible to manipulate. Let the rescue personnel do his job, and perhaps this train wreck can be saved!

Usually, it can. Somehow, with pure willpower and determination from both of you, total disaster can be averted and some semblance of a pirouette preserved.

No matter what, finish it off. Deciding when the pirouette's natural life span has been reached is another wordless dialogue, and a brief one, as you open your arms gradually to the sides to brake the momentum and he brings you to a smooth, clean stop, facing front, still perfectly, comfortably balanced on the center of your left leg.

But the pirouette hasn't ended, quite. He, ever the gentleman, wants to be of assistance in anything you may want to do, and getting off pointe is now on your mind. So: he will shift your weight slightly back, leaning your body toward his (you're still holding your stomach as strong as a board, but with graceful pliability in your upper back) so you can roll seamlessly down from the top of your pointe shoe. He'll keep firmly lifting your waist, easing your transition, and won't abruptly let go before he's certain you've found your own footing again. He'll offer his hand to you—not because you need it but because he's gracious—and together, you'll move on to whatever comes next.

Appendix 3

Places I've Performed

(Not necessarily in chronological order)

Macy's "Young Misses" department, Herald Square, New York City, circa 1985. As a ten-year-old student at the New York School of Ballet, I did a lecture-demonstration with my classmates of barre work, among the displays of girls' clothes. Why and how this event came to be, I don't know.

Symphony Space theater, Broadway and Ninety-Fifth Street, New York City, mid-'80s. My grade school, Columbia Grammar and Prep, mounted its annual musical revue. I sang and danced in sneakers and a neon sweatshirt.

New York State Theater, Lincoln Center, New York. As a School of American Ballet (SAB) student, performing in *The Nutcracker, A Midsummer Night's Dream, Coppelia,* and *Circus Polka.*

Stamford Center for the Performing Arts, Stamford, Connecticut. As a teenage student at SAB, performing adult corps de ballet roles in Stamford City Ballet's production of George Balanchine's *The Nutcracker.*

Many, many New York/New Jersey–area high school auditoriums and gymnasiums. With a group of my advanced classmates at the School of American Ballet, performing lecture demonstrations in public schools as part of SAB's education department.

Chateau St. Michelle Winery, Woodinville, Washington. My first appearance as a professional dancer.

Seattle Opera House, Seattle, Washington. Seven years as a member of Pacific Northwest Ballet.

Honolulu Performing Arts Center, Honolulu, Hawaii. On tour with Pacific Northwest Ballet.

Theaters in Phoenix, Arizona, and Tucson, Arizona. On tour with PNB.

Melbourne Opera House, Melbourne, Australia. On tour with PNB.

Costa Mesa Performing Arts Center, Costa Mesa, California. On tour with PNB.

Kennedy Center for Performing Arts, Washington, D.C. On tour with PNB and then again, five years later, as a dancer with the Suzanne Farrell Ballet.

New York City Center, New York, New York. On tour with PNB.

Sadler's Wells Theater, London, United Kingdom. On tour with PNB.

Edinburgh Opera House, Edinburgh, Scotland. On tour with PNB.

Southern Alberta Jubilee Auditorium, Calgary, Alberta. As a dancer with Alberta Ballet. "SAJA" was our home theater.

Northern Alberta Jubilee Auditorium, Edmonton, Alberta. But we spent nearly equal time performing in SAJA's identical twin, "NAJA."

Way too many theaters in towns and cities across Alberta, Canada, to remember. On tour with Alberta Ballet, we performed in venues ranging from college auditoriums to state-of-the-art concert halls.

Tampere Opera House, Tampere, Finland. The first stop on AB's first international tour.

Helsinki Opera House, Helsinki, Finland. Second leg of the tour.

Cairo Opera House, Cairo, Egypt. Third and final stage of the tour.

Spokane Center for the Performing Arts, Spokane, Washington. First stop of AB's annual four-week tour of *The Nutcracker*.

Royal Theatre, Victoria, British Columbia. Second stop on the *Nutcracker* tour.

McPherson Playhouse, Victoria, British Columbia. Third *Nutcracker* stop.

Queen Elizabeth Theater, Vancouver, British Columbia. Fourth and final stop.

Neptune Theater, Halifax, Nova Scotia. First stop on Alberta Ballet's tour of the Maritime provinces.

Various theaters in Moncton, New Brunswick; St. John, New Brunswick, Glace Bay, Nova Scotia. Continuation of Alberta Ballet's tour of the Maritime provinces.

Vaudeville theater outside Chicago, Illinois. A *Nutcracker* gig with a local ballet school in Downer's Grove, Illinois. The theater had been renovated to show movies after its vaudeville days were over but was rented out for *Nutcracker* performances every year. They sold popcorn during our shows as if a movie was playing.

High School auditorium in the Woodlands, Texas. Another *Nutcracker* gig; see "Boo Hoo, Jeremy Denk."

Keller Auditorium, Portland, Oregon. Oregon Ballet Theatre's home venue.

Newmark Theater, Portland, Oregon. Oregon Ballet Theatre's second home.

Newmark Theater Lobby Rotunda. Portland "First Thursday" open studio event. Once a month, art galleries and organizations in the downtown and arts districts open their doors for an evening, welcoming the public to stroll in, browse, and view a sampling or teaser of what's on offer. I danced a pas de deux from *A Midsummer Night's Dream* in this theater's lobby, in the round, on a tile floor, one cold February Thursday.

Lucas Theater for the Arts, Savannah, Georgia. On tour with OBT.

High School auditorium, Juneau, Alaska. Performing *The Nutcracker* on tour with OBT.

Atwood Theater, Alaska Center for the Performing Arts, Anchorage, Alaska. Performing *The Nutcracker* on tour with OBT. I spent five Thanksgivings on tour in Alaska.

Bluehour restaurant, Portland, Oregon. Dancing "The Man I Love" pas de deux from George Balanchine's *Who Cares?* at a birthday party for a friend of a friend. Because of the restaurant's parquet floor, I wore character shoes and my partner and I considerably altered the choreography. (Shh, don't tell the Balanchine Trust.)

Arlene Schnitzer Concert Hall, Portland, Oregon. When the Oregon Symphony presented an evening of Viennese ballroom music, they invited a small group of OBT dancers to bring it to life. Six of us danced in three pieces, sharing the stage with the musicians and conductor, dancing just inches from violin bows and the conductor's tuxedo tails. I led the Blue Danube Waltz with Paul Destrooper, the most perfect waltz partner I could dream of: smooth, sensitive, strong, and intensely musical, romantic, and gallant. He and I held our breath together through the waltz's opening moments of quiet suspension, building to its soaring, spinning peaks. His hand knew the exact groove at the small of my back from where to guide our waltzing, allowing and encouraging me to arch backward over his arm with abandon, freedom, and safety, spin away and retract, be lifted and twirled. We were in our own world for those nearly ten minutes of Strauss, broken only when we arrived at the conductor's side for a moment of Viennese graciousness: without pausing his baton, he turned to us for an exchange of slight bows with Paul and a whisper-light kiss on my gloved hand. We continued on our dreamy path, feeling the vibrations of the music through the stage's floorboards, hearing the coarse brush of horsehair on strings, the intake breaths of woodwind players, the conductor's shoes on the podium.

BodyVox Dance Center, Portland, Oregon.

Broderick Gallery, Portland, Oregon. Again with Paul Destrooper, accompanied by Scott Kritzer playing, on acoustic guitar, his arrangement of Puccini's *Nessun Dorma*.

Henry's living room, Portland, Oregon (see "Henry's Living Room").

Conduit Dance Center, Portland, Oregon.

Imago Theater, Portland, Oregon.

Coho Theater, Portland, Oregon.

Aladdin Theater, Portland, Oregon.

Disjecta Contemporary Art Center, Portland, Oregon.

Concert hall on the campus of University of Oregon, Eugene, Oregon.

Jamison Square, Portland, Oregon. Bastille Day festival, 2009. A fellow dancer and I did a short duet in the middle of the park's sprinkler-fountain (which was temporarily shut off). The concrete pavement tore my shoes to shreds and I momentarily blanked out the choreography.

Waterfront Park, Portland, Oregon. My second appearance with the Oregon Symphony, in September 2009. The Symphony's annual outdoor concert featured Tchaikovsky's *Serenade for Strings*. I, along with the entire female roster of Oregon Ballet Theatre, performed an excerpt of the first movement of Balanchine's *Serenade*, known as a plotless ballet that simply depicts the spare beauty of a group of women dancing together in the light of the moon. Indeed, we were just that. The night was clear and warm (the Oregonian rain had stopped earlier that day), the moon looked nearly full and shed its glow on us, though we were lit by stage lights as well. The nerve-wrackingly small platform, open to the skies, set up for us to dance on, was quite far from the symphony's covered stage, and the audience was spread out over several hundred feet of open lawn. As I stood along the side of our stage waiting for my entrance, I felt as if I could have been one of Balanchine's original dancers, performing this, his first work in America, at the country estate where it was first presented, a little haphazardly, open to and celebrating the elements of nature and music. But the strings, owing to the vast area their sound needed to reach, were amplified in our concert as they would not have been at the ballet's premiere. I craved hearing the raw music, not funneled through speakers—it hurt me to the core to know how close by the musicians were yet feel I was not allowed to directly hear them, to feel them playing. But I did feel the breeze on my bare skin as I danced (though not with the total abandon needed for this ballet, given how small the stage was and the danger of the unprotected drop-off on all four sides), and oneness with the air, as if there were no barrier between us.

Dean Richardson's roof deck, Portland, Oregon. On the occasion of a Dean's seventieth birthday, on a sweltering August day, I danced a lyrical jazz solo choreographed by a mutual friend as a birthday offering.

Southeast corner of Oregon Ballet Theatre's parking lot. The first annual "Fall For Dance" event, in the summer of 2009, was produced on a shoestring budget. A raised platform served as a stage underneath a large oak tree.

GAVIN LARSEN was a professional ballet dancer for eighteen years before retiring in 2010. Since then, she has written extensively for dance and literary journals including *Pointe, Dance Teacher, Dance Spirit, Dancing Times, Oregon ArtsWatch, Dance/USA's From The Green Room, Threepenny Review, Maine Review, Sunlight Press,* and *Artslandia.* She currently teaches and writes about dance from Asheville, North Carolina.